Between Contempt and Veneration . . .

Mary Magdalene

The Image of a Woman through the Centuries

Ingrid Maisch

Translated by Linda M. Maloney

A Liturgical Press Book

 THE LITURGICAL PRESS
Collegeville, Minnesota

Cover design by Ann Blattner. Illustrations of Mary Magdalene (left) by Paolo Veronese, 1528–1588, and (right) by Giovanni Bellini, 1430–1516.

This book was published in German by Verlag Herder GmbH & Co. KG under the title *Maria Magdalena: Zwischen Verachtung und Verehrung* © 1996.

1   2   3   4   5   6   7   8   9

Library of Congress Cataloging-in-Publication Data

Maisch, Ingrid.
    [Maria Magdalena.   English]
    Mary Magdalene : the image of a woman through the centuries /
Ingrid Maisch ;   translated by Linda M. Maloney.
      p.   cm.
    Includes bibliographical references (p.   ) and index.
    ISBN 0-8146-2471-5 (alk. paper)
    1. Mary Magdalene, Saint.   I. Title.   II. Title: Between contempt
and veneration—
BS2485.M3413   1998
226'.092—dc21   98-5542
 [B]   CIP

For Elisabeth Maisch and Hildegard Gollinger,
who have relieved me of so many
family and household obligations.

Contents

Foreword

And sank then, naked,
o'ercovered by her hair alone,
humbly at our feet . . .
She was the most glorious courtesan.
Her body was a precious vessel of joy;
nothing lovelier has this world beheld.

—Georg Trakl

Mary Magdalene is one of the best-known figures in the Bible, but close inquiry reveals that every man and woman carries a different image of her: the *prostitute* whose business was so profitable that she could spend a fortune on costly oils; the *friend, wife,* or *lover* of the prophet from Nazareth; the *disciple* who concealed her Easter vision out of fear; the *ecstatic* who brought the world (or women only?) a new God; the *repentant sinner* whose penitence was as measureless as her sin; the *saint* who was so highly revered by a medieval biographer that he would have liked to write her name in letters of pure gold.

She is a historical figure from the Bible who, in the course of tradition, became a myth of the feminine, and yet her greatest fascination derives from her fictional image as a beautiful sinner and great penitent. She became the symbol of all women whose fate she shared throughout history: honored, defamed, buried in silence, pushed to the margins, elevated to unreality, degraded to an object of lust. . . .

Reflecting on Mary Magdalene means looking behind the history of the influence of the woman from Magdala, but it also means inquiring about women in general, for the image of Mary Magdalene in every era is an indicator of the image borne by women at that time. This book is a report on that twofold search for those clues.

Merzhausen, January 1996   Ingrid Maisch

"St. Mary Magdalene"
Hans Baldung Grien (1512)
Historical Museum, Basel

"Mary of Egypt"
Hans Baldung Grien (1511)
Historical Museum, Basel

Chapter One

Mary Magdalene in the New Testament

Mary (or Mariam) is mentioned by name in all four gospels. In chronological order (with reference to the final redaction of the gospels) we find the following passages:

Mark 15:40-41 (*par.* Matt 27:55-56); 15:47 (*par.* Matt 27:61): crucifixion and burial of Jesus
Mark 16:1 (*par.* Matt 28:1; Luke 24:10): Easter morning
Luke 8:2: women disciples from Galilee
John 19:25: at the crucifixion
John 20:1-2, 11-18: Easter morning
Mark 16:9-11: Easter morning

In addition there are passages in which Mary's presence is presupposed:

Luke 23:49, 55-56 (*par.* Mark 15:40-41, 47): the women from Galilee at the crucifixion and burial of Jesus
Matt 28:9-10 (special material): Jesus' appearance to the women.[1]

At first glance this seems very little material, but in the context of the history of the time it does tell us something about this woman, her biographical background, and her place in the Jesus movement. Beyond that, these New Testament passages present a variety of problems and questions that touch not only Mary, but all the women in the Jesus movement and in the later Church.

1. The Woman from Magdala

Mary Magdalene bore a name that in her own time was popular in every segment of society; it goes back to Miriam, one of the leading figures of the Exodus. Miriam's song (Exod 15:21) celebrating the rescue from Egypt as a divine victory is one of the oldest texts of the First Testament. Something of Miriam's self-assurance was preserved in the New Testament Marys as well (cf. also Mary of Nazareth's Magnificat in Luke 1).

The derivation of the name and its original meaning are uncertain; suggested meanings include everything from "unruly" to "stout" to "child desired." In the LXX, the Greek translation of the Bible, the name was grecized to *Mariam,* and it later developed into the forms known to us from the New Testament period: *Maria, Mariam, Mariamne.* In the gospel manuscripts the method of writing shifts back and forth between *Maria* and *Mariam;* present-day editions of the text prefer the reading *Maria* (except for *Mariam* in John 20:18).

This woman, unlike others, is not called by the name of a man (whether father, husband, or son) but by the name of a place, something with which we are otherwise familiar only in the case of Jesus. This unique characteristic is apparently connected with her outstanding role in the Jesus movement both before and after Easter. The adjective "Magdalene," which has become her surname, points to her origins in the town of Magdala and should be translated "the woman from Magdala." The association of given name and surname varies: *Maria hē Magdalēnē* (Mary, the woman from Magdala, Mark 15:40, 47; John 20:1); *hē Magdalēnē Maria* (the woman from Magdala, Mary, Luke 24:10); or *Maria hē kaloumenē Magdalēnē* (Mary, called the woman from Magdala, Luke 8:2).

However, the gospels define Mary not only in terms of her place of origin; they also speak of her past: she is the woman from whom seven demons had gone out (Luke 8:2), or from whom Jesus had cast out seven demons (Mark 16:9). These were demons that caused sickness: Mary is depicted as a pitiable woman afflicted with a severe illness (the symbolic "seven" indicates strength and plenitude) who was healed by Jesus.

The victims of demonic possession are people who are alienated from themselves and cannot direct the course of their own lives. The causes vary. Sociological exegesis (Gerd Theissen) points to members of the middle class, threatened by economic and social downward mobility, who could not withstand the strain and in their distress sought refuge in illness. Psychological exegesis (Eugen Drewermann), by contrast, places more emphasis on causes peculiar to the individual, such as internal conflicts and anxieties. Possession involved types of illness that made those afflicted by them seem strange or monstrous; however, any "normal" illness could also be regarded as caused by demons (the fever in Mark 1:30-31 is attributed by Luke 4:38-39 to a demon that must be "threatened" as part of the healing process).

Mary's "demonically" caused illness can most probably be understood as a psychosomatic condition. It was only the later equation of these demons with "seven devils" that made Mary from Magdala an immoral woman overcome by sin (and made it easier to identify her with the "great sinner" whose story Luke had narrated immediately before Mary's appearance in the text).

Magdala is in Galilee, on the western shore of the Sea of Gennesaret. Modern travel guides emphasize the beauty and fruitfulness of the land and the wealth of fish in the lake. This situation would also have obtained in the first century, as we are assured by the Jewish writer Flavius Josephus.[2] This happy land belonged, after the death of Herod the king, to the district of his son Herod Antipas, who put his stamp on the landscape by an active building campaign. Tiberias in particular, a city near Magdala that had been chosen by the emperor Tiberius as the new seat of government, was famous for its handsome architecture. The city was built for a mixed population of Jews and Greeks; its synagogue and sports facilities were designed to meet the needs of Jews and non-Jews alike. However, other cities on the lake, including Mary's home town, could compete with the new capital in size and appearance.

An old tradition identifies the location of Magdala with the ruins of Migdal ("tower," Aramaic *migdal numaya*, "fish tower") and describes it as a fishing village. The gospels attest the existence of the place by their use of its name as Mary's surname, whereas it is found as a specific place name only in the manuscript variants of Mark 8:10 (instead of Dalmanutha) and Matthew 15:39 (instead of Magadan), where it replaces the names of places otherwise unknown.

Probably "Magdala" was the city otherwise known by its Greek name, Tarichea, mentioned by Josephus as already existing in pre-Christian times. Both the Greek and the Aramaic names indicate the drying and pickling of fish, a business that made the city one of the important industrial centers of the land, its exports being shipped as far as Rome.[3] Josephus, who was the military commander in Tarichea, speaks of it as a city (in contrast to villages), using the Greek word *polis,* with its own surrounding territory belonging to it. He lists it even before Tiberias, calling it a commercial city with a large population—though we should question the numbers he gives.[4]

Tarichea was a city with a Hellenistic character (cf. the hippodrome mentioned by Josephus, *Bell.* 2.21.3, §599). Its inhabitants are distinguished from the "people of the land" (*Bell.* 2.21.3 §602) and during the Jewish revolt they, together with the people of the other Galilean cities, sided with the Romans. Josephus gives a reasonable explanation for this: the inhabitants were concerned for their property and their city (*Bell.* 3.10.4 §492-3; Vespasian also considered "those that came out of the country" to be the cause of the revolt: *Bell.* 3.10.10 §532).

Such accounts, of course, are flavored by the tendency of the author to depict the native Jews to the Roman audience as reasonable and peaceable, and all radical groups as alien to the society; nevertheless his description of Tarichea could well be accurate. Places that worked with raw materials like salt (for fish packing) were wealthy, and people who cultivated vineyards lovingly and intensively for many years would not lightly surrender them. The well-to-do who have something to lose certainly value stable situations and shy away from the risks of revolt.

The New Testament reference to Mary's origins in Magdala/Tarichea is, on the whole, more than a simple indication of place and tells us that Mary, like the other women named in Luke 8:2-3, came from a city environment and therefore also from the realm of Hellenistic cultural influence. In the Jesus movement, when she was no longer living in Magdala, she was described by the name of her native city.

Was this done only to distinguish her from other Marys, or did it indicate a noteworthy woman shaped by her background? Was she unusual among the disciples as a city woman among Galileans of village origin, a well-to-do woman among the many poor, a member of a class influenced by Hellenism among more traditionally oriented disciples (cf. the later conflict between Paul and the Jerusalem authorities, which was also a matter of different cultural backgrounds)? Was she as a result emancipated enough to separate from her family and home and join the Jesus movement? The move to a different milieu presumes a strong personality, especially when it involves downward social mobility. Mary, like the artisan Jesus, came from the socially secure middle class and turned voluntarily, as did he, to the poor among her people. A beatitude for the poor does not emanate from below, but always from those who deliberately enter into solidarity with the poor (cf. Francis of Assisi or the theologians of liberation).

2. The Galilean Jew

The fact that Mary Magdalene was named in reference to a place and not, as usual, to a man suggests that she had no partner when she became a disciple of Jesus. Was she at that point already widowed or divorced? It is scarcely likely that she was still unmarried, since marriages were arranged by parents. The marriage of children was one of the parents' most important duties, although later rabbinic law, which regarded the young couple as parties to the contract, did require the consent of the woman if she had reached her majority (twelve and a half years). People married between the ages of twelve and fifteen. While betrothal was the basis of the marriage, the woman remained under the care of her father until she was conducted to her husband's house, and she could not leave her house and family.

In Mary's case, had her severe illness perhaps made it impossible for her to marry? The least contrived supposition is that Mary was married, and that she separated from her husband and family "for the sake of the reign of God" to join the Jesus movement. It is possible that she had a happy marriage, that she abandoned her children—all this is possible; we do not know.

In any case her joining Jesus cannot be automatically interpreted as a movement from patriarchal oppression to freedom, as is sometimes done. (Be it noted: patriarchal structures were not something peculiar to Judaism, but were the general rule in antiquity, as early Christianity itself shows!) What Mary did was rather to adopt a different ethos that included breaking with her family and was the same for men as for women, as the tense relationship between Jesus and his family makes clear.

The negative image of the status of Jewish women must, on the basis of what we now know, be much more sharply nuanced than what we find in some popular accounts of Jesus. The popular practice of contrasting negative statements in the Talmud with Jesus' free association with women is the basis for a number of false ideas.[5]

• Rabbinic statements from so-called "normative Judaism" are indiscriminately read back into Jesus' time, even though at that period there were very different opinions and it was only after the fall of the independent Jewish state (in 70 C.E.) that a certain conformity became necessary.

• The Talmud is the document of a highly developed culture of argumentative discourse, which is why the statements pro and contra on different themes were handed on. Consequently, when we find misogynistic statements we also find the contrary philogynistic opinions immediately cited. For example, to the question whether one should instruct a daughter in Torah the answers range from "it is an obligation" to "one may, but there is no obligation," to "one must not."[6]

• Repressive opinions about women are not to be read as the actual description of real conditions, but as an attempt to impose a contrary practice for ideological reasons. (The same is true, analogously, for Christian women's being forbidden to teach in 1 Tim 2:11-12.)

• Even when women are (apparently?) discriminated against in what men say about them these statements are to be read in the context of ancient culture and society. The much-quoted prayer of the Jewish man praising God for not having made him a Gentile or a woman or ignorant must be compared with corresponding Greek sayings (attributed to Thales and Socrates) in which the man thanks fate that he was not born a beast, a woman, or a barbarian.[7] In both cases the "I" of the speaker and his cultural identity are made the absolute; this does not mean that one may conclude that such a sense of superiority led to actual sanctions against women, Gentiles (non-Jews), or barbarians (non-Greeks).

• We should also consider that Christian scholars can only study Jewish sources from a distance while Jewish scholars read these texts on the basis of their experience of a living tradition. Thus Pnina Navè Levinson, who knows the ancient sources as a scholar and the situation as a woman, can speak quite freely of the "high value and estimation of women" in biblical and post-biblical literature—a conclusion that also applies to Christian authors insofar as this process of experience and learning can be applied to them.[8]

As regards the actual situation of Jewish women in the context of the Jewish-Hellenistic city culture of Galilee, the following observations may be of some help:

• Women could own or inherit property and could also control it. Women from the wealthier classes had an especially great degree of freedom in the economic sphere. Proverbs 31:10-31 presupposes that a woman can be active not only in her household but also in crafts and commerce, and that she can buy land and vineyards with her own money. The Galilean women mentioned in Luke 8:2-3 also appear to have had control of their own property.

• Women claimed the right to initiate divorce and to leave their husbands. The Jewish tradition based on Deuteronomy 24:1 did not prevent the parallel exercise of a different kind of practice that gave the woman broader rights. Such cases were known not only among the women of the Herodian family who were subject to strong Hellenistic influences (though their conduct may have influenced other families in the Galilean region) but are attested also for the marriage of Flavius Josephus, whose orientation was more to the Pharisees.[9]

• Women took an active part in religious life, not only in the house where many religious duties could be performed only by women, but also in public worship. For Galilean women the reading of the Scripture in the synagogue service is of special interest because they probably did not travel to Jerusalem for all three of the annual pilgrimage feasts. In the early synagogues men and women did not yet sit in separate areas. (The evidence for a women's gallery comes only from post-biblical times.) Women could be called to read from the Torah; they gave donations for the synagogue and could, according to ancient inscriptions, exercise offices in the synagogue. When a Galilean Jewish woman went to Jerusalem she could sacrifice in the Temple just as a man could, because in both cases "sacrificing" meant paying for the material of the offering (an animal or incense).

If we regard Mary Magdalene against this religious and cultural background in Galilee we see that multiple influences have to be taken into account. Mary was not an oppressed Jewess, but a Jewish woman who took charge of her own life and whose decision to separate from her family was respected by those around her (cf., in contrast, the aggressive reaction of Jesus' family to his departure: Mark 3:21). She never had it as bad in her Jewish past as she would in her Christian future.

3. The Disciple who Followed Jesus

In fifteen chapters of his gospel Mark tells of Jesus and those who accompanied him; many are named, and in several cases the story of their crucial encounter with Jesus is told (Mark 1:16-20; 2:14). We get the impression that this was a purely male movement. Then comes the thunderclap: not a single male disciple accompanies Jesus to his death—but there are *women* disciples at the cross! A few verses before the end of the gospel we learn that they have been among Jesus' followers from his earliest days in Galilee. Thus from the beginning there were women around Jesus, female disciples who remained faithful until his death and burial, and beyond.

The crucial text of Mark 15:40-41 reads, in as literal a translation as possible, "But there were women looking on from afar, among them Mary the woman from Magdala and Mary the (wife? daughter? mother?) of James the lesser and (the) mother of Joses, and Salome, who, when he was in Galilee, followed him [= were his disciples] and served him, and many other (women) who had gone up with him to Jerusalem."[10] Some of the "many" women around Jesus are mentioned by name.

The women are described, more precisely, in terms of four actions: (1) they looked on, (2) they followed, (3) they served, (4) they had gone up. The first and fourth are represented in Greek by a participial construction with the aorist, a temporal form that describes a single action concluded in the past; the second and third actions have the verbs in the imperfect tense, which describes a repeated and/or enduring action in the past. Thus the women's serving and following began earlier and, unlike the looking on and going up, were not single actions; they therefore guaranteed the continuity of the Jesus movement. The two verbs are also interesting, as to their content, in the overall context of Mark's gospel because Mark thus names two criteria for genuine discipleship:[11] *following* Jesus, even at the risk of one's own life (cf. 8:34-38) and, in the likeness of the servant Human One, becoming the *servant* of all (cf. 9:35; 10:42-45).

With these two terms, which in Mark are *termini technici* for the right relationship to Jesus, the author refers to experiences in the original Jesus movement, for "following" does not mean walking after Jesus as part of the mob, and "serving" does not simply mean lending a helping hand or caring for bodily needs. Instead, both expressions are descriptions of the life of the disciple that are mutually enhancing and explanatory.[12] In many translations this situation is obliterated when "serving" is translated by "care [for], support" and the like, and "following" by "accompanying, going with," and so on. *Following* in the sense of "discipleship" involves a change in one's living situation: those who traveled with Jesus abandoned home, family, property, and security.[13] In solidarity with the poor[14] they shared Jesus' propertyless existence and placed all their hope in the inbreaking of the reign of God. The consequence of this radical ethos of abandonment and letting-go within the community of disciples was the equality of all. The ethos of "above and below," fathers and children that stabilized secular society was no longer in force, but rather the sibling equality of all those who had become poor. *Service,* which was practiced by all disciples, male and female, was the surrender of time, strength, and abilities, solidarity with one's siblings in the reign of God; it could also consist of the abandonment and surrender of possessions, but before anything else it was service to the proclamation of the reign of God now close at hand,[15] including preaching, healing the sick, and the offer of divine peace (cf. Matt 10:7-8, 12-13; Luke 9:2; 10:5).

From the beginning this charismatic community inspired by Jesus included men and women. Even though the gospels, written later and from an androcentric point of view, have generally obliterated the memory of the women, we can still follow their traces. The image of an exclusively male discipleship is traceable primarily to Luke: while Mark 10:29 (*par.* Matt 19:25) presumes that a person abandons house and family, Luke 18:29 restricts discipleship by specifying that it involves a man leaving his wife. Correspondingly, he has eliminated the mention of the Galilean women's discipleship in the scene at the cross (Luke 23:49) and reduced their service (Luke 8:2-3) to material provision for the disciples.[16] Luke thus accommodated the role of the women to the later ecclesiastical idea of women and fixed their place in the Church for centuries to come. A similar procedure is found in Acts 6:1-7 where the division of labor between the groups of the Twelve and the Seven is described: an arrogant explanation is given (v. 2) for downgrading service at table in contrast to the service of the word.

The women under the cross (Mark 15:40-41) and in Galilee (Luke 8:2-3) are real disciples who traveled with Jesus,[17] responded to his call to discipleship, and followed him; we may think of them as proclaimers of the reign of God. Where traditional norms, the distinction between the propertied and the propertyless, and the tie to family were no longer in force, but rather the renunciation of possessions, sexuality, and security under the protection of an extended family for the sake of a higher goal, there men and women could assume the same roles. To put it another way, seen from outside, the Jesus movement was abnormal; seen from inside it was egalitarian.

Nevertheless, among these equals were some who were remembered as having had a special place: Simon whose other name was Peter, Judas, and Mary from Magdala. The synoptic lists[18] of the

names of the men who accompanied Jesus vary from the second position onward; the first and last, however, are always the same: Simon
and Judas (Mark 3:16-19; Matt 10:2-4; Luke 6:14-16). Even when a
group of only three or four is named, Simon is always first (Mark
1:16-20; 5:37; 9:2; 13:3; 14:3). The sequence in the first lists is the
expression of an order of rank connected with the behavior of the disciples after the death of Jesus. Simon, who fled like the other disciples
and even denied Jesus (Mark 14:30-31, 66-72) later returned to his
faith and played an outstanding role in the gathering of the male and
female disciples that made him, in the eyes of the others, the leader
among the disciples and "Peter," the rock (cf. 1 Cor 15:5). Judas, in
contrast, did not return to the community of disciples and in the eyes
of the others became an apostate and a scapegoat; his name was
handed down as a minatory example, given the last place and coupled
with a reference to his defection ("who betrayed him").[19] The English predicate "traitor" (Luke 6:16) is a further negative evaluation of
his action.

Parallel to the lists of the men, there are synoptic lists of women:

Mark 15:40: *Mary Magdalene,* and Mary [the mother] of James
the younger and of Joses, and Salome
Mark 15:47: *Mary Magdalene* and Mary [the mother] of Joses
Mark 16:1: *Mary Magdalene,* Mary [the mother] of James, and
Salome
Matt 27:56 (*par.* Mark 15:40): *Mary Magdalene,* and Mary the
mother of James and Joseph [!], and the mother of the sons
of Zebedee
Matt 27:61 (*par.* Mark 15:47): *Mary Magdalene* and the other
Mary
Matt 28:1 (*par.* Mark 16:1): *Mary Magdalene* and the other
Mary
Luke 8:2-3: *Mary,* called *Magdalene,* . . . and Joanna, the wife
of Chuza, Herod's steward, and Susanna, and many other
[women]
Luke 24:10 (*par.* Mark 16:1): *Mary Magdalene,* and Joanna, and
Mary [the mother] of James, and the other women.

According to these lists there were other Marys besides Mary
Magdalene, and they are related to various men; we also find Salome,
Joanna, Susanna, and other nameless women. Not only do the names
vary in the lists (some appear in only one list, for example Salome, Su-

sanna, and the mother of the sons of Zebedee), but the order of names varies as well. All the more important is the fact that Mary Magdalene appears in *all* the lists and that her name is always listed *first*.

This prominent placement cannot be accidental; analogously to the primacy of Simon, it must point to her importance in the community of disciples and her function in the origination of the Easter faith. Mary is connected with the Jerusalem tradition of the death, burial, and resurrection of Jesus, while Simon Peter first appears in the Galilean Easter tradition (cf. Mark 16:7), which may have been related to the so-called flight of the disciples. In the retrospective view of the early Christian communities that compiled and handed on such lists the *continuity* (Mary) and *new beginning* (Simon Peter) of faith and community were associated with these two names.[20]

4. The Apostolic Witness

Both the great gospel traditions—the synoptic and the Johannine—associate the continuity of the Jesus movement beyond the death of Jesus with the disciple from Magdala. She was present at his death, she remained true to the dead Jesus (a dangerous attitude toward one executed as a rebel by the occupying forces, as the gospels intimate!) and she became the first witness and messenger of the Risen One (cf. the pre-Johannine Easter account).

In John 20:1-18 a number of layers of tradition have been combined, as we can see from the discontinuities and contradictions in the text. Compare 20:1, where Mary comes alone to the tomb, with 20:2, which presumes the presence of several people ("we do not know where . . ."); at v. 13 Mary is alone at the tomb ("I do not know where . . ."). In vv. 14 and 16 Mary's turning twice does not make sense, and in vv. 3-10 there is a shift of interest to Peter and the beloved disciple.

John 20:1, 11-18 is a pre-Johannine narrative of the initial appearance of Jesus to Mary, which was then redactionally combined with a narrative about Peter (also pre-Johannine: cf. Luke 24:12 in which Peter goes to the tomb). The old Mary Magdalene narrative is not a historical account, but a revelation narrative; it nevertheless preserves the historical memory of Mary's visit to the tomb and/or the first appearance of Jesus to a female disciple (cf. Hubert Ritt, Raymond E. Brown, Eduard Schweizer, Martin Hengel, and others). Here "appearance" is to be understood as an experience (vision?) that was foundational for the Easter faith. While the Fourth Evangelist accepted the narrative of the appearance to Mary, he corrected the narrative about Peter by adding the figure of the beloved disciple, who comes to the tomb "first."

In the old narrative Mary is sent by Jesus to the other disciples and tells them: "I have seen the Lord" (John 20:18). This report from the pre-Johannine tradition is remarkable for a number of reasons including:

• Mary no longer calls Jesus "rabbi," or teacher, or master (cf. v. 16), but uses the *kyrios* title, "Lord," the divine name by which Jesus will be called henceforth.

• She speaks the apostolic formula, "I have seen the Lord," that Paul uses in 1 Corinthians 9:1 to legitimate his apostolic office, which in turn raises questions about Mary's position.

People who saw Jesus, who had died, as the Living One and proclaimed him thus to others are the ones we call "apostles." From the point of view of time Mary is the first to whom this title is owed. For us today the notion of a female apostle is still strange because we can only imagine the (male) bishops as the successors of male apostles. The NT authors saw it differently (cf. Junia in Rom 16:7), and so did the ancient tradition of the Church (cf. Mary Magdalene as "*apostola apostolorum*").

The problem seems to arise from the fact that the NT presents a number of different criteria for apostleship and from the circumstance that later the Lukan idea prevailed in the establishment of an ecclesiastical hierarchy.

Luke, in Acts 1:21-22, gives the following criteria: an apostle must be a man who was witness to the resurrection and who had been a member of the group of Jesus' disciples in the period from John's baptism to Jesus' being taken up into heaven. On the basis of these criteria he withholds the title of "apostle" even from Paul. However, on closer inspection we see that none of the so-called twelve apostles could lay claim to the title either, since none of them was numbered among Jesus' disciples at the time of his baptism by John; all the gospels, including Luke's, locate the call of the first disciples at some later point in time. The Lukan criteria are therefore wholly invalid, and they certainly say nothing against Mary.

Paul knows a different set of criteria (and his view was apparently shared by the early Christian communities): an apostle is someone who has seen Jesus and believes in him (cf. 1 Cor 9:1) and who was called and sent by God, or by Jesus (cf. 1 Cor 1:1; 2 Cor 1:1; Gal 1:1; Rom 1:1) to proclaim the gospel (cf. 2 Cor 10:14; Rom 1:1). These criteria apply to Simon Peter (cf. 1 Cor 15:5), to Paul himself (cf. 1 Cor 9:1), but apparently also to a number of others including Andronicus and Junia (Rom 16:7). On the basis of these criteria there can be no doubt that Mary Magdalene should be called an apostle. Having the title taken from her was a fate she shared with other women mentioned in the New Testament.

In translations of Romans 16:1-2, Phoebe is not allowed to appear as what she is: deacon of the church at Cenchreae and its presider; Junia was permitted to retain the title of apostle, but had to mutate into a man; and the prophet and teacher Jezebel (Rev 2:20-23) became a whore—a career that also awaited Mary Magdalene, as we will show.

Against the background of the late first century it is amazing that the Fourth Evangelist includes the appearance to Mary in his gospel; in this connection we should point to other stories of women in that gospel, for example the Samaritan woman in her role as preacher and missionary (John 4:28-29, 39) or Martha of Bethany who—instead of Peter, as in Matthew 16:16—is the first to confess Jesus as Son of God (John 11:27). In general women play a different role in the Fourth Gospel than in the non-Johannine communities where the beginnings of a hierarchical, institutional structure could already be detected (Matt 23:8-10 warns against titles and offices in the Church); such a structure had, for various reasons,[21] no place for women. The final redaction of the Fourth Gospel also swung in this direction and eliminated Mary Magdalene from the list of resurrection appearances (cf. John 21:14). The evangelist himself did not suffer from such anxieties: since he did not picture the Church in terms of institution and office he could edit the historical account of a woman as first witness to the resurrection into his gospel. The mediation of salvation was not accomplished through an institution but at the level of personal relationship with Christ. Consequently this gospel mentions the names of individual disciples, male and female, but does not name the "twelve apostles."

5. The First Witness of the Resurrection

In the Fourth Gospel Mary is, in terms of time, the first among the disciples to be led by a revelation to the faith in which the evangelist and his community also participate. This statement, derived from John 20:1-18, expresses the greatness and relative importance of Mary. Here, in contrast to the work of other New Testament authors, she retains the honor of being respected as the first witness to an appearance (protophany) of the Risen One, while at the same time her significance for the present is relativized. The "seeing" that in the past had been the expression of ecclesial legitimacy becomes secondary to the contrasting idea of "believing" that applies to individual Christians at every time. "Seeing" is, so to speak, a supporting aid by which Mary (vv. 11-18), the disciples (vv. 19-23), and Thomas (vv. 24-28) come to believe, but true believers are those "who have not seen and yet have come to believe" (v. 29). Thus the evangelist makes it possible for his community, for whom the Easter appearances are already far in the past, to believe without seeing. Their model is the so-called Beloved Disciple, who is sketched into the life of Jesus to serve as a figure of identification for the Johannine community: he sees (even without appearances) and believes. His introduction into the older narratives in John 20 had consequences for Peter as well as for Mary: their importance is in the past; now there are different routes to faith. In retrospect Mary is (only) the disciple with whom everything began and whose name has been preserved for future generations.

This relativizing of the appearance to Mary Magdalene, which the Fourth Evangelist accomplished by linking the story in John 20:1, 11-18 with other narratives, reaches its climax in the final redaction of the work. In John 21:14 the appearance to her is not even mentioned, as David Friedrich Strauss already pointed out in both versions of his *Life of Jesus.*[22]

The Fourth Gospel is the *only* canonical writing that recalls the protophany and apostolic service of Mary. It is also the *last* canonical writing to mention Mary Magdalene. From that point begins the history of her influence, both within and outside the Church. That her route was not foredoomed to lead into "heretical" communities is evident from a brief second-century text that in some manuscripts is placed at the end of the four gospels and in others at the end of Mark's gospel, and that is regarded today as the so-called "canonical ending" of Mark (Mark 16:9-20). This passage is an independent collection of a variety of appearance traditions, including the protophany to Mary Magdalene. The specific indication that "he appeared *first* to Mary Magdalene . . ." (v. 9) leads commentators to ask about the historical and literary value of this note, which is seen as competing with the Petrine tradition (1 Cor 15:5; Luke 24:34). The answer, much as with John 20, is to be sought on two levels: in its historical aspect this text retains the ancient (partly covered up, partly repressed) knowledge of the role of Mary (and other women?) in the origins of the Easter faith; from a literary point of view its significance in this context is minimized[23] because it is said that the whole set of appearances should be read as listed in order of ascending importance (cf. the missionary command to the eleven in v. 15). If the note is detached from its present context it still tells us that there were Christian groups in the second century who handed on the tradition of a protophany to Mary, even though they were aware of a contrary Petrine tradition.

This recollection of Mary Magdalene, still evident even at the end of the New Testament period, has evoked a variety of reactions:

• Her significance is *emphasized:* the apostolic Fathers called her *"isapostolos"* and she was known in Gnostic writings as the bearer of revelation.[24]

• Her significance is *relativized:* she shares the role of first witness with other women.[25]

• Her significance is *ridiculed:* Celsus charges that the truth of the Christians' faith rests on the witness of a crazy woman.[26]

The references in the New Testament and later reactions all show that Christians of the earliest period were aware of the importance of Mary Magdalene, a significance rooted in her role as the first witness to the Risen One and her resultant position in the post-Easter community of disciples.[27]

Notes

[1]There is an exegesis of the Mary-passages by Helen Schüngel-Straumann in her "Maria von Magdala—Apostolin und erste Verkünderin der Osterbotschaft," in Dietmar Bader, ed., *Maria Magdalena—Zu einem Bild der Frau in der christlichen Verkündigung* (Munich and Zürich, 1990) 9–32.

[2]Josephus, *Bell.,* 3.10.8 §516–9. References are to William Whiston, translator, *The Works of Josephus* (new ed. Peabody, Mass.: Hendrickson, 1987).

[3]Josephus, *Bell.,* 3.10.7; cf. also James F. Strange, "Magdala," in David Noel Freedman, editor in chief, *The Anchor Bible Dictionary* (New York: Doubleday, 1992) 4:463–4.

[4]Forty thousand from Tarichea are said to have engaged in a battle with Tiberias: in the course of the conflict Josephus captures the six hundred members of the city council of Tiberias and two thousand additional citizens and has them imprisoned in Tarichea, which raises questions about the size of the prison there (*Bell.*, 2.21.3 §595–613; 2.21.8 §634–46).

[5]For questions of method see also Bernadette J. Brooten, "Jüdinnen zur Zeit Jesu," in Bernadette Brooten and Norbert Greinacher, eds., *Frauen in der Männerkirche* (Munich and Mainz, 1982) 141–8.

[6]Brooten, "Jüdinnen" 144–5. For the religious and secular education of women, cf. Günter Mayer, *Die jüdische Frau in der hellenistisch-römischen Antike* (Stuttgart, 1987) 47–50.

[7]For the tension between the Greek sense of superiority and the Jewish consciousness of election that is expressed in such sayings, cf. Martin Hengel, *Jews, Greeks and Barbarians. Aspects of the Hellenization of Judaism in the pre-Christian Period,* translated by John Bowden (Philadelphia: Fortress, 1980) 55–66.

[8]Pnina Navè Levinson, *Einblicke in das Judentum* (Paderborn, 1991) 94–132 (ch. 3, "Die Rolle der Frau"); cf. Luise Schottroff, who points to the high estimation of this supposedly misogynistic Judaism by non-Jewish women in the ancient world: "'Leaders of the Faith' oder 'Just Some Pious Womenfolk'?" in eadem, *Let the Oppressed Go Free. Feminist Perspectives on the New Testament,* translated by Annemarie S. Kidder (Louisville, Ky.: Westminster/John Knox, 1993) 60–79.

[9]Mayer, *Frau* 79–81. For the right of divorce as an indicator of women's legal equality, see Monika Fander, *Die Stellung der Frau im Markusevangelium. Unter besonderer Berücksichtigung kultur- und religionsgeschichtlicher Hintergründe.* Münsteraner Theologische Abhandlungen 8 (Altenberge, 1898) 200–54; Ruthild Geiger, "Die Stellung der geschiedenen Frau in der Umwelt des Neuen Testaments," in Gerhard Dautzenberg et al., eds., *Die Frau im Urchristentum.* QD 95 (Freiburg im Breisgau: Herder, 1983) 134–57.

[10]Both in the manuscripts and in the commentaries on this passage the question of the relationship between the second Mary and James remains unresolved, as well as whether she is identical with the mother of Joses—that is, whether we should count three or four women in this list.

[11]For discussion of the question whether there were any women at all among Jesus' disciples and followers see (especially as regards Mark 15:40-41) Elisabeth Schüssler Fiorenza, *In Memory of Her. A Feminist Theological Reconstruction of Christian Origins* (New York: Crossroad, 1983) 316–23.

[12]Luise Schottroff, "Women as Disciples of Jesus in New Testament Times," in eadem, *Let the Oppressed Go Free,* 80–130, at 98–9, as well as "Mary Magdalene and the Women at Jesus' Tomb," ibid., 168–203.

[13]On the "itinerant charismatics" (as distinct from the settled "sympathizers") and their radical ethos, cf. Gerd Theissen, *Sociology of Early Pales-*

tinian Christianity, translated by John Bowden (Philadelphia: Fortress, 1977) 8–16.

[14]Not all Jesus' disciples came from the poorest class (Greek *ptochos*, Luke 6:20). Many "left everything" (Mark 10:28). "Here poverty was not only a fate, but a calling" (Theissen, *Sociology*, 13).

[15]Schottroff, "Women as Disciples," presumes that all disciples had the task of "preaching and healing" and adds with regard to Luke 8:2-3 that discipleship "involved . . . proclamation" (pp. 92–3). Similarly, for Susanne Heine, the concept of discipleship also means "proclaiming the reign of God near at hand" and cannot be reduced to "material support." Susanne Heine, "Selig durch Kindergebären (1 Tim 2:15)?" in Marie-Theres Wacker, ed., *Theologie feministisch* (Düsseldorf, 1988) 59–77, at 66.

[16]See Schüssler Fiorenza, *Memory*, 145, where she rejects the silent assumption that the Jesus movement consisted only of charismatic men; differently, Theissen, *Sociology*, 17, who only sees a few sympathetic women who supported Jesus.

[17]Fander, *Stellung*, however, reads Mark 15:40-41 as simply a redactional image of real discipleship without reference to historical reality (p. 347). She sees the women rather as among the sympathizers, the core of the later communities, while traveling women were "on the whole not a mass phenomenon" and were represented only by a few individuals (p. 335). At most she concedes that Mary, whose name "from Magdala" describes her as no longer resident in a place, may have been numbered among the itinerant charismatics (p. 320).

[18]On the correspondence of lists of names and order of rank see Martin Hengel, "Maria Magdalena und die Frauen als Zeugen," in Otto Betz, Martin Hengel, and Peter Schmidt, eds., *Abraham unser Vater* (Leiden and Cologne, 1963) 243–56; cf. Schottroff, who, however, does not read the listing as expressing hierarchy or prestige, but rather an authority arising out of work on behalf of the community: ("Mary Magdalene," 175–6).

[19]For the Judas problem see Hans-Josef Klauck, *Judas—ein Jünger des Herrn*. QD 111 (Freiburg im Breisgau: Herder, 1987).

[20]Schottroff gives a different evaluation of the two central figures in the Easter tradition; she recognizes a "failure" even on the part of Mary Magdalene. Both Simon and Mary were equally "witnesses of the resurrection" and "models of overcoming fear" ("Mary Magdalene," 185, 187–8).

[21]The communities had to defend themselves on two fronts: the danger of *Gnosticism* was avoided through a fixed church order and a moral code applicable to everyday life; against *pagan* criticism of Christian ideas of order the model of the ancient household with its prescribed image of women was adopted. Both tendencies, which culminate in the Pastorals, led to the deterioration of conditions for women in the communities. Cf. "Die Restauration setzt sich durch" in Susanne Heine, *Frauen der frühen Christenheit* (Göttingen, 1986) 146–54.

[22]David Friedrich Strauss, *Das Leben Jesu, kritisch betrachtet* 2 (Tübingen, 1836) 626; idem, *Das Leben Jesu für das deutsche Volk bearbeitet* (2nd ed. Leipzig, 1864) 291.

[23]Rudolf Pesch considered whether the note in Mark 16:9-18 should be seen in connection with pre-Lukan traditions. He suspects that behind Luke 24/Acts 1 there is a strand of tradition "that began with an appearance to Mary Magdalene, led by way of the Emmaus story to an appearance to the disciples, and included the pre-Lukan ascension story." In that case Luke would have erased the protophany to Mary, or rather replaced it by the story of the women in Luke 24:9-11 (Pesch, *Das Markusevangelium* 2 [Freiburg: Herder, 1977] 545).

[24]Martin Hengel, "Maria Magdalena," 251.

[25]Syrian *Didascalia*, 21: "He appeared to Mary Magdalene and Mary, the daughter of James." *Apostolic Constitutions*, 5.14.19: "He appeared first to Mary Magdalene and Mary of James" (cf. Pesch, *Markusevangelium*, 549). Hengel suspects that already behind Matthew 28:9-10 lies a tendency to "compel [Mary] to share with a woman possibly related to the Lord (!)" the honor of an appearance of Christ ("Maria Magdalena" 255).

[26]Origen, *Contra Celsum*, 2.55; cf. Hengel, "Maria Magdalena" 252.

[27]Note the connection between "seeing" and ecclesial functions in 1 Corinthians 9:1 (Paul), 15:5 (Peter), 15:7 (James). An exegetically based depiction of the issues surrounding women in the New Testament, including women's leadership functions, is found in Anton Vögtle, *Die Dynamik des Anfangs. Leben und Fragen der jungen Kirche* (Freiburg, Basel, and Vienna: Herder, 1988) 136–66.

Chapter Two

The Heiress of the Empire of Light:
The Gnostic Mary Magdalene

The latest canonical text that recalled the primacy of Mary Magdalene was written in the middle of the second century. It also noted
that her apostolic mission encountered disbelief among the other disciples; only Jesus himself was able to bring those disciples to belief
(Mark 16:9-14). About the same time a document with similar content was written, but with a different outcome. This was the Gnostic
Gospel of Mary, named for its central figure. The text, of which only a
fragment has been preserved, first tells of the disciples' despair after
Jesus' departure and how Mary encouraged them by recalling Jesus'
command to preach the gospel:

> "Weep not, be not sorrowful, neither be ye undecided, for his grace will be
> with you all and will protect you. Let us rather praise his greatness. . . ."
> (*Gospel of Mary* 9).[1]

In comparison to the canonical text the roles of Jesus and Mary are
reversed: it is not Jesus who confirms Mary's message, but Mary who
takes the place of Jesus in order to remind the disciples of their common assignment to preach. While in the canonical text she meets with
disbelief among the disciples, in the Gnostic text she is successful: the
disciples do in fact become active in doing as they were commanded
(*GMary* 19).

The comparison of these two texts makes it clear that in the second century there was a broad stream of tradition running alongside
the collection of texts designated in retrospect as the "canon" (=
norm). In that parallel stream themes and personalities were depicted

differently than in the New Testament, and this is especially true of the significance and function of the disciple called Mary.

Many of these "apocryphal" writings from the second and third centuries were created in Christian Gnostic communities.

The teachings of the Gnostics were known for many centuries only from the point of view of ecclesial authors, including Bishop Irenaeus of Lyons (ca. 177–202) and Tertullian (ca. 160–220). It was only the interest aroused by ancient papyri and their purchase by prominent museums in the eighteenth and nineteenth centuries, and above all the sensational discovery of a large group of papyri at Nag Hammadi (1945–6) that brought to public attention some Gnostic manuscripts of documents that originated in the second and third centuries and gave an authentic picture of the teaching and situation of Gnostic groups.

These writings were seen from the point of view of the developing "orthodox" Great Church as heretical or unorthodox; the same devaluation is retained in theology by describing them as "apocryphal." In retrospect we can understand this labeling, but it represents an anachronism in the context of the time when these documents were written because at that time it was by no means yet settled which side would ultimately prove to be orthodox or heretical. The very intensity of the battle against the "heretics" shows how strongly their attraction worked on the members of the Great Church. The Gnostics were part of a comprehensive movement out of which the orthodox Great Church crystallized in the course of the second and third centuries. Gnostic statements about Mary Magdalene must therefore be considered as a legitimate possibility for Christian expression about this biblical figure.

1. The Mediator of Revelation

The Gnostics, like many later "heretics," saw themselves as the true Christians. Against the Church's claims to truth they set up their own claims to apostolic tradition.[2] Some, in doing so, referred their claims to persons outside the circle of the Twelve—Paul, for example, or Mary Magdalene—while others asserted that the Twelve, to whom the Church referred its claims, had not yet received genuine enlightenment (= *gnōsis*); still others accepted the idea of a group of twelve but defined it differently from the Church's concept. Thus in *Pistis Sophia* Jesus says that at the command of the First Mystery he had taken twelve powers from the treasury of light and placed them in the wombs of women from whom were born the twelve disciples: that is, the Twelve did not belong to the evil earthly cosmos, but came from the sphere of the Redeemer (and thus were pre-existent). Only they could save the world.[3] The group of these twelve disciples or brothers, in spite of the masculine terms, comprised eight male and four female disciples, including Mary Magdalene.[4] Hence she also belonged to the group who, according to Jesus' promise, would sit on twelve thrones and judge the twelve tribes of Israel (*Pistis Sophia* 50; cf. Matt 19:28; Luke 22:30). Within this group, in fact, Mary has a special place, sometimes alone and sometimes together with others:

> But Mary Magdalene and John the Virgin will be superior to all my disciples. And all men who will receive mysteries in the Ineffable will be on my left and on my right. And I am they and they are I. And they will be equal to you in everything. (*Pistis Sophia* 96)

The next clauses are partly corrupted; according to the editor they read:

> except that your thrones will be superior to theirs, (namely those of Mary and John) and my own throne will be superior to yours.[5]

Mary Magdalene is frequently the spokesperson for the disciples as well; the frequency and quality of her questions, which advance central Gnostic themes, distinguish her from the others.[6]

This special position is acknowledged by the other disciples because Mary is in possession of special revelation that is hidden from the rest. Thus Peter urges her to speak the words of the Redeemer that are known only to her and not to the others (*GMary* 10); she then repeats the content of a vision. In Gnostic understanding it is precisely such secret revelations that bring salvation, not the teachings available to everyone, such as those found in the apostolic tradition of the Church; to that extent Mary, with her special knowledge, is the prime example of a Gnostic Christian. Although she is equipped with "*gnōsis*," that is, knowledge and wisdom (she speaks as "a woman who had understood completely"[7]) she has not acquired it through her own efforts, but because the Redeemer himself has filled her with knowledge and understanding (*GMary* 18).

The importance of Mary is evident especially from her closeness to Jesus, who "did love her more" than the other female and male disciples (*GMary* 10; *GPhilip*, Logion 55). The mutual relationship between Jesus and Mary is a "love affair," although it only appears to have erotic content. "Love" and "knowledge" are interchangeable concepts, as Levi's short saying about Mary shows: "Certainly the

Saviour knows her surely enough. Therefore did he love her more than us" (*GMary* 18).

Jesus knows and loves Mary and fills her with knowledge; in turn, Mary knows Jesus and hands on her knowledge to the disciples. In her position between Jesus and the disciples Mary Magdalene is both the recipient of revelation and its mediator.

2. The Life-Partner of the Redeemer

The *Gospel of Philip* goes beyond the functional description of Mary as mediator of revelation and gives her a place in the Gnostic myth: She is the companion or life-partner of the Redeemer, who loved her and often kissed her on the mouth.

This collection of sayings speaks in Logion 32 of three women who were always with the Redeemer: his mother, his (or her?) sister, and Mary Magdalene, "who is called his companion." The word "companion," which is repeated in the next sentence, indicates a female partner (in sexual intercourse) or the mythical "life-companion." This plays off the Gnostic concept of the syzygy, that is, the primal unity, its shattering (that is, the Fall as a division between the sexes), and its restoration. For this last act every pneumatic will constitute a "pair" or syzygy with his or her angel. The primal heavenly image of this union is the myth of the bridal chamber, the pairing of Christ and the (lower-ranking) Sophia, whose earthly figures are Jesus and Mary Magdalene. In their union the One is symbolically restored. At the same time, as a couple they are the primal image of the Gnostic sacrament of the bridal chamber (the earthly sacrament of the bridal chamber is the image of the bridal chamber above: Logion 76), and they perform (in figure, as do the believers) the kiss as symbol of the One:

> The perfect conceive through a kiss and give birth. Because of this we also kiss one another. We receive conception from the grace which we have among us. (Logion 31)

In this double sequence of primal image and figure the role of Mary Magdalene is especially emphasized because her partner is not an angel, as is the case with other people, but the Redeemer himself, as another saying tells:

> The Sophia who is called barren is the mother of the [angels] and the companion of the S[aviour] [Ma]ry Mag[da]lene. The S[aviour] lov]ed Mary more than [all] the disciples, and kissed on her [mouth] often. . . . (Logion 55)

Anyone who, like Mary Magdalene, has received the kiss is free from the deadly powers of the universe; he or she is redeemed.[8]

According to another interpretation Mary Magdalene is even identified with Sophia herself and in this role she can be understood, together with the Redeemer, as a part of the heavenly world of light.[9]

Expressions like bridal chamber, kiss, or (love-)partner, in spite of their erotic connotations, do not suggest libertine rituals such as have often been attributed to the Gnostics; as in other mystical texts they express spiritual things in erotic language. The same mythical subject (redemption) can be described in other terminology: when sexual differences are abolished, when male and female have become meaningless, then freedom from matter and the cosmos has also been achieved. Against this background as well Mary Magdalene is acknowledged as a model.

3. The Pneumatic Mary

Mary Magdalene achieved the goal of the Gnostic path to knowledge and redemption before all the other disciples: she became free of (evil) matter; she was spirit and no longer matter; therefore Jesus was amazed at her because she had "completely become pure Spirit" and he praised her as "thou pure spiritual one, Maria" (*Pistis Sophia* 87). Hence she was also no longer imprisoned in the earthly cosmos, in darkness, but had already made the transition to the new reality, the realm of light; this, too, is attested by a saying of Jesus in which he rejoices in her previous knowledge-filled words: "Excellent, Mariam, thou blessed one, who wilt inherit the whole Kingdom of the Light" (*Pistis Sophia* 61).

The aforementioned contrasting pairs describe the tension in the Gnostic worldview: the pure and the cosmic world, spirit and matter, light and darkness, male and female. Mary Magdalene always stands on the side of purity, spirit, and light. This in turn is the reason why she—although a woman!—had such a high position in Gnosticism: it was not her gender, which belongs to matter, that is significant, but her being filled with the Spirit; for everyone "in whom the power of his Spirit has welled up" (*Pistis Sophia* 36) may speak, whether man or woman, Peter or Mary.

Such statements are important when we consider whether the literary role of Mary Magdalene had any practical significance for the situation of women in Gnostic communities, for it was not as a woman, but as a pneumatic that she was honored. It is true, of course, that the outstanding position of Mary Magdalene as a perfect Gnostic could not have been "without influence on concrete social situations,"[10] but still we must maintain that in the Gnostic conception she became a model not *as a woman,* but *as a human being.* According to the *Gospel of Mary,* in fact, all the disciples, whether male or female, surpassed their gender because Jesus "made us ready, and made us to be [human beings]" (*GMary* 9).

Mary's function as model and its influence on the praxis of community life did not play themselves out in the realm of sexuality (that is, femaleness), but along pneumatic lines. Still, the consequences for female members of the community were positive nonetheless. Whether or not one posits a connection between religious theory and social praxis in this case[11] one may assume that the Gnostic communities were so attractive to women that women made up the majority of members.[12]

In the Gnostic communities it appears that the primitive Christian provocation of a situation in which "in Christ" there was no more male and female (Gal 3:28) remained in force. As (on the basis of this principle) there was a broad field of opportunity for women in the Pauline communities (cf. Phoebe, Prisca, Junia, and others), so also in the Gnostic communities that thus "had a closer relationship to the beginnings of Christianity than to their contemporary Christians of the third generation"; it was not the Gnostics who were the heretics, but rather in them "the orthodox were transformed into heretics."[13] As the developing Great Church distanced itself more and more from its egalitarian beginnings and adopted existing social norms in its own sphere (cf. the hierarchical structure of the community as figure of the ancient household, with primacy of the *paterfamilias!*), the Gnostics were less thoroughly adapted and thus more attractive to women.

Two contrary tendencies appear thereby to have been mutually supportive: against the loose organization in Gnostic communities the Church developed fixed functions, especially the unifying position of the bishop; in turn the Gnostic communities rejected a spiritual authority that, from their point of view, was derived not from God but from the demiurge, the creator of the evil world. The bishop, who in his own understanding was a representative of God, was for the Gnostics only the representative of the demiurge and could not expect obedience from the "initiated" believers. Hence Gnostic communities sought other community forms in opposition to the existing ecclesial structures. Irenaeus describes a group who revived the biblical practice of casting lots (cf. Acts 1:26) and distributed the necessary duties in their community life according to the luck of the draw.[14] If the roles of bishops, priests, prophets, or simple believers were newly allotted at every meeting, that procedure excluded any possibility that individuals could possess a particular office "in perpetuity." Irenaeus was as disgusted by this practice in the neighborhood of his community in Lyons as was Tertullian in a different location: the latter criticized the undignified meetings "without authority, without ecclesial discipline" and without distinction of functions.[15]

Besides the general "disorder" in the Gnostic communities it was especially the position of women and the opportunities made available to them that disgusted the men of the Church: "They [= the heretical women] are bold enough to teach, to engage in argument, to enact exorcisms, to undertake cures, and, it may be, even to baptize."[16] When such rights are accorded to women, clear words are necessary: "It is not permitted for a woman to speak in the church, nor is it permitted for her to teach, nor to baptize, nor to offer [the eucharist], nor to claim for herself a share in any masculine function—not to mention any priestly office."[17] The list of what is forbidden itself shows what was possible for women: teaching and administration of the sacraments including the confection of the Eucharist. These statements are confirmed by Irenaeus (women take the cup with the mixed wine and speak the thanksgiving); he adds prophecy as well.[18]

The appearance of women among the Gnostics corresponds to their refusal to accommodate to common social norms, while in turn the church communities very early conformed to the social conditions of the Gentile world, felt concern for their good reputation among outsiders, and therefore sacrificed the equality of women and slaves (1 Tim 6:1; Titus 2:5). If thus in the private sphere people were concerned to "take the wind out of the sails" of critical observers "by means of an orderly Christian household,"[19] how much more was that the case for the community in its public role. The pressure from outside and the resulting repression of women in the Church may also have "resulted from Christianity's move up the social scale from lower to middle class."[20] While women's labor was employed in the lower class, the middle order separated the public and private spheres: women were subject to the dependency of the patriarchally organized household, which also had consequences for the church communities. This view of church development has been generally accepted in recent scholarship; what remains controversial is the evaluation of the fact itself, that is, whether it was a matter of historical necessity or not.[21]

Gnostic communities did not surrender to the social pressure to conform; they preserved the primitive Christian freedom to have "chaos" in their meetings, and thus also retained a free space for women. Here (community) praxis corresponded to (theological) theory: "My Lord, my mind is understanding at all times that I should come forward at any time and give the interpretation of the words" (*Pistis Sophia* 72), says Mary Magdalene, and Jesus confirms her in this active role. Where polarity of the sexes was suppressed in favor of spirit-filled reason, as in the case of Mary Magdalene, the women of the community could be recognized as pneumatics with equal privileges.

4. The Rival of Peter

If ecclesial authors put special emphasis on the prominence of women as characteristic of heretical groups, the Gnostic authors react by personalizing the contrast in terms of symbolic figures. In a number of texts, therefore, Peter and Mary Magdalene are represented as rivals, thus embodying orthodox (and from a Gnostic perspective unenlightened) Christianity and their own superior position. In the *Gospel of Mary* she conveys to the disciples the secret words of the Redeemer that are hidden from them, and reports on a teaching that was given her in a vision; at first Andrew and then Peter register unwillingness to receive this teaching. Peter asks the other disciples: "Did he then speak privily with a woman rather than with us, and not openly?" (*GMary* 17). This position on the part of Peter contains two accusations that were leveled at the Gnostics by their ecclesial critics:

1. The Church derived its legitimation from what Jesus said "openly" to the apostles, which had been handed on to all the churches by their successors, even to the present, whereas the Gnostics put their emphasis on individual inspiration by the Spirit. This conflict between office and individual was presaged as early as the end of the first century in the so-called ecclesial redaction of the Fourth Gospel: with the transfer of office to Peter (John 21) the prior encounter between Jesus and Mary Magdalene was reduced to an event of purely individual significance. Here already the conflict between Peter and Mary was laid down.

2. The holders of ecclesial office were successors of Peter and the other (male) apostles. Female claims are decisively rejected by

"Peter," while his outraged questions, "Shall we turn about and all hearken unto her? Has he preferred her over against us?" (*GMary* 17) are, from the point of view of the Gnostic author and his communities, clearly to be answered in the affirmative.

Similar tendencies are evident also in *Pistis Sophia*. Peter complains to Jesus that Mary speaks too often (which, in the view of this document, attests that she is more intensely filled with the Spirit). Since Mary afterward keeps silent out of fear of Peter, Jesus himself urges her to speak for the following reason: "Everyone who will be filled with the Spirit of light to come forward and give the interpretation of those things which I say, him will no one be able to prevent" (*Pistis Sophia* 72).

Here again competing claims stand behind the figures of Peter and Mary Magdalene: the ecclesial officeholders and the Gnostics filled with the spirit of light, or in other words male and female claims. These and similar texts[22] reflect the then-current situation of the struggle between the Great Church and Gnosticism, in which the Gnostic community identified with the symbolic figure of Mary Magdalene. Peter in this connection embodies the Church, but also the mass of "ordinary" Christians, while Mary Magdalene stands for the elite gifted with enlightenment.

5. Mary as "Man"

The statement that Mary Magdalene is not respected in Gnostic literature as a woman, but as a pneumatic, should be critically examined. Gnostic anthropology, to put the matter in the simplest terms, rests on the idea of an original male-female unity (androgyny). Original sin consists in a disruption of that unity, and the goal of the path of redemption is seen as the removal of gender differences. According to the depiction in the *Gospel of Mary* all the disciples, male and female, have reached this state, for Mary says of herself and the other disciples, "He has made us ready and made us [human beings]," and Levi challenges the other disciples to "put on the perfect [human being]" (*GMary* 9, 18). But this is not true in all the documents. In the *Gospel of Thomas* there is a problematic passage dealing specifically with Mary Magdalene. Jesus replies to Peter's saying that Mary and other women are not worthy of life with the following "promise":

> Look, I will lead her that I may make her male, in order that she too may become a living spirit resembling you males. For every woman

who makes herself male will enter into the kingdom of heaven. (*GThom* 114).

In the background of this alienating passage is the idea of a double polarity: male/female, spirit/matter. Only when women divest themselves of their femaleness, that is, their (evil) material aspect, can they attain to the side of the Spirit. Therefore, while there was practical and cultic equality for women in Gnosticism, that status was not generally maintained at the ideological level, for the division of sexes, as an evil of the earthly sphere, began with the (culpable!) separation of the woman from the man (differently Gen 2:21-22) and therefore is clearly the woman's fault.[23] While in the *Gospel of Mary* women and men are equally challenged to surpass their gender in order to become perfect human beings, that expectation is only applied to women in the *Gospel of Thomas*.[24] In this process Mary Magdalene has a special position only to the extent that Jesus himself leads her on this way.

In connection with this idea of becoming male the texts about the "pneumatic Mary" also appear in a different light: her position in Gnosticism was dearly bought. If Mary Magdalene gradually declined in the orthodox Church *because of her femaleness,* her ascent in Gnosticism was achieved precisely *at the price of her femaleness.* Hence in the end it is questionable whether the Gnostic Mary Magdalene is really of any value as a model for today's women.

Notes

[1]The gospels of Mary, Philip, and Thomas are cited, when not otherwise noted, from Wilhelm Schneemelcher, ed., *New Testament Apocrypha I: Gospels and Related Writings,* translated by R. McL. Wilson (rev. ed. Louisville, Ky.: Westminster/John Knox, 1991, 110–33 *(GThom)*, 179–208 *(GPhilip)*, 391–5 *(GMary)*.

[2]Elaine Pagels, *The Gnostic Gospels* (New York: Random House, 1979) 22.

[3]*Pistis Sophia* 7. This work is cited from the edition by Carl Schmidt, with translation and notes by Violet Macdermot. The Coptic Gnostic Library 9 (Leiden: Brill, 1978).

[4]On this see Renate Schmid, *Maria Magdalena in gnostischen Schriften.* Material-Edition 29. (Munich, 1990), 46–7.

[5]Schmidt and Macdermot, *Pistis Sophia,* 96.

[6]Schmid, *Maria Magdalena,* 83–4.

[7]*Dialogue of the Savior,* 139, 8-13; quoted from James M. Robinson, ed., *The Nag Hammadi Library* (3rd rev. ed. San Francisco: Harper & Row, 1988) 252.

[8]Translation by Hans-Martin Schenke in Schneemelcher, *New Testament Apocrypha,* 1:179–208. For the connections, here described in very simple terms, cf. Schmid, *Maria Magdalena,* 32–9.

[9]This is suggested by Schneemelcher as probable: Mary Magdalene is the companion of the Savior (Logion 32); Sophia is the companion of the Savior (Logion 55).

[10]Schmid, *Maria Magdalena,* 89.

[11]Pagels, *Gnostic Gospels,* 60, in the affirmative; Susanne Heine, *Frauen der frühen Christenheit* (Göttingen, 1986) 191 n. 378, in the negative.

[12]Heine, *Frauen der frühen Christenheit,* 142.

[13]Susanne Heine, "Selig durch Kindergebären (1 Tim 2:15)?" in Marie-Theres Wacker, ed., *Theologie feministisch* (Düsseldorf, 1988) 59–77 at 75–6.

[14]Irenaeus, *Adv. Haer.,* 1.13.4.

[15]Tertullian, *De praescriptione haereticorum,* 41, quoted from *Bibliothek der Kirchenväter,* 24 (Kempten and Munich, 1915). On this, cf. Pagels, *Gnostic Gospels,* 28–47; she depicts the development of the monarchical episcopate as a political function of the theological doctrine of monotheism.

[16]Tertullian, *De praescr. haer.,* 41, quoted from Pagels, *Gnostic Gospels,* 60; cf. also Irenaeus, *Adv. Haer.,* 1.13.5, where he designates the attraction of women to Gnosticism as "defilement."

[17]Tertullian, *De virginibus velandis,* 9; quoted from Pagels, *Gnostic Gospels,* 60.

[18]Irenaeus, *Adv. Haer.,* 1.13.2–3. As early as the NT women's charismata of teaching and prophecy were suppressed; besides 1 Timothy 2:11-12 cf. also the denigration of the anonymous prophet and teacher dubbed with the negatively-colored name "Jezebel" in Revelation 2.

[19]Heine, *Frauen,* 143.

[20]Pagels, *Gnostic Gospels,* 63.

[21]Schüssler Fiorenza in particular (*In Memory of Her,* 82–3) defends against attempts to understand this development as "necessary" (as do Gerd Theissen and Elaine Pagels).

[22]That "Peter" tries to forbid women in general from speaking is evident from his request that women cease to ask questions and that they give way to the male disciples (*Pistis Sophia,* 146).

[23]On this cf. Kurt Rudolph, *Gnosis. The Nature and History of Gnosticism,* translation edited by R. McL. Wilson (San Francisco: Harper & Row, 1983) 270–2.

[24]There is a similar idea in early Islam as well: "If a woman follows the way of God as a man does, she cannot be called a woman." Quoted from Friedrich Heiler, *Die Frau in den Religionen der Menschheit* (Berlin and New York: Walter de Gruyter, 1977) 82.

Chapter Three

Mary Magdalene as Interpreted by the Medieval Mystics

Medieval scriptural interpreters had very little interest in the literal meaning of a biblical text. Such a literal understanding was regarded as characteristic of the uneducated; those with true knowledge advanced to the "real meaning" of what was written. This *sensus plenior* was discovered through allegorical interpretation, typological correspondences, popular etymologies, comparisons or practical moral applications in which the biblical passage was used as an inspirational or deterrent example. The idea of "multiple meanings of Scripture" as encountered in sermon texts, liturgical songs, or the illustrations in the so-called "poor people's Bibles" shaped the medieval image of Mary Magdalene and placed it within a rich relational context. She is not only a figure from the time of Jesus (see chapter 4 for an account of how she became confused with other New Testament women), but also is presented in various ways as model or image of the unity of salvation history. With Gregory the Great and the other Church Fathers ecclesiological correspondences are paramount (for example, Mary and the bride in the Song of Songs as images of the Church), while at a later period more individual comparisons were common (for example, Mary and the bride as images of the pious soul).

The multifaceted texture of images, only a tiny selection of which can be described here, shows that in exegetical and homiletic literature Mary Magdalene was not only an individual saint but a "theological figure" brought into play to support very different statements. An important initiator of all this was Gregory the Great, who on the one hand stood within a rich exegetical tradition, and on the other hand became an inspiration for later preachers and authors.

1. Bride and Church

Mary, who (in contrast to the flight of the male disciples) stood steadfast at Jesus' tomb, was held up for praise by Gregory, but not for her own sake: she was already prefigured in the bride of the Song of Songs and is at the same time, in a deeper sense, an image of the Church. As the bride goes about seeking the beloved in the nighttime (Song 3:1-2), so Mary remained by the tomb at night—not as an individual, but as the embodiment of the holy Church.[1]

The contrasting behavior of the fleeing male disciples and the faithful female disciple is also mentioned with praise in Odo's sermon on Magdalene, but because the connection to the Church is not drawn his reference to the bride's nighttime search (Song 3:1-4) is no longer unrestrictedly positive: the darkness at the tomb is a symbol of the heart that does not yet know of the resurrection; Mary sees the stone at the tomb but not the sun of the resurrection. Nevertheless, Odo does not entirely forget the connection to the Church: the confusion of the Lord with the gardener is still a sign of deficient faith, but the woman is not wholly in error because Christ is really the Lord of the garden that is the Church.[2] The high evaluation of the steadfastly seeking woman as epitome of the Church also occasions the preacher's reference to her gender; in connection with her being forbidden to touch the risen Lord he explicitly emphasizes that this has nothing to do with a depreciation of the female gender, and the contrary opinion that the Risen One did not wish to be touched by a woman is repeatedly denied.[3]

In the high and late Middle Ages the ecclesiological connection dissolved, but the typological correspondence of the bride with Mary Magdalene was retained, especially in the pictures in the "poor people's Bibles" of the thirteenth to fifteenth centuries. The "image" of Mary seeking Jesus in the tomb is coupled with the "model" of the woman who "with pious prayers" seeks the bridegroom; the "image" that shows Jesus and Mary in the scene of recognition is coupled with that of the bride and bridegroom.[4] These citations through pictures are usually accompanied by quotations from Scripture that explain the connection intended: the bride's and Mary's seeking and finding correspond to the texts "I sought him whom my soul loves; I sought him, but found him not" (Song 3:1-2) and "I found him whom my soul loves. I held him, and would not let him go" (Song 3:4). The *Salzburger Armenbibel (Salzburg Bible for the Poor)* adds the clarifying note:

> The bride is the model for Mary Magdalene, who sought her beloved, Christ, in the grave. . . . This bride means Mary Magdalene, who saw and wanted to hold fast to her beloved bridegroom, Christ.

Nevertheless, both the bride and Mary Magdalene are in turn "models" of the soul that seeks Jesus, her bridegroom.

2. A Church of Gentiles and Sinners

Mary Magdalene, who sinks weeping at the feet of the Lord as a repentant sinner, is widely held to be an image of the Gentiles, or rather of a Church made up of baptized Gentiles.[5] Gregory the Great took up this comparison and contrasted the Pharisee as image of the false righteousness of the Jewish people to the sinful woman as image of the converted Gentile world: while the Pharisees and the Jews refused to kiss the Lord, the sinful woman who represents both the bride of the Song of Songs (Song 1:1) and the converted Gentiles kisses him unceasingly.[6] At the same time a new connection appears in Gregory's work: the more infant baptism became the norm and the conversion of pagans the exception, the more the typological reference shifted. Increasingly the repentant sinner ceases to represent the Gentiles and stands instead for sinners within the Church who are prepared to do penance.

For Odo this idea is already a matter of course: the woman represents the Church.[7] This woman's tears of regret and penitence recall the water of baptism in which sins are washed away, and as repentance at that time had been fulfilled in literally following the Lord, so now it is completed in the imitation of his deeds.[8]

The same kind of typological thought is found also in ancient hymns in which Mary Magdalene is not yet personally addressed but, following Gregory, is represented as an "image" for the Church of converted Gentiles (the sinful Magdalene represents the "*proselytam ecclesiam*") and as a "model" for sinners within the Church ("*Haec sunt convivia / quae tibi placent*").[9]

As a supra-personal image she can even incorporate several aspects of salvation history and sometimes alter their meaning. In the sequence *Exsurgat totus almiphorus* by Hermann of Reichenau she appears as the image for three different collective entities: as sinner, convert, and recipient of grace she embodies unredeemed humanity (= Babylon), the converting Old Testament community (= Zion), and the eschatologically exalted Church (= heavenly Jerusalem).[10]

3. Witness to and Example of Divine Mercy

Mary Magdalene is not only a type of the Church as an abstract entity but also serves as an *example* to individual sinners of the value of penitence and conversion and as *witness* to divine mercy. Gregory was also the one who laid the foundations for this complex of meanings: according to him the woman embodies us, the sinners in the Church, when we repent from the heart, as she did, and imitate her penitence, and we may regard her together with Peter, Zacchaeus, and other repentant sinners as an example of the application of divine mercy.[11] In the future, whenever a sinner begs God for mercy he or she can call upon Mary Magdalene as a model.

In a tenth-century prayer Mary is mentioned first, together with the thief, David, Peter, and Lazarus as examples of the redeemed; the prayer asks that God, who comforted the weeping Magdalene, may also be merciful to us who pray:

> *Lacrimantem consolisti*
> *Mariam, te deprecantem*
> *Indulgentiam donasti:*
> *Misericors et nobis parce,*
> *Lux et lumen, deus.*[12]

4. Mary and Martha: The Perfected Christian Life

Since Mary of Magdala is equated with the woman with the same name from Bethany, the sisters Mary and Martha are also drawn into this typological interpretation: the two sisters are an image of the Church with Martha embodying the Church that receives Christ here on earth and works for him and Mary representing the same Church when it withdraws from material labor and devotes itself to the contemplative life.[13] At the same time the sisters are contrasted with one another as different models of Christian life. But according to Ambrose they may not be isolated from each other because otherwise action *(actio)* would be vain and attentive listening *(intentio)* feeble, so that Christian life is only embodied in its completeness by the two working together.[14] With Gregory, on the other hand, the preeminence of the contemplative life has already triumphed. In a letter to Gregoria he describes the model discipleship of the sinful woman:

> . . . she sat at the Lord's feet and listened to his words. Sunk in the contemplative life, she had already elevated herself above the active life still led by her sister.

This preeminence is connected with the objects with which one is occupied: Martha deals with visible, temporal, secular things, while Mary is concerned with the invisible, the eternal, the heavenly:[15]

> The contemplative Mary is first of all merely the image of the Church that withdraws from the active life to immerse itself in the divine mysteries; it is only the interest of the hagiographers in her personal life that takes its starting point here and describes the contemplative life of Mary Magdalene in her solitude.[16]

The primacy of the contemplative over the active (and secular!) life may correspond to the ideals of many priests and monastics, but there are wise religious who guard against despising secular life and automatically according monks a preeminence over people in the world;[17] references to Martha and Mary in particular are regarded as ideal for countering any kind of spiritual pride. An especially fine example of this kind is found in the "Fathers' Book" under the title "An Example from Mary and Martha" (V.2.989–20.256). To Abbot Silvanus and his brothers comes a stranger guest who is surprised that the brothers work so diligently to earn their living. He criticizes them because one should not work for food that passes, but—following the example of Mary Magdalene—only for the things of eternity:

> *Vil gar daz beste hat irkorn (= erwählt)*
> *Maria Magdalena.*
> *Der soldet ir nu volgen na.*
> (For Mary Magdalene chose the best part, and you should follow her.)

The wise abbot is silent, but when the brothers are called to their meal after work the guest is "forgotten." When he complains, he receives this answer: "You, after all, are a spiritual person to whom one should not offer earthly food; but we are earthly folk":

> *Du hast das beste gar irwelt*
> *Als (= wie) Maria Magdalena,*
> *Der du volgest vaste na:*
> *Stete an den buchen lesen*
> *Unde an dime gebet wesen.*

(For you have chosen the best, like Mary Magdalene, whom you ardently
follow, constantly reading books and concentrating on your prayers.)

You have books and constant prayer, so you need no earthly nourishment! The guest understands the teaching and repents of his pride,
but Father Silvanus instructs him: Mary cannot live without Martha;
her freedom for the contemplative life is only made possible by
Martha's efforts. Many who live quietly in imitation of Mary are just
lazy! Blessed the one who follows both: "homage there cannot be
without work."

5. Mary Magdalene as Antitype to Eve

The role of the witness to the resurrection led to some unusual
typological comparisons. The woman, who had been the primeval
source of guilt at the beginning *("auctor culpae"),* is now permitted
to be the first to see the resurrection; as she tasted death before the
man, so she is now the first to receive the remedy.[18] Through Mary
Magdalene who proclaims life to the disciples the guilt of Eve, who
offered death to the man, is removed.[19] Eve and Mary Magdalene
stand in contrast to one another as death and life.

In time the two women were reduced to mere "hands" or
"mouths" that as *pars pro toto* came to represent the original sources
of death (Eve) and life (Mary Magdalene). From the mouth of a
woman death took its beginning, and through the mouth of a woman
life was restored;[20] from the same hand that gave the man death to
drink he now receives joy and everlasting life.[21]

The primary interest in contemplating this event is not the fame
of the messenger of joy, but the praise of God who has taken away the
shame that had lain on the female gender since Eve: "It is a wonderful
providence of God's goodness that life was proclaimed by a woman,
for once in Paradise death came forth from a woman's mouth."[22] Because disgrace has lain on the female sex since Eve, so Odo tells us,[23]
God wanted to announce the joy of the resurrection to men through
a woman and so deliver the female sex from its disgrace; Mary Magdalene is, for him, the chosen instrument of this. At about the same period God was being praised in spiritual songs as well because of the
parallelism of the two women *(per stultam mulierem / per bonam
mulierem)* from whom have come death and life for the world.[24]

The examples here given, that see in Mary Magdalene the messenger of life and joy, are sustained by their opposite pole, the mes-

senger of death: the image of Eve, who had long since been made the original source of sin and death, was further cemented by these contrasts.

The thoroughly negative image attached to Eve since the beginnings of Christianity has always carried with it consequences for the image of women in general; in the typological exegesis of the patristic period and the Middle Ages Eve is regarded not as an individual but as the embodiment of the female sex. Tertullian provides an especially clear example of this; he consistently reveals his misogynistic tendencies. In impressive rhetoric he asks his "well-beloved sisters," "Do you not know that you are Eve?" in order then to tell them that God is against their gender because "you [i. e., women in general] are the devil's gate and you have destroyed the man, the image of God" (*Cult. fem.* 1.1.1.2). The woman is thus the origin of evil both in the human world (Gen 3) and in the heavenly world of the angels (Gen 6), for because of the beauty of women the sin of concupiscence even reached the angels (*Cult. fem.* 1.2.1; *Virg. vel.* 7.6-7). Because women are identified with Eve they all have reason to do penance throughout their lives.

Tertullian directs such statements at Eve and the female sex in general, not (as was the case with other ancient Christian authors) primarily at sexual intercourse; after all, Eve (and later the fair daughters of humanity) were virgins and not yet women "dishonored" by men (cf. *Virg. vel.* 5; 7.6-7).[25]

Only here and there do we find recollections of the New Testament idea that sin and death originated with Adam (cf. Rom 5:12-16). In this vein Adam and Mary Magdalene represent the turning points of salvation history in the hymn *Jesu Christe, auctor vitae.*[26] Adam stands at the beginning of the story of sin and Mary Magdalene at the beginning of the story of salvation that achieves a new beginning through the blood of Christ.

6. Miriam (Mary) and Mary Magdalene

Besides Eve (and Adam) as negative forerunners of Mary Magdalene there was also a positive precursor: Miriam with her tambourine, who led the song of thanksgiving. She is not only a singer but also a prophet; what is said of her in the literal sense, that she was health and salvation for bodies, means in a spiritual sense that she was health and salvation for souls in the water of baptism. The first Mary/Miriam is an image of the New Testament Mary, and as the former was considered a prophet, so the latter was called *apostola apostolorum,* a title due to her because she was the first to proclaim to the apostles the joy of the resurrection.[27] The typological association between Mary and Miriam lies here in their public proclamation; both scenes have a basis in profound joy.

There is a further correspondence between these two women: the scene with the penitent sinner who throws herself at the Lord's feet is also modeled on Miriam, who sinned against her brother Moses, was stricken with leprosy, and when she repented was healed through the intercession of Moses (Num 12:1-15).[28] The *Salzburger Armenbibel* says of this: "Moses, indeed, is a model of Christ who freed Mary Magdalene from all the impurities of her sins." Here, then, the commonality of the two women is seen in their bodily and spiritual healing; they are thus also a model for sinners who are comforted with references to these and other biblical passages.

7. Mary Magdalene and Her Male Models

The typological imagery is oriented not only to gender, but also to similar situations. Hence men of the First Testament could also be proposed as models for Mary Magdalene. In particular the "poor people's Bibles" show how particular contexts became fixed models, because the same images were used in different Bibles:

• The sinner is represented not only by the leprous Miriam, but also by King David, who repented of his sin after being accused by Nathan (2 Sam 12): "The repentant David indeed represents the repentant Mary Magdalene."[29]

• Mary Magdalene among the women at the tomb has a model in the figure of Reuben, who discovered the empty well after his brothers had sold the youthful Joseph (Gen 37): "This Reuben represents Mary Magdalene, who in great distress sought Christ in the grave."[30]

• Mary Magdalene on Easter morning is the bride who rejoices over the bridegroom; but she is also represented by the king from the book of Daniel who threw Daniel into the lions' den and rejoiced to find him alive (Dan 6: King Darius; Dan 12: Cyrus). Their joy over the living one unites Mary and the king: "This king is a model for Mary Magdalene. . . ."[31]

8. Mary and Mary

The similarity of the names of the two women who played a role at the beginning and end of Jesus' earthly life has occupied many authors and led quite a number to generalizing reflections on the female sex. Such thoughts are succinctly summarized in the *Golden Legend*: ". . . as womankind was not excluded from knowledge of the mysteries of the Incarnation and the Resurrection, neither was the angelic messenger excluded. God made both of these mysteries known through angels, the Incarnation to the Virgin Mary and the Resurrection to Mary Magdalene."[32] This very comparison between the two Marys demands emphasis on the apostolic significance of Mary Magdalene. Where the first Mary is the queen of the saints, the latter is their *apostola*.[33] Peter Abelard was apparently the first to use the title "apostle to the apostles" for Mary Magdalene (see n. 27), thus summarizing previous statements about her apostolic witness in a pregnant short formula, but as early as Odo of Cluny the presuppositions for the title were already at hand,[34] for he saw in Mary Magdalene not only the messenger *(nuntia)* but also the companion of the apostles *(apostolorum consors)*.[35] Her name, "Mary," is thus rightly interpreted as *stella maris* ("star of the sea"), for as the virgin Mary brought to the world the sun of justice, so Mary Magdalene was the first to reflect the light of the resurrection. At the end of his sermon Odo extends what he has said so far and applies the title of apostle to Mary Magdalene: as the disciples were called apostles because they preached the gospel to the world, the blessed Mary Magdalene was chosen by the same Lord for the office of apostle.[36]

Medieval preachers never tired of reflecting on this astonishing fact: the Risen One showed himself first not to his mother, not to the apostles, but to the sinful woman, and made her an apostle.[37] This apostolic role, however, had no consequences for the image of Mary Magdalene. She was certainly the teacher and *apostola* to the apostles, but her apostolate, unlike that of the male apostles, was exhausted in the carrying out of her assignment. She was *apostola* on Easter morning and that was that for the rest of the Church's history. The same is true of the comparison between the Marys: the honorific titles of the mother of Jesus became a matter of course (Virgin, Mother of God, Queen of Heaven), while the title *apostola* remained without consequence. Even the hagiographers who depicted Mary Magdalene as an eloquent preacher placed her after the "bishops" Lazarus and Maximus.

9. Mary Magdalene and the Mystery of the Incarnation

Since in medieval scriptural interpretation not a single word or phrase in the Bible meant only what the words in the text mean, but

were each overlaid by multiple meanings, apparently incidental remarks and marginal details could also point to deeper meanings. The
pursuit of such connections was such a joyful enterprise that the same
Bible verse could support numerous (often very different) interpretations. Thus allegorical interpretation of the stories of the tomb and
the anointing led, among other interpretations, primarily to statements about the progress of recognition of the incarnation: Mary
Magdalene thus "learns" to understand the mystery of the divinity
and humanity of Jesus:

• In John 20:12 the precise location of the two angels at Jesus'
tomb is given: the one is sitting where the head was laid, the other
where the feet had been. In Gregory's allegorical interpretation this
information is a reference to the doctrine of two natures: the angel at
the head represents the divinity (see John 1:1: the Word was God),
and the angel at the feet represents the humanity (see John 1:14: the
Word became flesh). This interpretation was taken over, almost word
for word, by many authors, but it did not exclude other interpretations: the angels can also represent the two testaments, both of which
proclaim the resurrection.[38]

• Because Mary Magdalene had already had a special relationship with the head and feet of Jesus she—on the basis of the three
anointings[39]—is seen especially as an image of progressive recognition
of Christ's true nature: the anointings progress from the feet (the
anointing by the sinful woman) to the head (anointing before the Passion) and finally to the whole body (anointing after the crucifixion, or
on Easter day). In the spiritual interpretation of these texts Mary is an
image of the way that every understanding must follow.

Here again additional meanings are possible: anointing by Mary
Magdalene is foreshadowed by the bride who sends forth a precious
aroma for the king (Song 1:12) and at the same time points to the
Church whose aroma consists of faith and devotion. Just as Judas
criticizes the woman's deed, the same befalls the Church, but the
works that are distasteful to its opponents are pleasing to God.[40]

At the end of this brief selection of spiritual interpretations we
may make several observations:

1. Medieval exegesis made *different and much more varied associations* with Mary Magdalene than we are accustomed to in the later
restriction of her image to that of a converted whore.

2. Mary Magdalene was seen by many authors as a (collective) *symbol* and not yet as a fixed and defined *person;* the image of the individual saint was only beginning to emerge.

3. The unified figure of Mary Magdalene thus described is in the strict sense not *biblical;* she is rather a *Christian* figure embodying an unsuspected spiritual wealth that should be preserved.

Notes

[1] *"Hinc est enim quod de eodem sponso Ecclesia in Canticis Canticorum dicit . . . id est sanctam electorum Ecclesiam. . . ."* Gregory the Great, *Homily on John 20,* MPL 76.1190.

[2] Odo of Cluny, *Sermo II in veneratione sanctae Mariae Magdalenae,* MPL 133.718–9, 720.

[3] Gregory, MPL 76.1193; Odo, MPL 133.720. This "prohibition on touching" presupposes the Latin translation, *"Noli me tangere!"* while in the original Greek text she is forbidden to hold him fast (after she has already succeeded in touching him).

[4] Karl Forstner, ed. *Die Salzburger Armenbibel.* Codex aIX12, Archabbey of St. Peter at Salzburg: Salzburg, n. d. Pictorial groups 28 and 29. Maurus Berve, ed. *Die Armenbibel. Herkunft, Gestalt, Typologie. Dargestellt anhand von Miniaturen aus der Handschrift Cpg 148 der Universitätsbibliothek Heidelberg.* Beuron, 1969. Pictorial groups 34 and 35. [Translator's note: where I have "image" and "model" the author writes "Bild" and "Vorbild," a play on words that cannot be reproduced in English.]

[5] Victor Saxer, *Le Culte de Marie Madeleine en Occident des origines à la fin du moyen âge* (Paris, 1959) 328, with reference to Hilary of Poitiers and Ambrose.

[6] MPL 76.1242–3.

[7] MPL 133.715.

[8] *"Dominum sequitur non gressu pedis, sed imitatione operis,"* MPL 133.715.

[9] Cf. the Christ hymn *Laus tibi, Christe* (11th c.) quoted from Wiltrud aus der Fünten, *Maria Magdalena in der Lyrik des Mittelalters* (Düsseldorf, 1966) 57–62.

[10] Ibid. 70–76; cf. also the sequence *Laudum Christi Praeconia,* where the sinful woman also stands for Babylon and Jerusalem: ibid., 133.

[11] Gregory, MPL 76.1242, 1196.

[12] From the hymn *Age, deus, causam meam,* quoted from Wiltrud aus der Fünten, *Maria Magdalena,* 52.

[13] Saxer, *Le Culte,* 336, with reference to Isidore of Seville.

¹⁴Ambrose, MPL 15.1616–7.

¹⁵Gregory, BKV 2nd. ser. vol. 4, 295; cf. Odo, MPL 133.716–7.

¹⁶According to Honorius Augustodunensis, after Pentecost she will no longer look on other men and will live only from the love of Christ; hence she retires to a hermitage (*Speculum ecclesiae*, MPL 172.807–1108.98)1.

¹⁷In the Middle High German "Fathers' Book" the monk Silvanus receives a corresponding lesson: he sees in a vision how monks are entering eternal punishment while virtuous seculars are achieving eternal joy (V.14.274–84). *Das Väterbuch,* ed. Karl Reissenberger. Deutsche Texte des Mittelalters 22 (Berlin, 1914).

¹⁸Ambrose, MPL 15.1936.

¹⁹Gregory, MPL 76.1194; Honorius, MPL 172.981, and frequently elsewhere.

²⁰Ambrose, MPL 15.1937.

²¹Otfrid von Weissenburg, *Otfrids Evangelienbuch,* ed. Oskar Erdmann (4th ed. by Ludwig Wolf, Tübingen, 1962), Book 5, 8.45–58.

²²Gregory, BKV 2nd ser. 4.296.

²³Odo, MPL 133.721.

²⁴Thus in the song *Hic est dies,* cited by aus der Fünten, *Maria Magdalena,* 51; cf. also the sequence *Adest praecelsa,* ibid., 93.

²⁵Tertullian, *La Toilette des femmes / De cultu feminarum. Introduction, Texte critique, Traduction et Commentaire* by Marie Turcan (Paris, 1971); Tertullian, *De virginibus velandis,* ed. Christoph Stücklin (Bern and Frankfurt, 1974). For the Christian image of Eve see the monograph by Helen Schüngel-Straumann, *Die Frau am Anfang. Eva und die Folgen* (Freiburg, Basel, and Vienna: Herder, 1989).

²⁶Cf. aus der Fünten, *Maria Magdalena,* 55.

²⁷Peter Abelard, *Sermo 13 in die paschae,* MPL 178.484–5.

²⁸*Salzburger Armenbibel,* pictorial group 12; *Heidelberger Armenbibel,* pictorial group 13.

²⁹*Salzburger Armenbibel,* pictorial group 12; *Heidelberger Armenbibel,* pictorial group 13.

³⁰*Salzburger Armenbibel,* pictorial group 12; *Heidelberger Armenbibel,* pictorial group 34.

³¹*Salzburger Armenbibel,* pictorial group 29, with reference to Daniel 6; *Heidelberger Armenbibel,* pictorial group 35, with reference to Daniel 14.

³²Jacobus de Voragine, *The Golden Legend: Readings on the Saints,* translated by William Granger Ryan. 2 vols. (Princeton, N.J.: Princeton University Press, 1993) 1.197.

³³Cf. the hymn *Maria, mater Domini,* quoted by aus der Fünten, *Maria Magdalena,* 86.

³⁴Cf. Saxer, *Le culte,* 344–5.

³⁵Odo, MPL 133.714.

³⁶Odo, MPL 133.721.

[37]Cf. Saxer, *Le culte,* 344–5.

[38]Gregory, MPL 76.1191; *Otfrids Evangelienbuch* V, 8, vv. 17-28.

[39]Cf. (Pseudo) Rabanus Maurus, *De vita beatae Mariae Magdalenae et sororis ejus sanctae Marthae,* MPL 112.1431–508, at 1480–1.

[40]Ibid., 1457–8; Honorius, MPL 172.981.

Chapter Four

Mary Magdalene as Saint:
The Middle Ages

A report from Mary Magdalene's home town can sharpen our focus on the development that her image underwent in the Middle Ages: long after the first millennium, pilgrims who had visited the most famous places in the Holy Land reported their trips to Magdala, the home of the disciple Mary, to Bethany, the residence of the other Mary, and even to Tiberias, where the unknown sinful woman appeared at the dinner, without ever making any connection among these women. In contrast, at the end of the Middle Ages people were shown the place in Bethany where Mary Magdalene did penance:

> In this chapel a cave has been carved in the stone, and it was the prison of Saint Mary Magdalene, where after the Lord's ascension she remained completely enclosed for seven years, while her sister Martha handed her bread and water through the window. Seven years' indulgence may be obtained there, but there is a plenary indulgence at the tomb of Lazarus.[1]

Here Mary Magdalene is the sister of Martha and Lazarus and she is a sinner who must do penance. How did this "mixed figure" come into being? In what follows I will not pursue an exegetical (or feminist) critique of the unified medieval picture of Mary Magdalene, but simply sketch the course of its origin and attempt to understand the reasons that motivated this development.[2]

1. From the Biblical Mary to the Church's Magdalene

In the ancient Church Mary of Magdala belonged to the group of *myrophores,* that is, the ointment bearers who went to the Lord's tomb on Easter morning. This reference contained both positive and negative elements: Mary was a part of salvation history and to that extent worthy of veneration, but she was not a saint with a personal biography.

Since the veneration of saints as a rule began with a local cult (at the place of martyrdom, the locale of the saint's death or tomb, or where the saint's relics were kept) it was not to be expected that there would be a cult of Mary Magdalene at an early date. Nevertheless, as early as the sixth century her tomb was pointed out in Ephesus and in the West her veneration is attested at the latest with the listing of her feast day (July 22) in Bede's martyrology (ca. 720).[3] The veneration of Mary Magdalene in both East and West cannot, however, obscure the fact that the women thus venerated were different: in the Eastern Church even today it is the *myrophora* who is honored, while in the Western Church questions regarding the identity of this biblical figure were raised at an early date.

In Latin patristics Mary—because of the commonality of names—was identified with Mary of Bethany, who anointed Jesus (John 12), and ultimately with other anointing women, especially the sinful woman of Luke 7. Alongside this development, which led to the confusion of different women, there was a countervailing tendency to separate the anointing woman of the Passion story (Mark 14) from the anointing sinner. Ambrose concluded from the observation that one woman anointed Jesus' head, the other his feet, that they could not be the same.[4] He even went a step further and divided the authentic Mary into two women:[5] one who was honored at the tomb with a vision of angels and brought the news of the resurrection to the apostles, and one who literally saw nothing and communicated this negative message; one who, together with the other women, fell believing at Jesus' feet, and one who saw him but did not know him and was not permitted to touch him. Here again the conclusion drawn was that there must have been two Marys from Magdala.[6]

It was only with the work of Gregory the Great that the unified figure began to prevail in the West: Mary Magdalene is the sinful woman of the town who later sat at the Lord's feet and listened to his words, who remained stubbornly at the tomb after the disciples had long since fled, who, weeping, sought the Lord at the tomb and was permitted to bring the news of the resurrection to the disciples; she was, finally, the woman who had suffered from seven demons.[7] It is true that Gregory did not invent this conflation, but he combined existing initiatives and thus created a unified figure that, thanks to his authority, was accepted in the Western Church. In this he did not argue as an exegete defending a scholarly theory; he simply took up statements made from time to time in different situations. This made his argumentation powerfully persuasive, for depending on the occasion the individual features of this "new" Mary Magdalene could be alluded to: the convert, the loving woman, the Easter messenger. The occasions were public homilies Gregory preached, each oriented to a particular pericope from the gospels (Luke 7, John 20), and in one case a very personal letter to Gregoria, a lady-in-waiting at the imperial court, who was concerned about the forgiveness of sins and assurance of salvation. In particular, his response to Gregoria shows that Gregory did not proceed in the manner of a systematic theologian, but simply reacted to the occasion. In answering this woman's scruples he cites Mary Magdalene as an example of the power of divine grace to forgive sins: "a woman who had fallen into the maelstrom of sin was, by grace, carried to the heights on the wings of love!" Gregoria's plea that she be given a revelation to confirm that her sins had really been removed was, however, refused: ". . . because you cannot be certain about your sins." Security would only lead to indifference. "Therefore during the brief time of this life your soul must be in fear, in order that afterward there may be no end to its joyful assurance."[8] The model of Mary Magdalene gives sinners hope of forgiveness, but it must not lead to any notion of automatic salvation; there is no assurance of salvation before death. With these remarks, shifting as they do between consolation and fear, the Pope touched a theme that would not leave people's minds for centuries: the question of pardon and the assurance of salvation remained an existential problem of medieval people until the time of Martin Luther. At the same time this letter begins to make clear to us the source of the power of the image of the *sinful* Magdalene: it was so influential not because it devalued a particular woman but because it relieved the anxiety of *everyone* about his or her soul's salvation. In the letter to Gregoria it is true that the sinful woman is more clearly described than in the homilies as "a woman who had been a great sinner in the town, whose sin-stained hands touched the feet of the one who sits above the choirs of angels at the right hand of the Father . . . a woman who had fallen into the maelstrom of sin . . ." and yet, here again, Gregory is not interested in the woman as a person, but in her function as a model and example: ". . . and I trust in his mercy that the mouth of eternal truth will speak over you the same judgment that was once spoken over a holy woman."[9] The accent is not on the sinful past but on the salvific present:

this woman is an image of the Church that trusts in the same divine mercy that placed the sinful woman in the way of salvation.

Gregory had no interest in Mary Magdalene as a person (and to that extent he is only indirectly the originator of her biography and of the later negative image of Magdalene!) but only in her significance as a unifying element between the biblical model and the ecclesial reality. Nevertheless, with this "artistic image" he created a Christian figure that little by little developed a power of attraction all its own.

2. The Beginnings of a "Biography" of Mary Magdalene

From about the eleventh century onward interest developed in the individual figure of this saint and she acquired a "biography," the elements of which were already present, in germ, in Gregory's work. As a result of her being combined with other women she had siblings (Martha and Lazarus) and both a town of origin and a residence (Magdala and Bethany); she was a sinful woman of the town, a whore who repented in tears and followed the Lord, but who also retreated into her house to listen meditatively to him, and who in the end went with other women to the tomb and became a joyful messenger, announcing the resurrection to the disciples. These events, originally connected to several different women, were brought into a sequence and thus constituted the preliminary stage of a biography of Mary Magdalene.

While in the ancient Church the martyrs were the prototypical saints, in the early Middle Ages the "noble saints" replaced them. Reference to noble birth became a regular *topos* in lives of the saints, with an obligatory note that a pious manner of life was more important than an aristocratic family background. Thus in the life of a Merovingian bishop we read: "he was through his parents a man of high position and nobility, and he was abundantly blessed with this world's goods, but it later became clear that he was far nobler and wealthier in Christian faith."[10] This ideal of aristocratic and wealthy noble saints remained the norm until the appearance of the "city saints" and those from the mendicant orders. A saint required a family background, for everyone, according to the thinking of that era, is not merely an individual but also a part of his or her family. Thus Odo of Cluny in the tenth century made the first references to the aristocratic descent of Mary Magdalene and explained the tradition of her name by the fact that ordinarily the names of wealthy and aristocratic persons were more likely to be handed down than those of the poor.[11] By giving Mary Magdalene a noble background Odo took the decisive step toward the development of her biography. Mary is at this point no longer an "image" of other things, but an individual person, as is apparent from the literary genre of Odo's text: it is no longer a homily on a particular gospel text like those of the patristic writers, but a sermon in her honor.

Odo's sermon pointed the way for the further embellishment of the Magdalene legend: various manuscripts incorporate the names of her parents (Syrus and Eucharia), and one even describes the exact location of the family property in Jerusalem, Bethany, and Magdala.[12] Other preachers know the details of her sin: according to Honorius she was married in "Magdalum," committed adultery, fled to Jerusalem, and became a public sinner *("vulgaris meretrix")*.[13] From this point on, such labels become a fixed part of her biography: "this same very lovely woman was a noblewoman in the worldly way and had been given into a blessed marriage, but she left her husband and became a public sinner."[14] Corresponding to the filling out of the picture of her sinful life was interest in her penitential sojourn in the wilderness: while Honorius only says that for love of Jesus she withdrew into isolation,[15] this quiet life, under the influence of other saints' lives (Mary of Egypt [see the illustration on p. x], Pelagia, and others), was transformed into an eremitic penitence. The picture of the penitent Magdalene in the desert is thus a relatively recent phenomenon! (The beginnings appear in Italy in the ninth to tenth centuries and the image spread quickly in Germany and England.) A number of factors may have contributed to its development, including:

- a widespread movement of eremiticism and penitential practice,
- the integration of demands for radical asceticism that dominated a number of heretical movements: cf. the "rise" of Mary Magdalene among the Franciscans (with a strong penitential impulse) and Dominicans (in their attack on the Cathari),
- the viewpoint of the hagiographers, who turned from the world and toward the monastic life, and
- finally, after the emergence of the French legends of Mary Magdalene, pilgrimages to Sainte-Baume, where the memory of her hermit life was promoted, and people were even shown the cave where she did penance.[16]

The final and decisive augmentation of the Magdalene legends came from France (Burgundy and Provence) and was connected with the battle over her relics, or rather the miraculous "discovery" of her bones in Vézelay (1265) and Saint-Maximin (1279).

The abbey of Vézelay in Burgundy was a famous place of pilgrimage: pilgrims bound for Santiago de Compostela stopped there; crusades began there; and in the eleventh and twelfth centuries the abbey itself became the goal of a pilgrimage for the veneration of the relics of Mary Magdalene. The (at first only asserted) possession of these relics was explained through the legends of her sea journey and fortunate landing in Marseilles, her life in the wilderness, her grave in Provence (according to some sources in Aix, according to others in Saint-Maximin), and the theft of the relics in 745 (or on March 19, 749) by the monks of Vézelay. In a period of decline at the abbey the saint's bones were "found" (with good public effect) and in 1267 they were solemnly venerated in the presence of the king.

In reaction to these events it was bruited about in Provence that the pious relic thieves had taken the wrong body in the wrong casket; the saint had been moved thirty-five years earlier, and her grave remained untouched. As a proof of the truth of this assertion, in the year 1279 the saint's bones were "discovered" and in 1280 they were shown to the faithful for their veneration. From then on pilgrims no longer went to Burgundy, but to Provence, where one may see the places where she worked and where she did penance as well as her grave. This sealed the religious (and economic!) downfall of Vézelay.[17]

Ultimately Mary Magdalene took over features of Saint Agnes and (like the latter) by divine grace grew hair over her entire body so as to clothe her nakedness; so was born the icon that was venerated above all others in the late Middle Ages: the woman with a hairy body, or entirely covered by the long hair of her head who, borne by angels, floats between heaven and earth (cf. Tilman Riemenschneider's sculpture, the inner face of the Tiefenbronn altar, and portraits by Albrecht Dürer and Hans Baldung Grien).

These various elements of the legends of Mary Magdalene were gathered together in Jacques de Voragine's famous collection of saints' legends, the *Legenda aurea (Golden Legend)*[18] and became throughout Europe part of the common wisdom about the saints. Mary Magdalene had now become a "real" saint whose life and works one could contemplate, who was close to those who venerated her at her grave and through her relics, and of whom, finally, miracles could be told (help in childbirth, healing of blind people, liberation from captivity, assistance at the time of death).

Poems in Latin and in various vernaculars were also based on this now authoritative life, as were the major picture cycles found especially in South Germany, for example in Tiefenbronn and Freising (fifteenth century) or in Donaueschingen and Rottweil (sixteenth century).

3. Saint Mary Magdalene in Spiritual Poetry

In the German-speaking regions the legend of Mary Magdalene left traces not only in the *Legenda aurea* and its translations, but also in spiritual poetry (rhyming sermons and collections of legends) in the twelfth and thirteenth centuries. The most important works were:

- *Des armen Hartmann Rede vom Glauben* ("The poor Hartmann's sermon on faith"), twelfth century[19]
- *Das Leben Jesu von Frau Ava* ("The life of Jesus by the woman Ava"), twelfth century[20]
- The *Väterbuch* ("Fathers' Book") and the *Passional* by the same author, ca. 1300[21]
- *Der Saelden Hort* ("The Treasury of Blessings"), ca. 1300.[22]

The Latin life attributed to Rabanus Maurus may also be from this period.[23] In these texts the "canonical" form of the legend speaks; only here and there do we find particular accents.

Fixed elements in the prehistory are the names of Mary's parents, her origins in an aristocratic family with landed property, and references to the beauty, wealth, and lively spirit that eventually bring the young Mary to ruin. Sometimes her sinful life is motivated by rage at Jesus' having prevented her marriage to John the evangelist: Lazarus had betrothed his rich sister to the poor but royal-blooded John, but when the bridegroom was called by Jesus during the wedding banquet and abandoned his bride, her social position was affected. She reacted not out of disappointed love, but because her honor was wounded. In accord with the feudal code of honor, the insult had to be avenged: people had been killed for lesser offenses.[24]

Mary begins a sinful life and because of it she loses her rightful name and is known only as "the sinner."[25] There is normally a discreet silence about the nature of her sins, but sometimes it is boldly stated (for example, "the chastity of her body was destroyed"). The author of the *Saelden Hort* has a different focus: since he had already said, in the context of Jesus' temptation, that unchastity was such an accursed sin that Jesus could not be tempted by it, he laid down a different course for Mary Magdalene: she was indeed wild and impetuous, but she did nothing obscene (that is, unchaste).[26] Her worldly aristocratic life alone was the ground for her later conversion.

The biblical texts are retold to narrate Mary's conversion, her participation in the Passion and Easter, the first appearance of Jesus and her sending to the disciples. At this point it becomes obvious how the ability of male scholars to perceive reality can be blocked. The author of the *Passional* entitles his second book "the book of the apostles" or "the book of the messengers" and lists among the "messengers" about whom he will write: the apostles, angels (*angelus* means messenger), John the Baptist (as precursor, messenger who goes before), and Mary Magdalene, who was sent by God to the apostles "as a messenger." Whereas this role as messenger was for the poet, as for modern readers of the Bible, a part of the authentic picture of Mary Magdalene, one of the earliest scholars to examine the *Passional* explained (on the basis of the image of Mary Magdalene current in the nineteenth century) the motives for the inclusion of this single female saint in the book of messengers as "really and truly far-fetched."[27] This androcentric perspective prevented him from perceiving the messenger-function as the common feature of all the people named in the book, including Mary Magdalene.

Another fixed element is a reference to the threefold accusation against Mary (by Simon the Pharisee, Martha, and Judas) and Jesus' defense of her:

> "Drey stunt ich sie gestrafet las:
> Judas daz eine was . . .
> Den phariseum ouch virdroz . . .
> Daz dritte ir swester Martha . . .
> Hie von was ir vurspreche (= Fürsprecher)
> Cristus gein disen allen drin
> Unde lobete wol Marien sin."
> (Three hours [= times] I let her be accused:
> Judas was one . . .
> The Pharisee another . . .
> The third her sister Martha . . .
> Her advocate in the face of this was
> Christ against all these three
> And praised his Mary well.")[28]

In addition, biblical texts were expanded so that Mary Magdalene also had a place in them:

• she is present at the ascension as well as at Pentecost, where she receives the Holy Spirit with the other disciples;[29]

• after the ascension the rich siblings sell their property, lay it at the feet of the apostles, and choose to live as poor apostles, "as twelve messengers, male and female."[30]

Among the post-biblical scenes in the life of Mary Magdalene are the voyage across the sea in a rudderless boat, the miraculous landing in Marseilles, her preaching there before the people and the nobility (her sermon, the "speech sweet as honey" was so pleasant because "the mouth that gave such sweet and tender kisses to the feet of our Lord" could speak nothing but sweet words),[31] and certain incidents involving a noble couple in which for the first time Mary Magdalene appeared as a helper in various kinds of difficulties. Finally, for love of Jesus she retired for thirty years of solitude to a place prepared by the angels; there she was carried up to heaven seven times a day (at the customary hours of prayer) and was sustained only by heavenly food. In addition to the popular notion that at that place there were "neither a source of water nor the pleasure of trees and grass" there was another tradition according to which she did take nourishment because near her cave there was "water" and a "fruit tree," apparently representing the water of life and the tree of life, and thus both the earthly and the heavenly Paradise (Gen 2; Rev 22:1-2).[32]

At the end of her life she was swept up by angels and carried into a church, her face already shining like the sun, received holy communion from the hand of her old companion Maximinius, and died at the altar; for seven days a sweet smell filled the house of God as a sensible sign of her reception in heaven.

4. The Sinful Saint and Sinners

The newly awakened interest in Mary Magdalene as an individual saint found eloquent expression in spiritual songs. But while in the eleventh century she was still cited as a witness of God's mercy (*"testis enim Maria Magdalena"*), soon afterward the roles were reversed: God is witness to her model behavior (*"testante Domino"*).[33] Accordingly, no longer is God praised or implored for mercy for the saint's sake; she herself is called on as an advocate and helper (*"ergo Maria, precare Deum / Nostra precata ferens ad eum"*) and she herself is praised (*"Pange, lingua, Magdalenae / Lacrimas et gaudium"*).[34]

As saint she is a bond between God and the petitioner; as model she shows that the way of the sinner (and everyone in the Middle Ages understood himself or herself as a sinner!) does not automatically lead to eternal damnation. As advocate she guarantees hope for pardon and redemption, even if the works of penance are far beyond the abilities of the individual. At the end of the Middle Ages this idea becomes even stronger: the despairing petitioners not only immerse themselves in pious contemplation of her life, but identify with the sinful woman in order, like her, to be redeemed *("O peccatorum spes, / Exemplar desperatis, / Magdalena. . . .").*[35]

Mary's part in the Passion and Easter events was never completely lost sight of, but her role as a repentant sinner became increasingly important because it was only in that role that she could fulfill her function as a support and advocate for sinners. Very few authors (including, however, Ava and Christine de Pisan) avoid mentioning her sinful life; a few, like Peter Abelard, interpret the "tears" that are a fixed part of her image as tears of longing and love and not as the sinful woman's tears of penitence.

It is also important in contemplating the medieval image of the saint to consider the company in which she appears: for Gregory her companions were Peter, Zacchaeus, and the crucified thief; Honorius mentions figures in whom God's mercy was especially prominent: David, Peter, Paul, Cyprian, Theophilus, Mary Magdalene, Maria Aegyptiaca, and Thais. Of particular interest is Hartmann the Poor's connection of three men and two women, in each case one New Testament example (the thief is associated with Mary Magdalene) and two later saints (Theophilus, Peter Thelonarius, Afra, Maria Aegyptiaca).[36] Common to all of them are their sinful past, their repentance and conversion, their acts of penance, and finally their publicly visible redemption.

All the sins that were treated in the theological catalogue of vices (pride, ambition, apostasy, murder, adultery, incest, et cetera) were represented among the saints, and each in turn points to a biblical model. Saintly lovers, male and female, correspond to Rahab and David in the First Testament and Mary Magdalene in the New Testament, whereby (especially for the promiscuous women and their New Testament prototype) there is a kind of mutual influence:

• The life of the repentant sinful women is stylized according to the model of Mary Magdalene; thus it is said of the sinner Pelagia that she fell at the feet of Bishop Nonnus as once Mary Magdalene fell at the feet of Jesus. Against the objections of a pious woman the bishop defends the sinner by saying that Pelagia, like Mary Magdalene, had chosen the best from God.[37]

• In turn, elements from the lives of the saints slipped into the biography of the New Testament saint: for example, her strict life of penitence in the wilderness and her thirty-year fast from earthly food, both of which are taken from the life of Maria Aegyptiaca. That sinner did penance in the desert for her sins for forty-seven years; for seventeen of those years she nourished herself with three loaves she brought with her, and in that period she also suffered the attacks of the devil. For thirty years, however, she lived entirely without food and remained free from temptations.[38] Mary Magdalene is, then, not just any saint, but one of the many sinful saints who were presented as hopeful examples to the eyes of the disheartened. The *Golden Legend*[39] summarizes these ideas succinctly:

> Before her conversion she remained in guilt, burdened with the debt of eternal punishment. In her conversion she was armed and rendered unconquerable by the armor of penance. . . . After her conversion she was magnificent in the superabundance of grace, because where trespass abounded, grace was superabundant.

The elaboration of her "sinful career" was not for its own purpose, but was directly related to the fundamental problem of the people of the Middle Ages: the question of the possibility and the certainty of salvation. As we have seen, the imperial lady-in-waiting Gregoria, like so many later people plagued by anxiety over their sins, was comforted with the example of the saintly sinner, Mary Magdalene. Her figure was also used by Hartmann the Poor as an example of the "conditions" for forgiveness, including love for God, faith, repentance, and trust (5.2194–7, 2230–3). Those who orient themselves to this model conduct of the saint will be saved as she was.

This idea had consequences that found both liturgical and social expression:

• While the liturgy ordinarily honors the saints only on the anniversary of their death, it devotes an additional feast day to each of two sinful saints, a man and a woman (Paul and Mary Magdalene), as a commemoration of their conversion.[40]

• Medieval veneration of the saints always had practical effects as well, extending into daily life. The saints do not stand around idly before God's throne; as "patrons" they have very concrete tasks in the realm of daily life: for example, St. Hubert (patron of the hunt), St. Florian (protection against fire), St. Anthony (in charge of finding lost objects), and so on. Such patronal tasks were also derived from the *vita* of Mary Magdalene; she was, for example, the patron of hairdressers, ointment makers, and cosmeticians.

• Mary Magdalene's relationship to prostitutes had an immediate social consequence. In the Middle Ages prostitution was closely associated with the beginnings of urban culture as a new form of community life alongside the feudal courts and monasteries. The whores made up a separate profession; although it was one of the "dishonorable" callings its members nonetheless were regarded as a necessary part of the urban community. As a recognized "profession" it was, like all occupations, concentrated in particular streets and residential quarters; it was only when sexually-transmitted diseases began to be feared that this spatial segregation took on a clearly negative association.

The Church also tolerated the whores. Their activity was not reckoned among the sexual sins, but was regarded as work, and therefore as having a claim to a just wage. It was only morally reprehensible if a whore sold her body "for her own pleasure." Besides the officially recognized, well-to-do whores there were poor itinerants who, like beggars, criminals, lepers, and the like, found themselves on the outer fringes of society.

While the cities and the nobility (both secular and ecclesiastical) regarded the brothels as important sources of income (they paid taxes!), prostitution was regarded by others as a religious and moral problem. In the wake of a general penitential movement the conversion of fallen women and girls and the protection of those in danger was seen, especially in the twelfth and thirteenth centuries, as a religious and social duty. Ultimately this led to the foundation of special monasteries and religious houses: particular mention should be made of the movement led by the penitential preacher Robert of Abrissel (d. 1115) and the Order of Repentant Women or "Penitents of Saint Mary Magdalene" confirmed by Pope Gregory IX in 1227. The conversion movement swept through all social classes and affected not only penitent prostitutes but even noblewomen. For both groups the sinful penitent, Mary Magdalene, was the image on which they could orient their lives.[41]

For the prostitutes, as for every person, it was true that everyone has a chance. For centuries people drew strength from the contemplation of Mary Magdalene and all the saints who had once been sinners and were now models of conversion and advocates before God. The moral and religious perfection of the saints and their heroic lives as martyrs or ascetics were certainly admirable, but to know that sinners had been made saints was not only comforting but indispensable: no one must remain what she or he is, namely a sinner; everyone can change, just as the saintly sinners did!

5. The Blessed Mary Magdalene: A Different Image for Sainthood?

The picture of the comforting sinner-saint thus developed is based on depictions by *male* authors. The question therefore arises whether *women* authors perhaps placed their accents somewhere else. Did the women poets liberate the saint from her connection to the sinner, as is sometimes asserted?

Hrotsvitha of Gandersheim, who wrote in Latin, did describe in her poems the conversions of Mary, the niece of the hermit Abraham, and Thais by the hermit Paphnutius: both of them repented in tears of their sexual sins and did penance in isolation; but she did not connect these two penitents with Mary Magdalene. That connection was made only by a modern editor of her works.[42] Whether the educated canoness, who must have known the Church's mixture of imagery from literature and liturgy, avoided any reference to the ancient figure of the converted sinner so as not to weaken the model function of her heroines, or whether she deliberately set out to remove Mary Magdalene from the context of sins against chastity—these are questions for which we can scarcely offer any answers. In contrast, we can say something more definite about the intentions of the two younger women who wrote in the vernacular (Ava and Christine de Pisan).

Ava (see n. 20 above), an *"inclusa"* (enclosed woman) of Melk Abbey, first mentions Mary Magdalene by name under the cross. However, in light of her entire work it cannot be maintained that Ava made a strict distinction between Mary Magdalene and the sinful woman.[43] The question is not whether Mary Magdalene is identical with the sinner (for poets rooted in tradition and liturgy she is certainly that), but where emphasis is placed and what elements are left in the background. It is only by such placement of accents that the individual poet can be distinguished from the general and unified view. We should also keep in mind that medieval poets did not strive for individuality and originality, but were embedded in the fundamental consensus of tradition and sought an artistic rendition only within that framework. With respect to Ava's depiction of the life of Jesus this means that she did *not* undertake to equate Mary Magdalene with one of the women appearing in every imaginable episode (the sinful woman, the sisters in Bethany, the raising of Lazarus, the anointing before the Passion), but she probably presumes such an equation as a matter of course. This she shows at the end of the poem, where she speaks of the gifts of the Holy Spirit bestowed on repentant tears, which we should shed as once did blessed Mary when she washed the feet of Jesus with her sweet tears (V.2317–22). However, in retelling the New Testament stories she speaks of such an act at only one point: when the sinful woman washed Jesus' feet with her tears (V.851–3). Thus, for Ava, quite as a matter of course Mary Magdalene is the sinful woman (V.845), the public sinner (V.866); but by omitting her name in this episode she hints at a modified image of Magdalene: before all else she is the co-sufferer at the cross:

> "Owi, Maria Magdalena,
> wie gestunte du ie da, /
> da du dinen herren guoten
> sahe hangen und bluoten"
> (Alas, Mary Magdalene,
> how you stood precisely there,
> where you saw your good Lord
> hanging and bleeding)
> V.1693–6.

She is the one healed (V.1823–5) of evil spirits (not sins!) and the woman who, after the protophany, speaks the sole Easter confession in the poem: "Iz sahen miniu ougen, ir sult iz wol gelouben, / surrexit dominus, daz ist: erstanden ist unser herre Jesus" (I saw with my eyes, that should you then believe / *surrexit dominus*, that is: our Lord Jesus is risen) (V.1923–6).

Ava knows of Mary Magdalene's sinful past, but she apparently has no interest in elaborating the point. The same is true of Christine de Pisan, who in her *Book of the City of Ladies* in 1405[44] also merely hints at Mary Magdalene's role as a sinner while putting her accents elsewhere.

Mary Magdalene is, as a matter of course, the sister of Martha and Lazarus; her tears are tears of sorrow over her dead brother and later tears of repentance. Christine, whose whole book is a defense of women against male prejudices, in this connection defends women against the ironic proverb that "God made women to speak, weep, and sew" and turns the barb around: "What special favors has God bestowed on women because of their tears!"—for the tears of the two sisters caused Jesus to raise Lazarus, and he accepted Magdalene's tears "and forgave her sins, and through the merits of those tears she is in glory in heaven." Even "gossiping" is—from God's point of view—not to be condemned, as men think, because otherwise the Lord Jesus would not have ordered "the blessed Magdalene" to announce the mystery of the resurrection. Therefore praise is due to God "who, among the other infinite boons and favors which You have bestowed upon the feminine sex, desired that woman carry such lofty and worthy news." Preachers who ridicule the first appearance before a woman by saying that God took into account the tendency of women to gossip in order to make the mystery known "more rapidly" are called "foolish" and sharply criticized for thus speaking "even in jest."[45]

The key word "tears" thus leads the thought to the sinner, Mary Magdalene, even if her sins are not emphasized. On the contrary, in connection with the legend of Saint Afra, a woman who had led a sinful life but then converted to Christianity and refused to take part in the pagan sacrifice, the sinful woman from Luke 7 is mentioned without reference to Mary Magdalene,[46] while the latter is considered primarily as a woman enthroned in heaven. In the third part of the book where Mary, as queen of heaven, enters the city of ladies, her sisters and the "blessed Mary Magdalene" take the first places in her train.

These two authors (Ava and Christine de Pisan) do not directly attack the mixed figure of Mary Magdalene, but neither do they emphasize her equation with the whore or her sinful life. That could be related to their gender: these are women writing, full of understanding (Ava) and enthusiasm (Christine de Pisan), about another woman, in contrast to the men previously considered (even if they were sometimes very well-meaning men). Probably, however, another common feature was more important to the two authors: both had been or still were "in circulation," knew the realities of daily life, had children, cared for their families (Christine had to earn her family's living by her writing; Ava, although as an enclosed woman she was now in religious life, was "the mother of two children"). The male authors, in contrast, whether preachers or poets, were all religious who knew secular life only "from without" and often regarded it as a "temptation." In particular the male religious who wrote in the vernacular were pursuing pedagogical ends: for the honor of God and the salvation of their readers they wanted to present models for a life withdrawn from the world *(Väterbuch, Passional)* and at the same time to suppress popular secular romances like Wigoleis or Tristan *(Der Saelden Hort)*. Hence they presented Mary Magdalene primarily in the context of penitent desert saints like Pelagia or Maria Aegyptiaca, or depicted her as a beautiful noblewoman who fell victim to the fascination of secular and feudal life.

The secular attachments of the two women poets preserved them from the fantasy-laden image of the sinful Magdalene, but nothing more! They could ameliorate the contribution made by Luke 7 to that image, but they did not deny it. The time for teasing out the threads of the Magdalene tapestry had not yet come, even if an initial doubt about the "sinful" Mary Magdalene was already making itself heard, as in a Copenhagen manuscript of 1431 where we find in connection with the legend of her conversion the following surprising note: *"Nota, aliqui volunt, quod Maria Magdalena non peccavit."*[47] On the whole the penitent Mary Magdalene was still useful—especially for the baroque era and the Counter-Reformation!

Notes

[1]Clemens Kopp, *Die heiligen Stätten der Evangelien* (2nd ed. Regensburg, 1964) 249–51 (pilgrim accounts); cf. Herbert Donner, *Pilgerfahrt ins Heilige Land. Die ältesten Berichte christlicher Palästinapilger* (Stuttgart, 1979).

[2]For the medieval Mary Magdalene see V. Saxer and U. Liebl, "Maria Magdalena," *Lexikon des Mittelalters* 6 (1993), cols. 282–4; Victor Saxer, *Le Culte de Marie Madeleine en Occident des origines à la fin du Moyen âge* (Paris, 1959).

[3]For the beginnings of liturgical veneration of Mary Magdalene see Saxer, *Le Culte*, 32–45.

[4]Ambrose, *Expositio Evang. sec. Lucam*, MPL 15.1758.

[5]*"Nescit una Maria Magdalene . . . scit alterna Maria Magdalena,"* ibid., col. 1936; cf. also col. 1934.

[6]*"Ergo plures Mariae, plures fortasse etiam Magdalenae,"* ibid., col. 1936.

[7]*"Maria Magdalene, quae fuerat in civitate peccatrix . . . Nam postquam venit ad monumentum . . . Hanc vero quam Lucas peccatricem*

mulierem, Joannes Mariam nominat, illam esse Mariam credimus de qua Marcus septem daemonia ejecta fuisse testatur" (Gregory, *Hom. in Luc. 7,* 33, MPL 76.1238–46; cf. *Hom. in Joann. 20,* 25, MPL 76.1188–96; *Letter to Gregoria* in BKV, 2nd ser. 4 (Munich 1933) 295–7.

[8]*Letter to Gregoria,* 296–7.

[9]Ibid., 295.

[10]Quoted from Klaus Herbers, "Die deutschen Heiligen im Mittelalter," in Régine Pernoud, *Die Heiligen im Mittelalter. Frauen und Männer, die ein Jahrtausend prägten* (Bergisch Gladbach, 1988) 298–348, at 309.

[11]Odo, MPL 133.714. The "castle" of "Magdalum" also belonged to this noble family.

[12]Hans Hansel, *Die Maria-Magdalena-Legende. Eine Quellenuntersuchung* (Bottrop i. W., 1937) 109. The reference to royal birth and the names of her parents appear first in the twelfth century in the Martha legends; cf. ibid., 111.

[13]Honorius, MPL 172.979.

[14]"Diu selbe vil liebe frouwe diu was nach der werlt ein edil wip unde heten si ir friunt zelicher hirat gegeben, da liez aver sie den ir echarl unde wart ain offeniu sundaerinne." From a sermon by the priest Konrad on the feast of Mary Magdalene; quoted from Hansel, *Die Maria-Magdalena-Legende,* 87.

[15]Honorius, MPL 172.981.

[16]Cf. Saxer, *Le culte,* 59, 337–40; Hansel, *Die Maria-Magdalena-Legende,* 18, 99.

[17]On the competing loci of the cult in Burgundy (Vézelay) and Provence (Saint-Maximin, Saint-Baume), cf. the thorough discussion in Saxer, *Le Culte,* especially 89–108, 137–41, 185–227, and Susan Haskins, *Mary Magdalene: Myth and Metaphor* (New York, San Diego, and London: Harcourt, Brace & Co., 1993) 98–133, also based on Victor Saxer's research.

[18]Jacobus de Voragine, *The Golden Legend: Readings on the Saints,* translated by William Granger Ryan. 2 vols. (Princeton, N.J.: Princeton University Press, 1993). The chapter on Mary Magdalene is at 1.374–83.

[19]Friedrich von der Leyen, ed., *Des armen Hartmann Rede vom Glouven. Eine deutsche Reimpredigt des 12. Jahrhunderts.* Germanistische Abhandlungen XIV (Breslau, 1897).

[20]Friedrich Maurer, ed., *Die Dichtungen der Frau Ava.* Altdeutsche Textbibliothek 66 (Tübingen, 1966).

[21]Karl Reissenberger, ed., *Das Väterbuch.* Deutsche Texte des Mittelalters XXII (Berlin, 1914); K. A. Hahn, ed., *Das alte Passional* (Frankfurt, 1845).

[22]Heinrich Adrian, ed., *Der Saelden Hort. Alemannisches Gedicht vom Leben Jesu, Johannes des Täufers und der Magdalena.* Deutsche Texte des Mittelalters XXVI (Berlin, 1927).

[23](Pseudo)-Rabanus Maurus, *De vita beatae Mariae Magdalenae et sororis ejus sanctae Marthae,* MPL 112.1431-1508.

[24]"Von minren sachen / vil lutes ist zu tot erslagen," *Hort*, V.7384–5; for the betrothal cf. also the *Passional*, 369.56–69 (leaving open the question whether the tradition is correct), and *Legenda aurea*, 481 (rejecting this opinion as improper).

[25]*Passional*, 370.4–6; cf. *Hort*, V.7484–90; *Legenda aurea*, 472.

[26]*Hort*, V.4579–99, 7491–8.

[27]*Passional*, 154.59; 155.7–10, 39–47; 367.35–87. Friedrich Wilhelm, *Deutsche Legenden und Legendare. Texte und Untersuchungen zu ihrer Geschichte im Mittelalter* (Leipzig 1907) 89.

[28]*Väterbuch*, V.20.165–20.182; similarly *Legenda aurea*, 472; (Pseudo)-Rabanus Maurus, MPL 112.1485.

[29](Pseudo)-Rabanus Maurus, MPL 112.1484; Honorius, MPL 172.981.

[30]*Hort*, V.10.259–71; cf. *Legenda aurea*, 471–2; (Pseudo)-Rabanus Maurus, MPL 112.1487–8.

[31]*Passional*, 376.1–3, 61–9; *Hort*, 10.415–20; *Legenda aurea*, 473.

[32]*Legenda aurea*, 477; *Passional*, 384.22–5.21 (without food); *Passional*, 384.92–5.4 (with the food of Paradise).

[33]Quoted from Wiltrud aus der Fünten, *Maria Magdalena in der Lyrik des Mittelalters* (Düsseldorf, 1966) 64, 86.

[34]Ibid., 116–7, 143–9.

[35]Ibid., 190.

[36]Honorius, MPL 172.809, 881; *Des armen Hartmann Rede vom Glouven*, V.1843–2353.

[37]*Väterbuch*, V.29.893–5; 30.321–3.

[38]Ibid., 35.21ff.; in the *Legenda aurea* the thirty years represent only the period she was free from temptation (p. 288). For the depiction of the saintly sinners cf. Erhard Dorn, *Der sündige Heilige in der Legende des Mittelalters* (Munich, 1967) 52–80.

[39]*Legenda aurea*, 1.375.

[40]Regional saints' calendars from southern Germany assign Mary Magdalene both March 10 and April 1: cf. Saxer, *Le culte*, 324; Hansel, *Die Maria-Magdalena-Legende*, 126. The late medieval legend *Conversio beatae Mariae Magdalenae* may also be connected with the conversion feast; it goes back to monasteries in the Netherlands: cf. Hansel, *Die Maria-Magdalena-Legende*, 114–27.

[41]For this section cf. Shulamith Shahar, *Die Frau im Mittelalter* (Königstein/Taunus, 1981) 181–6; Peter Dinzelbacher, "Rollenverweigerung, religiöser Aufbruch und mystisches Erleben mittelalterlicher Frauen," in Peter Dinzelbacher and Dieter R. Bauer, eds., *Religiöse Frauenbewegung und mystische Frömmigkeit im Mittelalter* (Cologne and Vienna, 1988) 1–58; K. Elm, "Magdalenerinnen," *Lexikon des Mittelalters* 6 (1993) col. 71; G. Gieraths, "Magdalenerinnen," *LThK* 6 (1961) 1270–71.

[42]H. Hohmeyer, *Hrotsvitha von Gandersheim: Werke in deutscher Übertragung. Mit einem Beitrag zur frühmittelalterlichen Dichtung* (Munich,

Paderborn, and Vienna, 1973) 222–37 (Abraham and Mary); 238–58 (Paphnutius and Thais); for the Magdalene motif cf. the editor's introduction, 222, 238.

[43]Elisabeth Gössman, "Maria Magdalena als Typos der Kirche," in Dietmar Bader, ed., *Maria Magdalena—Zu einem Bild der Frau in der christlichen Verkündigung* (Freiburg, 1990) 51–71; for Ava, 63–8; contrast Eoliba Greinemann, *Die Gedichte der Frau Ava* (dissertation Freiburg, 1968), who vigorously defends the thesis that the Marys and the sinful woman are one and the same for Ava: especially pp. 81, 85, 115.

[44]Christine de Pizan, *The Book of the City of Ladies,* translated by Earl Jeffrey Richards. Foreword by Marina Warner (New York: Persea Books, 1982).

[45]Ibid., I.10.3–5, pp. 27–9.

[46]Ibid., III.17.1, pp. 250–1.

[47]("Be it noted that according to others Mary Magdalene did not sin.") Cf. Hansel, *Die Maria-Magdalena-Legende,* 114.

Chapter Five

The Penitent Magdalene: A Symbol of the Baroque Era

By happy accident three versions of Magdalene imagery from three different centuries came together on my desk; they illustrate the path followed by Mary Magdalene through history far better than any theoretical discussion could.

1. On the exterior of the wings of the great altar of the last judgment by Stephan Lochner (ca. 1440: the altar was disassembled in the nineteenth century; the wings are in Munich, other sections in Frankfurt and Cologne), Mary Magdalene can be seen together with other saints: on the right wing we find Catherine, Hubert, and Quirinius, on the left Mary Magdalene, Anthony the hermit, and Pope Cornelius. The pictures represent male and female, secular and religious, young and old saints; while Catharine is depicted with flowing hair and a crown, Magdalene, her hair partly covered by a veil, models the adult woman. Each of the saints bears a lightly painted halo, and all six can be recognized by their attributes: for Magdalene this is the ointment jar that she bears in her hands since Easter morning.

Before each group of three kneels a donor who (unlike the saints) has individualized features. The increasing self-awareness of city dwellers is unmistakable, and yet the differing size of the figures makes it clear that we are still in the Middle Ages: the saints claim the entire vertical dimension while the donors, especially as kneeling figures, occupy only about a quarter of the height. The power of the holy patrons and advocates is unbroken even in the waning years of the Middle Ages. The saints depicted are those to whom these citizens have a special relationship, who reflect their history, and on whom they rely in crises. Magdalene is one of the saints with whom the city (in this case Cologne) and its residents could identify.

2. The next picture brings us to the sixteenth century: it is the Mary Magdalene of Lucas Cranach the elder (found in the Wallraf-Richartz Museum in Cologne). We behold a young woman in a peaceful pastoral scene with a city and steep cliffs in the background. Her gown of expensive materials and its modish design are more reminiscent of a young Renaissance noblewoman or the daughter of a patrician family than of a saint. Here again she can be recognized by her attribute, the ointment jar. There is also a reference to her legend in the left upper border of the picture: sustained by angels, she ascends to heavenly glory. This halo-less saint could step out of the picture and mingle with the viewers; nothing recalls the saintly aura except the pictorial reference to her elevation.

3. A completely different view appears in the Magdalene of the great painting "Christ and the Repentant Sinners" by Peter Paul Rubens (ca. 1620: Bayerische Staatsgemäldesammlungen, Munich). The powerful saint has become the deeply bowed sinner: Magdalene kneels before the transfigured Christ of Easter. The space allowed her by the painter is limited by the body and outstretched arm of Christ, and this is underscored by her bowed head.

This Magdalene is almost naked; her gown and hair are designed more to reveal and suggest her body than to cover it. Her hair falls wildly and unbound over her shoulders. Her hands are crossed on her breast but the fingers of the left hand are so cleverly spread that the viewer's eye is drawn irresistibly to her nipple. Everything about this figure—its body language, the swing of the hair, the sensual mouth— is movement, surrender, longing, sensuality. She could never step out of the frame like Lucas Cranach's Magdalene and move about in the real world; on the contrary: she stands in complete contradiction to everything the viewers approve for themselves.

If one compares the "normal" apparel of a lady of the baroque period[1] with this unclothed Magdalene one notices that the noblewoman's natural bodily shape was rendered unrecognizable by hoop-skirts; for women of the upper classes generally the same purpose was accomplished by loose overgarments. Neck and breast were covered by starched collars; the hair was combed and shaped and hidden under various kinds of headdresses; the face was withdrawn from direct view by being covered with powder and beauty spots. Above all the fashion of hoopskirts, deriving from Spain, matched the moral conceptions of the Counter-Reformation, which "not only covered the woman's lower body to an extreme degree, but also in fact denied its natural shape."[2] Nothing of the body was visible unless it was ennobled by the art of the tailor, the hairdresser, and other masters. Anything natural was to be abhorred; only artistically shaped nature, which had overcome the raw and sensual, could express perfection. What we know of tastes in gardening, whereby it was not a hedge in itself but only a hedge shaped and clipped into an artistic form that responded to the aesthetic demands of the period, was true also for people: we learn nothing of their natural bodily shapes, their hair, their gestures and facial expressions; everything is shrouded by fashion and ceremonial. The portraits of the baroque period do not show people, but the significance they had or wished to have. The naked body became a problem, for it revealed no distinctions of status. In a strongly hierarchical society a body covered with brocade and lace is significant because only in that way was it useful as the substance indicating power and wealth.

Court preachers like Abraham a Sancta Clara or the authors of city sumptuary laws struggled unavailingly, for ethical and social reasons, against the profligate expenditure dictated by fashion. Only when the fashion of decolletage emerging from France led to an immense consumption of Venetian lace for scarves and neckcloths, or when other foreign products had to be imported, were state fashion regulations passed with the deliberate aim of maintaining the advantage in foreign exchange. But when local manufacturers could produce the required luxury articles they, or the corresponding fashions, received public subsidies because they provided work and wages for many citizens. The elaborate fashions of the upper classes had become an economic factor. Moral objections or social-critical ideas were suppressed.

Against this fashion background the Rubens Magdalene is offensive for a number of reasons: she is a piece of uncontrolled, raw, formless nature and thus embodies everything the viewer of the picture abhors. In her nakedness, with no indication of her social station, she is a nobody in a period when clothes made the person. Nakedness and nature were no longer the essence of ideal beauty as they had been in the previous generation (cf. the depiction of the nude and the cult of antiquity in the Renaissance); they were instead the expression of raw matter that must be artistically ennobled in order to reveal the significance of its owner.

The artist shows a woman who contradicts all the norms of society. No woman looking at the picture, even if she were filled with pious ecstasy and love for Christ, could desire to slip into the role of this saint. As for the male viewers, they saw what must not be; their eyes beheld the half-concealed and their fantasies could go still farther. The woman is not depicted here in chaste nudity; in an artistic play of concealment and revelation she is handed over to every shameless and calculating eye.

The portrayal of Magdalene by Peter Paul Rubens reveals the fine line between religious and erotic art. Even today, when advertising deals very freely with women's bodies, it would present some problems, because at least some advertising sectors (the cosmetic industry, for example) maintain a rule for presentation of the female upper body: "frontal nudity is all right, but only if the nipples are covered, for example by the woman's arm; breasts may be shown from the side without covering."[3] In contrast Rubens has the fingers spread at the "right" point to emphasize the erotic allure of the woman's body. Magdalene, the repentant sinner, is at the same time a skilled seductress!

When a contemporary eye shifts back and forth among the three depictions of the Magdalene and recognizes each as typical of its era it becomes more than clear that in the baroque era the image of Mary Magdalene underwent a fundamental change. The medieval Magdalene was a (former) sinner, but that aspect of her legend was only important insofar as through it sinful people were brought to salvation. She was honored because she had overcome sin. Now, however, she was interesting precisely as an exciting, seductively beautiful sinner. What people wanted was no longer the patron and advocate, but the loving and penitent sinner. This was true in all the Counter-Reformation lands, especially France and the Catholic principalities of southern Germany.

It is true that Mary's old significance as a sinner's saint endured here and there in poetry and the plastic arts well into the eighteenth century, especially when she was portrayed together with other saintly sinners as in the confessional figures of the Salem minster (Joseph Anton Feuchtmayer), at the sides of the Lady Chapel of the Fulda cathedral (penitent Peter and penitent Magdalene), or in a small group of figures by the Breisgau artist Matthias Faller (Peter and Magdalene, in the Augustinermuseum in Freiburg). The New Testament's saintly sinner also played an occasional part in poetry:

> Look graciously on me
> As you did on Peter.

> Let me, like Magdalene,
> go comforted from here.
>
> As for Matthew at the tollbooth
> And Zacchaeus full of hope,
> And to the thief, so be gracious to me
> And forgive all my sins.[4]

But her true task was no longer that of the advocate; she had become a symbol reflecting the fragility of life and the world. Humanism and the Renaissance had placed the human being at the center of things, but now the people of the baroque era discovered how uncertain their existence in the world was. They experienced the temporality of all things (hence their fondness for clocks in churches and castles, mechanical toys that were at the same time warnings about the transitoriness of all things). Everywhere they encountered the signs of death; they turned to penitent thoughts and penitential acts and fled to ecstatic forms of religion; they dreamed of flight from the world and covered their fear of death with orgiastic feasting. The dubious symbol of this experience of the world and of life was the sinner Mary Magdalene in her varied roles: as a hermit in flight from the world, as a penitent, as a great lover who transferred her formerly sinful love to Jesus. These sometimes new associations that were attached to Mary Magdalene in the seventeenth and eighteenth centuries can be seen in buildings, pictures, and texts that reflect the spirit of their time.

1. The Hermitages in Baroque Parks

Every epoch has roles and figures in which it expresses its special character: in the seventeenth and eighteenth centuries the prince or ruler was emblematic of the time. The most obvious example is the young Louis XIV, who in 1653 in the "Ballet of the Night" danced the role of the *Roi Soleil*, the royal sun, and from then on dominated the entire epoch as the "Sun King." In centralized France it was the king who radiated the light of this sun; in other lands the role was played by a number of lesser princes. The prince stood at the center of things, and this was visibly reflected in the layout of palaces and estates: the streets of the city and the allées in the estate park radiated like rays from their center. This was true especially of cities and palatial estates newly established by rulers, such as the city of Karlsruhe or the palace and park at Nymphenburg near Munich.

The baroque prince was not a private person, but a representative of a public idea; his palaces were not primarily places to live in, but representative structures. The baroque palace had no cozy rooms because princely life knew no intimacy (cf. the *lever* that regulated every phase of arising, dressing, breakfasting, or the "bedding" at royal weddings). Ceremonial encompassed life just as the hoopskirt covered the figure or the gardener's shears shaped natural growth.

In this period of high artistry and formalization of court life the garden also served the purpose of representative exhibition of splendor, but where representation was the principal aim of palatial and garden architecture, the desire for an opportunity for retirement was also evident. In the baroque garden, away from the principal axis, there appeared various tiny palaces whose names revealed their purposes: *Mon Repos, Mon Plaisir, Solitude, Sans-souci, Eremitage:* places of retreat, of quiet, of pleasure. At times these buildings imitated foreign styles (cf. the fondness for East Asian or Turkish architecture) or ancient forms (cf. the artificial ruins), corresponding to the taste of the time and pleasure in the exotic and bizarre. Religious needs played little or no part in most of these constructions (cf. the buildings in Potsdam or the Württemberg palace in Basel with its artificial hermitage) unless the person who ordered the designs was an ecclesiastical nobleman (cf. the hermitage of the Prince-Bishop Damian Hugo of Schönborn in Waghäusel). These hermitages, unlike the decorative structures in landscape gardens, had a real purpose: for the hunt, ball games, or adventurous "gallantry."

Quite different were the hermitages in estates in southern Germany that were known as "Magdalene cells" (for example, Favorite at Rastatt, or Nymphenburg). These cells were not placed at the site of a lovely view but in a place symbolizing wildness and distance from the world. Their very exteriors demonstrate vulnerability and surrender to nature (cf. the bark siding of Favorite or the artificial rifts in the walls at Nymphenburg). Unlike the hermitages in landscape gardens they were not intended to awaken feelings and moods; they are not window-dressing. They were meant for the use of the prince: for meditation, penance, religious contemplation, as expressed in the verses of a late baroque poet penned at about the same time: "Drop, you worn out garment (= the body) / decay brings perfection."[5]

The dedication of such places to Mary Magdalene and with it the association of the saint with places of penitence and self-humiliation documents her dominant image in the baroque era: that of the penitent sinner, combined with the idea of the transitoriness of life.

Buildings in which destruction by the passage of time was already incorporated as part of the original style were perceptible reminders of that transitoriness. The absolutist prince who, turning his back on the splendid facade of his palace, leaves the geometrically ordered garden to enter on the path of unordered nature and penetrate the wilderness, is reminded at first sight of such a cell of his own vulnerability and mortality.

The two hermitages connected with the saint's name which we will examine more fully here (Nymphenburg and Favorite) belonged to Catholic rulers who were strongly affected by the spirit of the Counter-Reformation: Elector Max Emanuel of Bavaria (1662–1726) and Margravine Sibylla Augusta of Baden (1675–1733).

> The Magdalene cell in Nymphenburg was built between 1725 and 1728 according to a design by Joseph Effner. It was completed by Elector Carl Albrecht and solemnly dedicated on April 4, 1728, by his brother, Clemens August, archbishop of Cologne.

> The hermitage at Favorite was built in 1717–8 by Ludwig Michael Rohrer. In 1722 the margravine saw the Pagoda castle with its octagonal plan during a visit to Munich; hence we may presume immediate influence from that on Rohrer's work in Rastatt and Waghäusel, but the cell in Favorite, also a round structure, follows other models to be found in Rohrer's home district of Bohemia.

Common to both these members of the nobility is also that they were directly affected by the military events of the seventeenth and eighteenth centuries (the wars with the Turks, the wars of the Spanish and Palatine successions, and so on); they were moved by the fickleness of earthly happiness to turn to the enduring values contained in religion. The Elector was on the "wrong" side of the War of the Spanish Succession, supporting the French against the Habsburgs, and was forced to spend the period from 1704 to 1715 in exile, part of the time in the Netherlands and part in France. The Margravine had a still more difficult fate as wife and ruler in a land impoverished by warfare.

Sibylla Augusta,[6] Princess of Sachsen-Lauenburg, grew up on the family estates in Bohemia; after the death of her parents she and her older sister were placed under the care of the emperor. The sisters' claims to female succession to Sachsen-Lauenburg was rejected; instead these two wealthy heiresses quickly found themselves at the center of a miserable haggling over their marriages. Finally Margrave Ludwig Wilhelm of Baden-Baden ("Louis of the Turks") won the rich heiress as his bride; she was the financially strapped emperor's payment to his general, who urgently needed money for his war-ravaged land. In Baden, since the Margrave was still in the imperial service, she undertook the duties of ruling the land until, after the death of her husband in 1707, she received the official title of Regent for twenty years. Sibylla Augusta proved herself a prudent and active regent who brought the despoiled land back to order. In her private life as well she had to accept many blows of fate.

The Margravine's life is only sketchily documented, but her buildings permit us to discern the typical features of a baroque ruler in whom secular magnificence combines with serious religious feeling. As the governor of her land she followed the ceremonial lifestyle the role demanded, but she asked her confessor to treat her like "a common, poor beggar woman."[7] Her profound piety was demonstrated in numerous pilgrimages, devotional foundations, and membership in religious societies. After her death she was buried in the robe of a Carmelite under the doorsill of the palace church at Rastatt so that everyone who entered might tread upon her.

Both these hermitages were conceived as dwelling and chapel combined. The building at Nymphenburg,[8] consisting of a grotto room, a chapel, and a simple apartment with four dwelling rooms for the prince, was furnished for living, sleeping, eating, prayer, and contemplation. Although it was "conceived as a hermit's dwelling"[9] the princely dignity of this hermit was not overlooked, as the costly table service indicates. The internal decorations were meant to warn in their different ways of the Last Things; these included ceiling pictures and paintings of scenes from the life of the penitent Mary Magdalene as well as a statue of the saint above a fountain pool (the water was meant to symbolize her tears of remorse and was supposed to have power to heal diseases of the eye). Her attributes here are a crucifix and a skull.

While this Magdalene cell was regarded as "one of the most important religious hermitage structures of the waning baroque era"[10] the baroque ideal is still more highly developed at Favorite: here the hermitage is much more modest, even in its external dimensions,[11] as a contemporary traveler wrote: "This hermitage is the very opposite of the one at Nymphenburg, which has something grand about its hidden splendor, as one might say," whereas the one in Baden, in its natural simplicity, had more the character "of a comfortable retreat for spiritual contemplation."[12]

The structure is on an octagonal plan with the Magdalene chapel in the center. The remaining space contains a dining room with statues of the Holy Family and a seat for the Margravine as well as a bedroom and a kitchen that was probably not used. The present furnishings include an oil painting, "Mary Magdalene Beneath the Cross" (eighteenth century) and a so-called "Memento Mori" (eighteenth century), a skull inlaid with precious stones. The exterior of the building is covered with real bark and the interior walls and ceilings are painted to resemble bark; this, with the tiny windows, heightens the appearance of frugal poverty.

Still, the special feature of this hermitage is its chapel, in which life-size wax figures depict the life of the saint: (1) Mary Magdalene anointing the feet of Jesus; (2) the weeping Magdalene beneath the cross; (3) the tomb of Jesus; (4) Christ as a gardener appearing to Magdalene. On the walls are instruments of torture recalling the Passion. Probably the skull now displayed in the bedroom was part of a no-longer-extant scene with the penitent Magdalene.

The purpose of this chapel goes far beyond its use for formal worship services. The Margravine's prie-dieu beside the tomb of Jesus and the lifelike facial features of the Magdalene figures, perhaps "even displaying features from the Margravine's own portraits,"[13] indicate that this room functioned as a "religious theater" with the Margravine as "role-player" of the sorrowing and penitent Magdalene. Today this kind of "play" may seem tasteless, but for a person of the baroque era to whom the world appeared as theater and the theater as symbol of the world, the connection between religion and theater, serious penance and play had a deeper meaning; that is why the theater was also a preferred medium of instruction, frequently used by the teaching orders (including the Jesuits and the Piarists) to make faith an experience of the whole person.

Connections to the Piarists are especially easy to establish in the case of the Margravine: probably the Princess was taught by Piarists, and it is certain that she brought members of the order to her city of residence, Rastatt; it was also Piarists who prepared the festivities for the birthdays of the Margrave and Margravine's family. The preparation and presentation of court feasts was taken so seriously by the princely families that only the best artists—from Rubens to Goethe—or educated and artistically knowledgeable members of the religious orders were entrusted with the task. As a true child of the baroque the Margravine also loved the game of dressing up and slipping into mythological or biblical roles. When the line between the religious and the secular is blurred the "play" can be continued in the chapel and the cell.

It is of course true that the roots of this type of piety, especially in Sibylla Augusta's case, go much farther back: in the Middle Ages it was Franciscan devotion more than any other that imitated scenes from the life of Jesus with all the appropriate tools and scenery. Of this Saskia Esser remarks: "In the powerful movement of the Counter-Reformation, particularly marked in Bohemia, this mystical devotion, marked by a strong degree of realism and the longing for immediate participation, enjoyed a rich revival; Sibylla Augusta's piety should be understood against this background."[14] The Margravine herself became a figure in the religious drama as the penitent Magdalene. In humility, self-abnegation, and meditation, but also in her practical readiness to lend assistance, especially to the ordinary people, she expressed her penitent spirit. Her "humility" culminated in the epitaph she desired for herself: "Pray for Augusta, the great sinner!" This expression, and knowledge of the penitential cell in the palace park later led to some rather different reactions:

In his 1826 travel narrative Karl Julius Weber described the structure and its features in a tone of ironic distance: "Here the last Margravine of Baden-Baden, the last princess of the house of Lauenburg, and widow of the heroic Louis, the sinful Sibylla [here there is a gap in the manuscript] portrayed the penitent Magdalene,"[15] while among the people, who had no access to the park and the cell in the nineteenth century, the memory of a dim, strange, ghostly building lingered.[16]

However, for the princess subject to the ideas of her time the penitential play was a genuine, deeply felt expression of her piety, which is why the ordinary people of her time also looked up to her with great admiration. Certainly the emphasis on her outstanding role as a penitent makes it clear that this was something exceptional: "normal" women had no opportunity to express their religious feelings with such intensity. Their lives were much too harsh to permit them such extravagant religious exercises; one may recall, for example, the newly-established factories that could not have survived without the work of women in homes and in the factories themselves, the girls in agricultural industry or the female personnel in city households who had no time for extended religious exercises. Even the Princess's penance was a privilege of her exalted social position.

2. Magdalene the Penitent as Symbol of Temporality: Reflections on a Painting by Januarius Zick

Nothing was so certain for the people of the baroque era as the temporal nature of the world and all that pertains to it; nothing endures, everything is vanity, appearance, mask, dream, and frivolity. Behind the beautiful, healthy body stands its death, behind time, a reality made up of superficial appearances, stands eternity. The title of Calderon's drama, "Life is a Dream," could stand as a motto for the entire epoch, for the hero's final words of instruction were valid for everyone: "that the happiness of all human beings vanishes like a dream." This conviction was matched, on the one hand, by the mysticism of the afterlife and longing for death; anyone who has heard a Bach cantata will recall petitions such as "If only the wind were already blowing over my tomb, my grave" (BWV 57) or "I rejoice to think of my death; oh, had it already come to pass" (BWV 82). The other side of the coin is the rejection of the world as *vanitas* (nothingness, vanity), a conviction voiced again and again, with ever new variations, by countless poets and agreed upon by everyone in spite of the disparity of confessions: for example, the Protestant Andreas Gryphius:

> When you look, you see only vanity on earth.
> What this one builds today, another tears down tomorrow,
> Where countless cities stand will one day be a meadow,
> Where a shepherd's child will play with the flocks.[17]

or the Catholic Angelus Silesius:

> The world and its desires pass away,
> The beauty of the flesh cannot last,
> Time can bring to ruin everything
> That human hands have built.[18]

These words from the seventeenth century had lost none of their poignancy a hundred years later, as we see in the warnings of the mystic Gerhard Tersteegen:

> Lose yourself, with the world and time,
> And sink into eternity,
> Believe me, in that way, day and night,
> You will spend your time the best you can![19]

The painting of the "Penitent Magdalene" by Tersteegen's contemporary Januarius Zick can be seen as a pendant image to his poem. The artist, son and student of the painter Johannes Zick, was born in Munich in 1730 and died in Ehrenbreitstein in 1797. Most of his education took place in Paris and Rome, where he devoted himself to the study of baroque style. From about 1760 onward he was court painter to the Elector of Trier, and it was during this period, in 1765, that he painted the "Penitent Magdalene." (Staatliche Kunsthalle Karlsruhe, Inv. Nr. 1480; cf. Plate 8.)

This small-format painting (46x35.2 cm) shows a deeply meditative woman who has turned from the world (following the poet's counsel) and immersed herself in eternity. This is neither an altar picture for a public church space nor a representative object designed for a secular space; it is an intimate painting intended for the private contemplation and observation of its owner, probably a man.[20]

What does the observer see? first, a young woman deeply immersed in reading. Her upper body and legs are naked, her hair uncovered; this woman has fled from the world and has put aside everything that could indicate her position in society. At her feet is a simple dish recalling the necessities of earthly life. In her lap she holds a skull. The woman, the skull, and the book are bathed in bright light that spills over into the background. The group warns of the temporality of life, a theme underscored by the contrast of youth and the skull. The scene is characterized as a religious *memento mori* by the cross pointing steeply upward and to the right. In this context the crucifix represents both love for Christ and immersion in his suffering and death, just as the skull, in addition to the general reference to death, recalls the skull of Adam depicted in many crucifixion scenes: human subjection to death (= Adam) is transformed into life through the cross.

The woman is seated on a heap of stones, the crumbling remnants of a wall or a well. The picture does not depict a naturally growing wilderness, but indicates a cultural landscape given over to decay: what people have made will be destroyed in the course of time; everything constructed breaks apart. The ruin thus fulfills the same function as the artificial ruins in eighteenth-century gardens: it is a symbol of the passage of time. Even the book, the vehicle of enduring ideas, is old and worn; its borders show traces of decay. The picture could be read as a timeless allegory of mortality were it not for the vessel in the background that is one of the constant attributes of Mary Magdalene: the ointment jar, together with the cross, identify the woman as Magdalene.

Its title and iconographic program locate the painting within a long tradition, for as early as the sixteenth century there emerged a type of picture showing a variety of holy penitents and hermits (Anthony, Jerome, Magdalene, and others) in wild mountain and desert landscapes. The "modern" artists who had just discovered the depiction of nature indulged in wildly romantic landscapes that filled most of the canvas; the hermits themselves were, as a rule, only visible at the extreme edge of the picture. In addition to the indications of hermits' cells, symbols of death and transitoriness were part of the program of these pictures. In the motif of the *Magdalena poenitens,* which endured into the nineteenth century, the cross, book, skull, and ointment jar were fixed attributes, while others (such as an hourglass or the instruments of martyrdom) could augment the traditional ensemble.[21]

The message of this kind of picture, "which must emphatically be called a key theme of baroque painting,"[22] is clear: penance is a precondition for the heaven-centered ecstasy into which baroque piety resolved itself. The suppression of earthly and sensual life and an exaggerated longing for eternity were inseparable. That this was not merely a matter of theoretical considerations is evident from a glance at the history of the religious orders and saints of the period. In Catholic lands such as France, Spain, or Italy there was a strong movement of turning away from the world in the sixteenth and seventeenth centuries; this was connected with the foundation of new orders (such as the Ursulines of St. Angela Merici in the sixteenth century) or the reform of existing orders (the Carmelites, reformed by St. Teresa of Avila in the sixteenth century; the Trappists by Armand-Jean de Rancé in the seventeenth) that soon spread far beyond the lands of their origin. (Significantly, the new orders included the "Sisters of the Order of St. Mary Magdalene," founded in the seventeenth century for the improvement of fallen girls.) Women of the upper classes especially were inclined to abruptly abandon their superficial life in society and seek a rational alternative in cloistered communities. The rapid spread both of strictly contemplative and of socially-engaged women's orders would not have been possible without the spiritual and financial support of prominent women in society.[23] These men and women followed the same idea of penance and turning away from the world that formed the governing ideal of the representations of the penitent Magdalene. Something similar is true of the canonizations of the period: thus in 1728 Margaret of Cortona (thirteenth century) was canonized; after a sinful relationship followed by severe penance she entered the canon of saints under the titles "the Penitent" and "the Second Magdalene."[24] This saint, whose piety was shaped by eternity from the twofold aspects of penance and surrender to the afterlife, also fully matched the ideal of sanctity that is expressed in the now canonically correct image of the penitent Magdalene, for those who have correctly grasped the teaching of the instability of all earthly things will ultimately "bid farewell to the world in repentance and rejection" and conclude their lives as hermits or in the cloister "in contemplation of the things that do not pass away."[25] Saints and rogues, religious and princes, ladies and gentlemen found their model in the figure of the penitent Magdalene.

Nevertheless, for this world-averse penitence it is also true that nothing is so serious that it cannot become a game. Many ladies of the court—princesses and mistresses—as well as the *demimonde* "played" the penitent saint and had themselves painted in this pose, which had the advantage of permitting a liberal display of the female body.

Januarius Zick took up the typical image of the penitent Magdalene, but also altered it. Whereas the high baroque smothered the knowledge of the vanity of earthly life in splendor and festivity, surrendering itself to a mood somewhere between libertinism and penance, the rococo preferred more muted tones; ecstatic gestures gave way to silent resignation. Zick's intimate rococo version of the theme shifts the woman from the margin to the center of the picture, makes the grandiose wilderness an idyll, and by adding a border of flowers and leaves deprives the whole of its threatening character. Contrary to the title, this is not a "penitent" Magdalene; rather the woman is seated in an attitude of pensive, tranquil meditation and invites the observer to regard his or her own mortal life from the perspective of eternity. Only in this way will the viewer recognize what the lyricists and storytellers repeatedly emphasize: that all earthly things last only for a time.

Zick's Magdalene points to a further motif context: the biblical figure is replaced (as I have already hinted in describing the picture) by the allegorical figure of Melancholy. A corresponding depiction by Domenico Feti, "Melancholy" (ca. 1613, Paris, Louvre) shows a young woman deeply immersed in the contemplation of a skull and surrounded by objects that indicate the futility of earthly learning: old books, an ancient torso, a variety of tools, a globe. The background shows an old building falling to decay. The idea of melancholy, a resigned contemplation of the nothingness of the world and earthly life, suffuses the depiction of the penitent Magdalene, "who heedlessly thrusts aside the signs of human activity" and, sunk in "meditation on death and hope for the afterlife" gives valid expression to the attitude toward life typical of the age.[26] In her transformation into the figure of melancholy Magdalene has lost her halo and has herself become a symbol of *vanitas.*

3. Sinful and Penitent Love

The pictorial motif of the penitent Magdalene so strongly shaped the image of sanctity in the baroque era that on the one hand other saints—contemporaries or the newly-canonized—were measured by it, and on the other hand the topos "penitent woman" for Magdalene gradually became an empty formula. Even authors whose intentions were quite different were unable to avoid occasional references to the blessed, tearful penitent (cf. the "penitent Magdalene" of Friedrich Spee). With others (artists as well as authors) one even gets the impression that Magdalene's love, which is primarily "penitential love," is only interesting because it draws its intensity from the sinful love that has been overcome. At any rate, according to the ideas of the time Magdalene is the sinful woman who appeared at the banquet of Simon the Pharisee to weep over Jesus' feet and anoint them—a scene immortalized by painters in countless versions. Certainly she is not depicted as a remorseful penitent—something that would only detract from her youthful beauty—but as a seductively beautiful lady who caresses one of Jesus' bare feet and whose appearance as much as her tender act sets the respectable company at table in an uproar. The intimate association of sensuality and divinity increases the allure of such depictions, especially when they present such subtle hints of the woman's sinful past as in Jean-Baptiste Jouvenet's "Christ and Mary Magdalene at the Banquet of Simon the Pharisee" (seventeenth century; Staatliche Kunsthalle Karlsruhe),[27] where the beautiful sinner is surrounded by carefully strewn and broken blossoms. The presence of such banquet scenes especially in refectories or convent drawing rooms made the sinful woman the representative of an earthly and sinful world that simultaneously disturbs and fascinates.[28]

Only as this sinful woman with her worldly experience can she say through her tears:

> Jesus, accept a heart that is no longer worthy of you because it has belonged to others rather than to you; but at least it is a heart that has this advantage from its evil experiences: in the depths of its emotion it is convinced that you are the only one deserving of love (p. 16).

This quotation is taken from the work of an unknown French author that Rainer Maria Rilke translated into German: "The Love of Magdalene." A French sermon taken by Abbé Joseph Bonnet from Manuscript Q I, 14 in the Imperial Library of St. Petersburg."[29] According to Rilke, then, this is a text discovered in St. Petersburg by Abbé Bonnet and published in Paris in 1909. For the most part Jacques-Bénigne Bossuet (1627–1704) is suspected as the author; he was active as politician and bishop under Louis XIV and was particularly famous as a preacher.[30]

Rilke (1876–1927), who translated a number of works from foreign languages, completed this translation in Paris in 1911. The poet, exhausted from work on his novel, *Die Aufzeichnung des Malte Laurids Brigge*, endured a period of doubting his own creative abilities and until the outbreak of war undertook a number of commissions, including the translation of this tractate that had recently appeared in Paris publication. From the practical point of view it was a piece of work done to earn his living, but the figure of Magdalene, with her limitless love, moved seamlessly into the continuing series of women conjured up by the poet, women whose love surpasses that of men and beside whom men always fail (Marianna Alcoforado, Louise Labé, Gaspara Stampa, Heloïse, Bettine Brentano); in particular, individual passages in the *Malte* novel read like an anticipatory commentary on "Magdalene."

The tractate describes the threefold form of Magdalene's love, as the introductory lines announce: "Magdalene, the saintly lover of Jesus, loved him in his three conditions. She loved him as a living man, she loved him when he was dead, and she loved the Risen One" (p. 9). The first form of her love, devoted to the present Jesus, was the bold tenderness of penitent love that draws near to the beloved or the bridegroom and at the same time withdraws from him in order by that very act to be held fast by his love. The author is "never tired of contemplating the miraculous relationships of our holy penitent" (p. 13). Page after page he describes the passionate and tender game of love, Magdalene's sighs and tears at Jesus' feet. Jesus' brutality appears to him all the more alienating ("What an unpleasant game you play with the hearts that love you!" [p. 19]); it culminates on the cross: a good word for everyone, but none for the loving woman under the cross. The second form of love belongs to the dead and consists in a patient waiting at the tomb; the third form is revealed in rage and in the excesses of love abandoned. Jesus ascended is the cruel lover who tortures beyond all measure the loving woman left behind. Her despair borders on madness: "In this condition of love everything becomes horror and disgust" (p. 27).

This third form of Magdalene's love, her waiting and longing for the return of her bridegroom, is illuminated by the Song of Songs and at the same time reflects the Church. The beloved in the Song sometimes thinks she is being put to shame; she withdraws into the desert and hides in the cliffs, seeking consolation in the wilderness—so also Magdalene: "What else was it that drove Magdalene into the horrors of that haunted desert and the silent fearfulness of the dim caves in which she reproached her heart for its rage at her abandoned and surrendered love?" (p. 25). The laments of this lover are also the laments and sighs of the Church, who after Jesus' disappearance remains as an "unconsolable young widow" (p. 23). Like the bride of the Song, like Magdalene, so also the Church groans "because she is deprived of her bridegroom" (p. 23). Thus the "Song of Songs of the synagogue," who has not yet seen the beloved, is transformed by way of the "Song of Songs of penitent love" with which Magdalene embraced him into the "Song of Songs of the Church," who has seen and touched him and ceaselessly calls out to her divine bridegroom:

> Toward this second appearance of Jesus Christ all the inmost parts of the beloved burn, but the period of waiting for this reunion is a single pain. . . . In truth it is the intention of this holy bridegroom to keep us continually waiting, attentively waiting in an anticipation that groans and longs for him (pp. 23–4).

What is imaged in the Song of Songs and became reality in Magdalene is the mystery of love that is accomplished in the Church through the centuries: "Such is the nature of the love of those who are on the way: God is communicated in it only by concealment" (p. 29). The divine love will be accomplished for Magdalene, as for the Church, only after a period of exile, in the fullness of time.

The tractate adopts the traditional image of Mary Magdalene (the sinful woman, the sister of Martha) and also stands within the tradition of typological interpretation of biblical texts as applied to the Church; it is completely untouched by the biblical criticism that was then in its infancy (something that also favors the supposed authorship of Bossuet!). Nevertheless, the text sketches the image of that "other" Magdalene projected by European painting in so many banquet scenes: she is the charming penitent who is only interesting because her past as a sinful woman is presumed. Here love, despite its passionate content, is depicted from a cool distance; her penance—this courteous, penitent love (p. 11)—is not the revision of a failed life, but a cover for her "charming tendernesses" and "the holy gallantries of repentant love" (p. 15) by means of which the new lover is ensnared; even the penitent gestures described in the gospel are erotically reinterpreted: "Loose your hair, Magdalene, and so bind the feet of Jesus. . . . How shall he disentangle his feet from the net of your hair?" (p. 14). The love of this Magdalene ultimately lacks the existential seriousness with which the real penitents of the period devoted themselves to reforming their lives; despite this emphasis it is only dalliance without obligation, a game from a courteous age.

The little tractate takes on an especially piquant note if we detach it from its spiritual-typological scheme and connect it to secular reality as a sermon preached to a court society in which the royal mistress had her official place. (Jouvenet's Magdalene, too, is not so much bowing in penitent humility as executing a courtly curtsy!)

In the French text, as in the pictorial images of the period, Mary Magdalene certainly embodies the humble sinner (and the passionate penitent beneath the cross), while Easter scenes featuring her (cf. the older *noli me tangere* motif) recede to a striking degree. She thus becomes a sister to those noble courtesans who populate eighteenth-century literature.[31] Through genuine love for a noble man they are converted to a virtuous life at his side, or they renounce his love so as not to stand in the way of his future. The reformed courtesan as a type (cf. A.-F. Prévost d'Exiles' *Manon Lescaut,* 1731) associated both by authors and by their audiences with the penitent Magdalene, lives beyond the novels of the eighteenth and nineteenth centuries (cf. Dumas' *Camille*), beyond the opera (cf. Verdi, *La Traviata;* Puccini, *Manon Lescaut*), and beyond the movies made of this literary and operatic material well into the present; it continues also to have a reverse effect on the image of the biblical Magdalene.

In retrospect Mary Magdalene is seen as a perfect symbol of the baroque: ardor and playfulness, earthly and heavenly love, penance and longing for heaven, elevation toward the life beyond, and finally, melancholy and resignation as well: she incorporates all the important themes of the baroque. Only she herself, Mary from Magdala, who attracted all these associations to herself—she remains out of the picture and is completely obscured by the flood of images she called forth. She is a time-bound symbol that endures only in partial aspects: the beautiful sinner as object of male lust. The depictions of the naked penitent or the groveling sinner fit seamlessly within the thought of the period that feared woman as "witch" and at the same time reveled lasciviously in her perverse games of love.

Notes

[1]For the fashions of the baroque era cf. "Das Kostüm" in Richard Alewyn and Karl Sälzle, *Das grosse Welttheater. Die Epoche der höfischen Feste in Dokument und Deutung,* vol. 92 (Hamburg, 1959) 33–8, and "Damen und Kleider" in Helga Möbius, *Die Frau im Barock* (Stuttgart, 1982) 178–200.

[2]Möbius, *Die Frau,* 184.

[3]*Brigitte,* 3/1995, 90.

[4]Angelus Silesius, *Heilige Seelenlust oder Geistliche Hirtenlieder* in idem, *Sämtliche poetische Werke in drei Bänden,* edited by Hans Ludwig Held (3rd rev. ed. Munich, 1949) 2.127.

[5]Wilhelm Krämer, ed., *Johann Christian Günthers Sämtliche Werke 2: Klagelieder und Geistliche Gedichte, in zeitlicher Folge* (Darmstadt, 1964) 235.

[6]For the Margravine's biography cf. Saskia Esser, *Leben und Werk der Markgräfin Franziska Sibylla Augusta* (Rastatt, 1983), and Hans-Georg Kaack, *Markgräfin Sibylla Augusta. Die große badische Fürstin der Barockzeit* (Constance, n. d. [1983]).

[7]Esser, *Leben und Werk,* 21. Now and then the Princess's piety took on peculiar features under the influence of a fanatical confessor, as when "offensive" pictures worth 50,000 gulden were burned at the palace in Rastatt: cf. Kaack, *Markgräfin,* 195.

[8]For the description cf. Elmar D. Schmid, *Nymphenburg. Schloß und Garten, Pagodenburg, Badenburg, Magdalenenklause, Amalienburg* (Munich, 1979) 64–71, and Gerhard Hojer and Elmar D. Schmid, *Nymphenburg. Schloß, Park und Burgen, Amtlicher Führer* (Munich, 1989) 70–5.

[9]Schmid, *Nymphenburg,* 64.

[10]Adrian von Buttlar, "Der Nymphenburger Schloßpark," in Harri Günther, ed., *Gärten der Goethezeit* (Leipzig, 1993) 240.

[11]For a description cf. Walther Schwenecke and Wolfgang Wiese, *Schloßpark Favorite und Eremitage.* Kurzführer der Staatlichen Schlösser und Gärten Baden-Württemberg (Karlsruhe, n. d. [1994?]).

[12]Johann Georg Keysler (1729), quoted by Kaack, *Markgräfin,* 183.

[13]Wiese, *Schloßpark Favorite,* 40. This is all the more the case because other "roles" of the Margravine are documented: for example, she was Saint Helena at the palace church of Rastatt. Cf. idem, "Die Magdalenenkapelle und die kostbaren Wachsfiguren," in *Schlösser* (Baden-Württemberg, 1993) 1/2, pp. 12–5.

[14]Esser, *Leben und Werk,* 46.

[15]Quoted in Kaack, *Markgräfin,* 165.

[16]Anna Maria Renner, "Die Einsiedelei im Park von Favorite," *Die Pyramide,* 21 (1932) 19, pp. 75–6. The impression conveyed at that time is confirmed by historical perspectives from the early twentieth century, whereas the renovated cell surrounded by newly planted trees presents instead a kind of friendly and inviting appearance!

[17]The text of the sonnet, "Es ist alles eitel," is printed, together with an interpretation by Erich Trunz, in Benno von Wiese, ed., *Die deutsche Lyrik. Form und Geschichte* (Düsseldorf, 1962) 1.145–51.

[18]Angelus Silesius, *Heilige Seelenlust,* 162.

[19]Gerhard Tersteegen, *Geistliches Blumengärtlein inniger Seelen.* (2nd printing of the new edition Stuttgart, 1969) 38.

[20]The typical image of the penitent Magdalene with the repentant woman completely or partially nude led gradually from the field of ecclesiastical art into private use; cf. Marga Anstett-Janssen, "Maria Magdalena," *Lexikon der christlichen Ikonographie* (Rome et al., 1974) 7, cols. 516–41, at 520. The commissioner and/or first purchaser of Zick's picture can no longer be identified. (Telephone communication from Dr. Dietmar Lüdke of the Staatliche Kunsthalle, Karlsruhe.)

[21]A (blood-spattered) scourge as indication of the seriousness of the penance is found in "Magdalene's Night Vigil" by Georges de la Tour (17th c., Paris, Louvre; cf. Plate 7).

[22]Möbius, *Die Frau*, 140.

[23]For the close connection between female orders and ladies of high society, especially in France, cf. Möbius, *Die Frau*, 135–40.

[24]In a vision before her death she heard Christ say of Mary Magdalene, "this is my beloved daughter"; cf. Walter Nigg, *Das Buch der Büßer* (Olten and Freiburg, 1970) 81–103.

[25]Richard Alewyn, Afterword to Johann Beer, *Das Narrenspital*. Rowohlts Klassiker der Literatur under der Wissenschaft 9 (Hamburg, 1957) 147.

[26]Möbius, *Die Frau*, 32. The picture of "Melancholy" is in the same work, figure 92.

[27]Inv. No. 1096, canvas, 101 by 162, 5 cm. This is the replica or a school copy of a larger work (390 by 624 cm.) originally intended for a Paris church. The picture was published in Jan Lauts, ed., *Französische Meister. Aus der Staatlichen Kunsthalle Karlsruhe* (Karlsruhe, 1963) figure 12 (section).

[28]The reference to the sinful world that bursts in with her is especially evident when the banquet scene is set within the picture as a secular pendant to the spiritual Last Supper scene; cf. Gerhard Neumann, "Gedächtnismahl und Liebesmahl. Das Bildprogramm des 'Fürstensaales' von St. Peter," in Hans-Otto Mühleisen, ed., *Das Vermächtnis der Abtei. 900 Jahre St. Peter auf dem Schwarzwald* (Karlsruhe, 1993) 149–84.

[29]Rainer Maria Rilke, "Die Liebe der Magdalena," in *Die Liebenden*. Insel Taschenbuch 355 (5th ed. Frankfurt and Leipzig, 1992) 7–31. The page references are to this edition.

[30]For this suggestion cf. the monograph on Rilke by Hans Egon Holthusen, *Rainer Maria Rilke, in Selbstzeugnissen und Bilddokumenten*. Rowohlts Monographien 22 (Hamburg, 1958) 119; and Wolfgang Leppmann, *Rilke. Sein Leben, seine Welt, sein Werk* (Bern and Munich, 1993) 334.

[31]Cf. Elisabeth Frenzel, "Die selbstlose Kurtisane," *Motive der Weltliteratur* (3rd ed. Stuttgart, 1988) 434–51.

Chapter Six

Mary Magdalene
Between Religion and Aesthetics

In the literature of the seventeenth and eighteenth centuries, between the baroque and the classical periods, we find surprising images of Magdalene in the work of two major poets; these depictions dispense with the well-known features of the sinner or the penitent. In the seventeenth century Friedrich Spee wrote his great Magdalene poem, and in the eighteenth century she is celebrated in Friedrich Klopstock's *Messiah* as a disciple of the divine friend of humanity. Certainly the presuppositions and intentions of the two poets could not be more at odds: whereas Spee's literary activity grew out of a deep devotion and complemented his ecclesial duties as priest and teacher, Klopstock's work is the expression neither of personal nor of church-connected piety, but represents a modern cultural Christianity in which the deep inwardness of pietism is aesthetically secularized. The same is true of the biblical texts: familiarity with them derives not from participation in worship; it is simply part of the educational canon of the period, to be learned just as one learned the stories of the Greek, Indian, or Nordic gods.

1. The "Spouse of Jesus" (Friedrich Spee)

Friedrich Spee of Langenfeld (1591–1635) wrote a poem on Mary Magdalene that can be found not only in his collection *Trutz-Nachtigall* (1649) but also in the *Güldenes Tugend-Buch* (a Paris manuscript of 1640).[1] It is a great poem not only because of its length

82

(472 verses in 59 strophes), but primarily because of the qualities of its form and content.

The context and title differ in the two versions:

(a) In the *Güldenes Tugend-Buch,* which is divided according to the three supernatural virtues of faith, hope, and love, the poem is placed in the second part entitled "Hope, or Love as Desire." In the introduction, where he describes how he envisions the book being used, Spee followed scholastic theology in distinguishing two kinds of love: "love as desire" *(amor concupiscentiae)* and "benevolent love, or love of friendship" *(amor benevolentiae);* the first longs for what one does not yet have, the second wills good to the other from the heart.[2] Among the exercises of "love as desire" are poems in which the spouse of Jesus (that is, the soul that loves God) sighs for her bridegroom[3] and cries out with longing until her throat is raw, until at last she finds a point of rest:

> Before your cross, by day and by year
> Will I sit with Magdalene.[4]

The Magdalene poem is the conclusion and climax of this series; its baroque title makes the connection once again to the second part of the book: "Other works of hope or love / of desire / of / Mary Magdalene when, after the / Jewish Easter feast or Great Sabbath / she sought early in the morning / her Jesus at the tomb."

(b) While Mary Magdalene here appears as prototype of hope, in *Trutz-Nachtigall* her function has shifted. This poem follows numbers 2–10, each of which is entitled "Love Song of the Bride of Jesus." It is number 11 and is entitled "Mirror of Love; or, Of Mary Magdalene . . . ." Mary Magdalene has changed her virtue, so to speak, for "the love of friendship, however, is the third supernatural virtue and is rightly or wrongly called simply 'love,' because the name fits it better than it does the love of desire, or hope."[5]

Mary Magdalene's shift from image of hope or seeking love in the *Güldenes Tugend-Buch* to epitome of true and genuine love in *Trutz-Nachtigall* can be very clearly seen in one of the few alterations in the text itself; while in the *Tugend-Buch* Spee still wrote "the one she seeks there, but does not find," the passage in *Trutz-Nachtigall* is much more pointed: "The beloved she does not find."[6]

The Magdalene poem in the *Trutz-Nachtigall* version is an Easter song; both versions clearly presume the situation depicted in

John 20 (Mary at the empty tomb with no other women present); so
Strophe 1:

> The sun with its steeds
> late easterly drunken
> Yet flooded with sleep
> and unwilling to waken:
> Then found I already
> Mourning at the tomb,
> Preparing her salves and boxes,
> the weeping Magdalene.

The poem begins with a depiction of nature: the sun and its rays are
still drunk with sleep. In this early dawn begins a dramatic event that
leads from sorrow to jubilation. The poetic means Spee uses to shape
this introductory strophe are typical for him; compare only the first
strophe of the well-known "Song of Sorrow at Christ's Suffering in
the Garden on the Mount of Olives":

> In the stillness of the night
> In the first watch
> A voice began to lament.
> I took note
> Of what it said;
> Went there with heavy eyes.[7]

Both strophes reveal a combination of report and personal testimony
of the poet: ("I found" / "I took note") and use a description of the
natural world to express a particular mood (the sun that is reluctant
to give light / the deep night as image of sorrow). The same is true
of the masterful depiction of the contrast between nature and the
human: on the one hand the ruling sun with its glorious chariot
drawn by horses, on the other hand a picture of misery, the weeping
woman (or the deep silence of the night out of which a sound of
lamenting gradually arises). Here a new, modern tone in German lyric
poetry makes itself heard, one that perhaps came to its fullest flower-
ing in Goethe's nature poetry.

Not only are specific features of this poem's content significant,
but so is its placement in the overall cycle of poems in *Trutz-
Nachtigall.*

(a) With regard to *content* what is especially striking is what is *not*
present: Mary's lament is entirely one of love and not, as in the me-

dieval Easter plays, regret for her sinful past. An older Magdalene lament[8] that, like that of Spee, presumes Magdalene's discovery of the empty tomb ("Ah what tidings / ah, what a pitiable cry / The tomb is empty . . .") gives Magdalene's repentance as the reason for her lament:

> Where is now my consolation,
> the one who redeemed me from sins,
> I, poor wretch, was lost,
> he was born for my salvation.

Here the sinful woman has lost her savior and has thereby fallen back into her old lost state. Friedrich Spee's Magdalene, however, is no sinner. It is true that at one point she is called "the weeping penitent" (strophe 42), but this is said only in passing, like the name used in another poem (and quite out of place there), "penitent Magdalene," or her mention together "with the repentant King David," where she is awkwardly introduced, apparently only because of the male/female address that follows: "O sinful man, O sinful woman!"[9] Of course Spee was also aware of the many-faceted figure of Mary Magdalene, as a reference to Mary of Bethany in the Magdalene poem shows ("the best part chosen," strophe 29); but what is most striking is the fact that he does not take further notice of the penitential aspect of the figure. When Spee is specifically intent on presenting a New Testament example of sin and right penitence he looks elsewhere: to, of all people, the holy apostle Peter, who weeps and does penance day and night in a cave near Jerusalem, while Mary Magdalene in the same chapter, although weeping ("Mary Magdalene weeps copiously"), does so not because of her sins but out of sympathy with the martyred Jesus.[10] The same is true of the Magdalene poem: Mary Magdalene in Spee's work is not at all the regretful, weeping penitent who laments her sins, but the woman who weeps for her beloved.

(b) The fact that the poet does not intend to put this woman (or women in general!) in the role of sinner is shown also by the *placement* of the poem within the framework of *Trutz-Nachtigall*: it is not one of the songs of remorse and penitence, but instead it concludes the series of love songs addressed by the spouse (= bride) to Jesus the beloved. Mary Magdalene is the embodiment of this bride, but unlike her model from the Song of Songs she is not only the woman as counterpart to the man; the "spouse" stands for the "soul," that is, for every human being, male or female, in relationship to Jesus. Mary

Magdalene is, in this context, the human being as such. She represents every person who seeks life in Jesus. Therefore in other passages all the souls who take part with "my beloved Mary Magdalene" in the movement of love's seeking are called blessed.[11]

Spee's surprising image of Mary Magdalene did not appear out of the blue: he shows himself in his other works as well to be an advocate for women, for example in *Cautio criminalis,* first published in 1631, where he bravely stood up for women accused of witchcraft although he must have known that in doing so he was jeopardizing the security of his own life and of his career as a professor of theology, or in his *Güldenes Tugend-Buch,* which contains advice for women who desire to live a spiritual life in the world outside the cloister or cell. This second book also gave offense by addressing itself to people who were not even supposed to exist, for in the wake of the Council of Trent the Church made strenuous efforts to direct women with a spiritual calling into the cloister, the habit, and the Latin liturgy of the hours.

The negative effects were evident in the succeeding centuries in women's humiliating struggles to obtain Church recognition of female congregations. We may mention as examples two founders who followed the example of St. Mary Magdalene in their work of education, care for children, and charitable work: Julie Françoise Cathérine Postel (1756–1846, canonized 1925), who chose "Maria Magdalena" as her name in religion, and Catharina Damen (1787–1858), who was called Sister Magdalene.

Since women who were members of papally recognized orders were forbidden to leave the cloister, apostolic activities were not possible for women, or, in other words, women who proposed to live an active religious life were not recognized as nuns according to canon law. The grinding struggle of these two founders is revealed by, among other things, the fact that Sister Magdalene was only permitted to assume her religious name at the age of 49, and Sister Maria Magdalena Postel at 51. In writing their rules as well the two were subjected to many forms of ecclesiastical pressure; the result for Sister Maria Magdalena was that at the age of 82 years she was forced to undergo a second novitiate and religious profession. We can only guess at the degree of strength required of women to withstand ecclesiastical suspicion of their desire to shape their own lives and be active.[12]

In contrast, Father Spee wrote his spiritual exercises and meditation texts for "secular" women;[13] he used the German language they could all understand and emphasized regular, brief meditations (fifteen minutes per day!) that could be carried out even by women with household obligations, women who were wives and mothers. It was

Group of Three Myrophores, *from Henry II's Pericope Book*
p. 116 v. (11th c.)
Bavarian State Library, Munich

Plate 1

"Mary of Magdala and the Risen One,"
Billerbeck Altar (ca. 1640).
Westphalian State Museum, Münster

Plate 2

"Mary Magdalene as Apostle to the Apostles"
Illustration from the Albani Psalter, Hildesheim (12th c.)
Herzog August Library, Wolfenbüttel

Plate 3

"Mary of Magdala Announces the Risen One to the Apostles"
from the Misereor Hunger Cloth
"Biblical Women—Guides to the Reign of God"
by Lucy D'Souza
© *1990, Misereor Medienproduktion und Vertriebsgesellschaft Aachen.*

Plate 4

"Magdelene with the Jar of Ointment"—The Patroness
Master of Moulins (end of the 15th c.)
Louvre, Paris

———————

Plate 5

"Saint Mary Magdalene Borne Aloft by Angels"
Tilman Riemenschneider (ca. 1490)
Bavarian National Museum, Munich

Plate 6

"Magdalene's Night Vigil"
Georges de La Tour (mid-17th c.)
Louvre, Paris

Plate 7

"Penitent Magdalene"
Januarius Zick (1730–1797)
State Art Gallery, Karlsruhe

———

Plate 8

specifically for that group that he suggested exercises of active love of neighbor (for example, care of the sick, charitable acts for the poor and prisoners, scholarships for schoolchildren). This kind of secular spirituality is still modern even today.

It is noteworthy that a professor of theology gave any attention at all to the education of women, especially when Spee's work is contrasted with the following remarks about women, their character, and their capacity for education taken from a book that was highly popular at the time:

• Women are credulous "and since the chief aim of the devil is to corrupt faith, therefore he rather attacks them."

• Because "women are naturally more impressionable" they also have less faith, and this observation can be based even on the etymology of the word *femina* (woman): "for *Femina* comes from *Fe* and *Minus*" (*fe* = *fides,* faith; *minus* = less, so that *femina* = one who has less faith)," since she is ever weaker to hold and preserve the faith."

• Women are by nature easily influenced.

• Women have been evil ever since Eve (but because of the transformation of *Eva* to *Ave* one should be careful how one preaches on this topic).

• Women are stupid, for "as regards intellect, or the understanding of spiritual things, they seem to be of a different nature from men."

• Women are weak in faith, for the natural evil of the female is shown in the fact that she is "quicker to waver in her faith, and consequently quicker to abjure the faith."

• Women, even saintly ones, are quarrelsome, as one can see from the behavior of Martha toward Mary Magdalene (!) in Luke 10.

To complete the measure of their misogyny the authors affirm that they have written all this "without in any way detracting from a sex in which God has always taken great glory that His might should be spread abroad"; they even recommend that this should be preached "for the admonition of women . . . so long as it is set forth with discretion."

This is the image of women presented by the *Hammer of Witches:*[14] evil, thoughtless, witless. Spee, in contrast, describes his women readers as reverent, pious, and intelligent.[15]

In fact it is only possible to understand Spee's different image of women if one sees it as a mirror of his different image of God: His

God is "a kind and loving mother," a God who has a "tender and more than motherly heart," and in his own spirituality he affirms that the all-powerful God "is truly such a mother. He himself, God the Father, Son, and Holy Spirit, is such a mother, and we are his children."[16] In the Catholic Church (unlike pietism) it was a very long time before a pope, the gentle John Paul I, shocked the faithful with a similar expression. That Spee affirmed the right of "normal" women to spiritual instruction against the ecclesiastical tendencies of his time, and that he even thought them capable of dealing with theological discussions when all the witch hunters knew for certain that women are stupid, wicked, and weak in faith, sheds a special light on his Mary Magdalene, who, though she is "without understanding," nevertheless goes her way *out of love,* and in fact *out of love and strength of faith.* This Mary Magdalene is the embodiment of a protest against all the disparagement of women in Spee's time.[17]

The quality of this image of Mary Magdalene was unfortunately ignored in the years that followed; it deserves to be rediscovered.

2. The Disciple of the Divine Friend of Humanity (Friedrich Klopstock)

In the mid-eighteenth century two intellectual currents that cannot always be clearly distinguished shaped the literary climate in Germany: the Enlightenment and Sentimentalism. The one movement was grounded in philosophy, the other in a variety of movements of "awakening" (pietism); both were also concerned with religion, either (on the one hand) to purify it from dogma and irrationalism or (on the other) to liberate it from dogma and ritualistic rigidity in favor of a deeper inwardness.

The most important representative of Sentimentalism was Friedrich Gottlieb Klopstock (1724–1803), whose principal work was *The Messiah* (1748–73).[18] His influence on the development of the German language and poetry can scarcely be overestimated, even though modern readers find his work difficult of access. It is necessary to consider that the pathetic style of emotional language that leaves us cold today moved the poet's contemporaries to tears.[19] Lessing's hostile and distant saying, "Who would not praise a Klopstock? But will everyone want to read him? No!" may be accurate, but it is still true that *The Messiah* was in its time a work that influenced a broad, though not always literarily educated audience and evoked some poetic imitations, set standards for the future, and—in deliberate imita-

tion of ancient literature—laid claim to equality with the Greek literature that was acknowledged as a model. Its educational claim touched
readers whose own educational program included the reading of
Greek texts and who in recognizing ancient models in the unexpected
clothing of their own language experienced aesthetic pleasure and
proudly acknowledged that the German language could also be laced
within the corsets of the ancient verse rhythms (although this required
the creation of new words and the abandonment of some rules of
grammar).

This self-asserted claim is supported even by the famous introductory verse, which establishes the "high" tone that will be sustained
through twenty long lyric poems:

> Sing, O immortal soul, the redemption of sinful humanity.

In its imitation of the opening verses of the *Iliad* ("Sing, goddess, the
anger of Peleus' son Achilleus") and Odyssey ("Tell me, Muse, of the
man of many ways") the claim of the poet to be the German Homer
is as clear as it could possibly be. The classical challenge to the self to
sing is frequently repeated, and the great *leitmotif* of the epoch is thus
announced: "Sing, my song / . . . let my song flow with sensitivity
and simplicity" (XII, 254–7). The poet, or rather the poetic "I" is thus
not a speaker or a writer, but—again indebted to the heritage of
antiquity—he is the singer with the harp, the rhapsodist (cf. VII
817–8; XVII, 178–9). No mortal could dare to describe the great
drama of the divine friend of humanity that unfolds between heaven
and hell; but instructed and led by the Muse, consecrated and inspired,[20] the poet-singer can dare to sing his song.

The matter to be communicated is so sublime that the chosen
singer can only receive instruction in it during specially "consecrated
hours" (XI, 1567), and he in turn can only approach his object when
he accomplishes his work as a new creation in adoration and imitation
of the Creator Spirit (cf. I, 8–12). This attitude does not arise out of
religious vision but belongs to an aesthetic program whose goal is not
religion (in the Church's understanding of it) but humanity, for the
religion of the educated is humanity and its opposite is delusion, su-
perstition, and infatuation (X, 950–8); a harsh judgment will strike
those who have debased what is most holy in the human being, the
image of God: *reason* (XVIII, 375).

This reflects the optimism of the Enlightenment that places its
hopes in "education" to bring the whole person to perfection. The

expression of this ideal is the sympathetic heart imbued with great *emotions*. The poet's educational program is the same as that followed by the divine Master: to cause "emotion" to flow "into the heart" of the human being and to develop a heart full of feeling (cf. III, 119; XI, 1–2).

The content of Klopstock's *Messiah* is the passion, death, and resurrection of Jesus, his post-resurrection appearances, and his ascent of his throne. Within this brief time frame, by means of recollections of the past and visions of the future, he incorporates the whole broad sweep of creation and the history of humanity from the beginning to the final judgment.

Mary Magdalene stands against this grandiose background. In depicting her the poet uses biblical foundational elements that he himself develops further; it is interesting to note which elements of the traditional picture stand out and which ones retreat into the background. For Klopstock she is Magdale Maria or Maria Magdale, or simply Magdale; these versions of her name distinguish her from the many other Marys. He excludes the assimilation to Mary of Bethany that is so often found in Catholic tradition because he provides Martha's sister and Lazarus with biographies of their own. The two women are friends, but they are not the same person (XII, 787–8). Klopstock also avoids the other equation of Mary Magdalene with the prostitute of Luke 7 that is so fixed in the tradition that even today it can scarcely be uprooted; her "sins" are not named. The pious voyeurism that is often found surrounding the figure of Mary Magdalene is completely absent. Instead, Mary Magdalene is the *forgiven* sinner. This aspect of her image appears in a number of places, with the accent always on grace. It is not the poet who describes her sins and repentance; characters within the history of salvation reminisce, in meaningful contexts, on the "sins" that led to Jesus' preferential choice of this woman disciple. Even Jesus' mother hopes to receive the same favor that had been accorded to Magdalene: in the turmoil of the passion, with her son's death before her eyes, she has only one wish: to be able to fall weeping at his feet as once Magdalene had done (IV, 898–900).

Later Magdalene, in a duet with Mary, recalls the past that had become her salvation: "I, the sinner, sank at his feet in silent repentance, and he had mercy on me . . ." (XIX, 420–1). When Peter hears of the angel's message that the Risen One will appear to the disciples, and particularly to him, he cannot believe it. In comparison to Magdalene, who had failed as he had, the coming grace seems to him still more improbable: "But Magdale sinned, too! When did she sin? Before she knew him! And have I loved as Magdale loved?" (XIV, 383–4).

The "sin" of Magdalene, which in contrast to Peter's failure is not depicted, is here only the moment that occasions mention of the loving gesture of humility, for the parallel with the Beloved Disciple shows that her tears at Jesus' feet are not so much tears of repentance as the expression of the most tender love:

> Then John came near . . .
> Cast himself at Jesus' feet and kissed them, weeping,
> Then dried the tears with his cascading curls. (IV, 1166–68)

Nowhere in the book is Mary Magdalene reproached for her previous sin; her rank among Jesus' friends is unimpaired. But what distinguishes her from all others, and what is emphasized in Klopstock's poem, is the preference she receives on Easter morning: she, true to the biblical picture, is named first among those who go to the tomb; she sees the angel and then the Risen One, and she (differently from John 20:16-17) holds "the divine feet with wavering hand"; the words forbidding her to touch him are softened by the promise of Jesus' presence and a future encounter with him. Finally, she is permitted to bring the "news of bliss" to the others in Jerusalem (XIV, 1–133). Again differently from the biblical model, her place of primacy founded on receiving the first appearance is acknowledged even by Peter and is repeatedly emphasized:

> " . . . here we all stand, the nine!
> Magdale then! then I! . . ." (XIV, 799–800)
> "Magdale saw him first, and alone; then the nine saw him, . . .
> Then he appeared also to me . . ." (XIV, 1155–57).

The event at the tomb that distinguished the loving woman from all the disciples is told several times (sometimes in the same words), first to Portia, the wife of Pilate, later in a child's song of praise, and finally Jesus' mother recalls the event in a conversation in which Mary Magdalene considers whether she will one day give "the great testimony" of martyrdom: Mary promises her that then, in all her suffering, she will be able to draw strength and consolation from that memory.

The Protestant poet, bound by no dogmatic strictures, was able to praise in Mary Magdalene the beginnings of the knowledge of God that will spread itself like a life- and shade-giving tree over the nations of the earth (XIX, 537–8, 543–5). This statement remains as the last word about her and need not, as in the biblical and extra-biblical traditions, be later retracted in favor of Peter and the primacy associated with his reception of the (first) appearance of the risen Christ.

Klopstock in his epic describes not "real" people in their development, but characters in their ideal aspect. What would be deadly in a novel (especially one that depicts development of character) constitutes here the urgent aesthetic impact. Mary Magdalene is *the model human being* who, certainly accompanied by deep emotions, goes her way, undeceived and undeceivable. Her life is completed; her image is fixed from the beginning: the depiction of a later revision of her life in penitent retirement would contradict the once-for-all achieved perfection of the "beautiful soul."

The almost incidental references to Magdalene's "sin" and "quiet repentance" and the omission of pathetic penitential exercises make her a sister of the canoness whom Goethe memorialized with the "confessions of a beautiful soul" in the sixth book of *Wilhelm Meister*. She rejects the practices of some conversion and awakening movements designed to put sinners in a mood of fear and horror in order to cause them to recognize their sinfulness and to experience fear of hell before their pardoning. The deeply emotive "beautiful soul" needs neither fear nor repentance because it constantly senses the nearness of the invisible divine friend.[21]

The reader of Klopstock's *Messiah* retains the image of a woman who is characterized by repose, exaltation, confidence, and unshakable trust, and who rests in perfection (cf. XIV, 362–5):

> " . . . She smiles at the storm
> That rushes upon her in the nocturnal depths of the valley of death!"

Notes

[1]Theo G. M. van Oorschot, ed., Friedrich Spee, *Sämtliche Schriften. Historisch-kritische Ausgabe.* 1. *Trutz-Nachtigall* (Bern, 1985) 55–70; 2. *Güldenes Tugend-Buch* (Munich, 1968) 535–45. For the editing and textual history of the *Güldenes Tugend-Buch* see the editor's notes on pp. 565–72 and 669–74.

[2]*Güldenes Tugend-Buch*, 26–7.

[3]Ibid., 218–48.

[4]Ibid., 229.

[5]Ibid., 29.

[6]Ibid., 536; *Trutz-Nachtigall,* 57.

[7]The "Song of Sorrow" is found in *Trutz-Nachtigall,* 182–5 and *Güldenes Tugend-Buch,* 171–3.

[8]"Magdalene's Lament," quoted from Friedrich von der Leyen, ed., *Deutsche Dichtung des frühen und hohen Mittelalters* (Darmstadt, 1962) 742–3.

[9]*Güldenes Tugend-Buch* 174–5, 327.

[10]Ibid., 398 (Peter); 403 (Mary Magdalene).

[11]Ibid., 273.

[12]For the biographies and influence of the two founders see Magdalena Padberg, *Maria Magdalena Postel. Du hast mich gerufen, hier bin ich!* (Meschede, n. d. [ca. 1975]), and Angelita Cools and Hildegard van de Wijnpersse, *Sein Werk—nicht das meine. Mutter Magdalena Damen und ihre Kongregation der Franziskanerinnen von Heythuysen im neunzehnten Jahrhundert* (2nd ed. Aachen and Kevelaer, 1992).

[13]For Spee's spiritual method cf. *Güldenes Tugend-Buch.* Auswahl, Bearbeitung und Einführung von Anton Arens. (Freiburg, 1991).

[14]*The Malleus Maleficarum of Heinrich Kramer and James Sprenger,* translated with introductions, bibliography, and notes by Montague Summers (New York: Dover, [1971]). The statements collected here are found in Part I, Question 6 on pp. 42–5.

[15]*Güldenes Tugend-Buch,* 127, 298, 125.

[16]Ibid., 11.

[17]For the personality and influence of the poet and theologian Friedrich Spee, cf. the collection edited by Michael Sievernich, *Friedrich von Spee. Priester—Poet—Prophet* (Frankfurt, 1986), as well as Christian Feldmann, *Friedrich Spee. Hexenanwalt und Prophet* (Freiburg, Basel, and Vienna, 1993).

[18]Friedrich Gottlieb Klopstock, *Ausgewählte Werke* edited by Karl August Schlieden (Darmstadt, 1962): "Der Messias," 195–770; editor's notes on *The Messiah* 1263–93. All quotations are based on this edition.

[19]Cf. F. G. Jünger in the Afterword to the edition cited, 1335–69, 1338–9.

[20]Klopstock traced the original idea for the work to a dream that he interpreted in an autobiographical poem as a poetic consecration: cf. his letter to K. W. E. Heimbach, ibid., 1180–1, and the poem "An Freund und Feind" ["To Friend and Foe"], ibid., 127–9.

[21]The idea that Goethe's "beautiful soul" represents not the perfected human being but only a stage in the education of Wilhelm Meister is a point that cannot be pursued here.

Chapter Seven

A Pearl More Precious than All Others: Magdalene in Brentano's Jesus-Novel

1. The Book

In the great work of his mature years, *Lehrjahre Jesu (The Youth and Education of Jesus)*—originally inspired by the visions of the nun Anna Katharina Emmerick, who bore the stigmata—Clemens Brentano (1778–1842) describes a vision of Magdalene dated to 30 July 1821:

> Look now, I see her standing there above her castle. Behind her breaks forth a brightness like that of the moon, but before her there seems to be a dark mountain; she must put it beneath her feet, then she will be safe.—She is barren. . . . When she had known Jesus and done penance she bore many children in the Spirit (I, 51).

The text reads like a prefatory summary of all the subsequent "communications" about Magdalene: her sinful period (a dark mountain, her barrenness); her conversion (the brightness behind her); her future (penitential life, spiritual fruitfulness). It is an image that sums up the saint's whole life.

The work from which these lines are drawn is almost unknown today. But unlike Klopstock's *Messiah*, which was praised when it appeared and then quickly forgotten, Brentano's Jesus book was not subjected to being forgotten because the poet suppressed the work during his lifetime and permitted his heirs to publish only a "censored" version.

Soon after Clemens's death his pious brother Christian promised that "he would take care that after his death no one else would get hold of these papers because they would only provide occasion and nourishment [!] for sectarianism and every kind of spiritual upheaval."[1] Christian's desire in this matter was satisfied for more than a century!

Among Brentano's spiritual sympathizers and later editors this work (like the other manuscripts from his Dülmen period, *Bitteres Leiden,* 1833, and *Marienleben,* 1852) was the subject of controversy. Some called it a work of (divine) inspiration, others (human) fantasy. The three-volume *Life of Jesus* ultimately published by Father Schmoeger between 1858 and 1860, still read as an edifying book today, is in any case not identical with Brentano's text; it is a version adapted to the tastes of the time and the Church's teaching.[2] The final edition of the *Lehrjahre,* prepared by Brentano himself and completed by 1838, is only now appearing as part of a critical edition of Brentano's complete works prepared by the Freie Deutsche Hochstift in Frankfurt, which has held the manuscript on loan since 1969.[3]

In the course of the work Brentano's role as "writer" of the visions and biographer of the nun shifted: he became the creative shaper of his material. Unlike the nun, who (in accord with her stigmata) saw in her visions primarily the passion of Jesus, the writer was interested in the entire life of Jesus, including its pre- and post-history,[4] and by means of suggestive inquiries made use of the nun as a source of inspiration for his "historical" interest. Walter Frühwald, who sees biblical criticism and study of the life of Jesus as central problems illuminating the intellectual (not theological) history of the nineteenth century, includes Brentano's work within this context, as did Albert Schweitzer[5] before him.[6] As liberal life-of-Jesus research attempted to get behind the dogmatically influenced gospels, so Brentano, with the assistance of the nun, tried to discover the true history of Jesus behind the gospels. What the gospels ignore or report only briefly he desired to describe in exact detail, for behind historical reality shone absolute truth. Recourse to visions was intended to assume the function of a fictive guarantee for the truth content of his fantasy.[7] In light of Brentano's claims to truth present-day readers will be well advised to keep in mind the judgment of his nephew, Lujo Brentano, on another Emmerick work as a hermeneutical aid: he called it "one of the greatest poetic creations of world literature; but obviously it contains no historical truth."[8]

Within the framework of this "poetic" depiction of Jesus, Magdalene occupies a significant place: her "historical" life is a "symbol" or, to use Brentano's words, she is not important as an individual, but as a genus—for the words noted on 31 July 1822 concerning Dina, the woman from Samaria, are true also of Magdalene: "I have always felt and recognized that the persons with whom the Redeemer had to do were not simply individual human beings; they were also at all times a complete image of an entire genus of people" (I, 463).

Let us see what kind of human being Magdalene represents in this work.

2. Magdalene in the *Lehrjahre Jesu*

Background and Family

In the Romantic conception of history all human beings are connected through a primeval family; Brentano had already made use of this idea in a detailed narrative of a family and its sins in his *Romanzen vom Rosenkranz ("Romances of the Rosary"),* and he also applies it to the people around Jesus: his followers all belong, through complex relational ties, to his extended family (especially through the three marriages of his grandmother, Anne). By means of this Romantic conception Magdalene is made part of Jesus' natural environment from the beginning.

Lazarus's family history is developed according to the materials of ancient legend: his father is a Syrian nobleman who, through his military service, has acquired property in different parts of the land, including Bethany and Magdala; his mother is a respectable Jew. Magdalene thus comes from a rich and noble family. The importance of this description of her background is evident from the contrasting figure of Judas, who is negatively characterized by his illegitimate birth, the unstable life of his parents, and his father's and mother's occupations (as soldier and dancer, respectively).

Brentano solves the problems that could arise from identifying Mary of Magdala and Mary of Bethany by giving Lazarus three sisters: (Mary) Magdalene, Martha, and the silent Mary who cannot separate earthly from heavenly things and therefore is regarded by other people as "stupid": this sister dies during Jesus' public ministry "from anguish over his great suffering, which she saw beforehand in the spirit" (I, 130–2, 365). She combines the images of the biblical Mary of Bethany and the visionary who suffers in sympathy with the Passion of Christ. By the introduction of this sister, Magdalene is more sharply profiled as a woman of the world (and less as a listener of a meditative nature); noble background and external beauty are aspects of her image: "She was taller than the other women, strong, well-fleshed but slender, she had very thin(!) and beautifully pointed fingers, small but slender feet, a noble carriage, very lovely, rich, long hair" (II, 371).

Magdalene's "Possession"

This theme is prepared by a number of notices: Magdalene has a devil, lives a despised and profligate life, was "at one time living quite a luxurious life" (I, 63); but her later conversion is also indicated beforehand (I, 51).

The consequences of her diabolical possession are reflected in her social decline, imaged in the condition of her palace and garden and the nature of her surroundings. First it is said of her house and garden that they are "neglected, and appeared to be falling into decay, except for the rooms in which she dwelt" (I, 426). Later, when she is already possessed by seven devils, the decay is progressive, just as her behavior is going gradually downhill. In the beginning it is said of the people with whom she associates that they are "not respectable people, but artists, officers, and adventurers" (note: all three categories are included in Judas's ancestry!). This first stage of her decline (I, 425) is quickly followed by a second: now her environment consists of "respectable common sinners who live according to the flesh and cover their shame and abomination with handsome clothing and dainty manners, but they were much lower than Magdalene's earlier associates . . ." (I, 440). While it was said in connection with her previous environment that her reputation was "somewhat lowered" (I, 425), the text speaks later of her social "decline" (I, 440). The lowest level of her fall is prostitution: "She is wholly in the hands of the evil man who lives with her, and he lives on the fees of her clients" (II, 489).

Her vain manner of dress is another indication of her fall into demonic possession. Even the women of Herod's court had a better reputation: they were richly but nobly gowned, while Magdalene, by contrast, "was more fantastic in her finery" (I, 67). Again and again her striking dress, her jewels, her pearls, or her coiffure are depicted always with a negative undertone; from time to time there is also a disapproving remark on the fact that she does not wear a veil. Her unfettered external appearance describes her internal state, her possession. Before her second encounter with Jesus, when she has arrived at the nadir of her life, her washing, anointing, hairdressing, robing, and adornment are described at extreme length, down to the last detail (II, 526–8). What is true of her hair ("indeed, not much could be seen of her hair, it was so bedecked with ornament") is true of her whole person: at the climax of her possession Magdalene disappears completely behind her vain adornment. The fact that clothing is also representative of the (sinful) human being is likewise clear from the example of an adulteress who after reconciliation with her husband burns "many beautiful silk dresses in which she had paraded her vanity before her lovers" (II, 248).

The ambivalence in the description of Magdalene (between refinement and vanity, of noble birth yet threatened by social decline) is especially obvious in some scenes involving dancing. The negative evaluation of dancing appeared earlier in the case of Judas's mother, and the same is true for Magdalene. Dancing is not bad in itself; it is a regular feature of festive occasions. When it is done in a fitting way—as at the marriage feast at Cana or at other such feasts—the dancers do not touch hands, "but grasp the ends of scarves held in their hands" (II, 518; similarly I, 267). But some surrender themselves to other forms of dancing: on the name-day of a nobleman the dancing women are dressed in such a way that during the dance one "saw all too well the shapes of their bodies," and as a result there was considerable opportunity "to regard [one another] and give room to evil thoughts" (I, 137). On the birthday of Magdalene's lover the dance takes place in a hall in which the dancers can see themselves in mirrors[9]—something that marks them as sinful people in love with themselves. This dance also expressed "every kind of passion and foolishness and was a continual display of and enticement with the body." Magdalene permits this dancing in her house, although it is expressly stated that she does not join in the dance (I, 439–40). Her libertine life and her moral failings are discussed in the *Lehrjahre* but they are not described, or only with great reticence. In contrast, the descriptions of her extravagances in clothing and behavior, her emotions, and her compromising conduct are given broad scope. On closer inspection Magdalene is found to embody everything Brentano criticized in women, as shown especially in his letters to his younger sister, Bettine. She was also accused of explosions of emotion, bold conduct, or what her brother considered bad behavior, and the noble virtue of rational bourgeois life was held up to her as an ideal. She is frequently admonished not to despise ordinary middle-class life, for sensation, education, or the arts often serve only to uncover one's own nakedness, as is "very often the case among women." Anything extravagant, anything that could be summarized as "sentimentality," is dangerous, for the "possessed people and witches" of the past were also "hypochondriac personalities."[10] Brotherly advice culminates in the formula: be kind and gracious "without being noticed."[11]

Bettine defended herself against the attempts of her family and her brother to tame her: "But my soul is a passionate dancer. . . . All cry that I should be still, and you too, but . . . if the dance were over, it would all be over for me."[12] We hear, like a late echo of this confession of passionate emotion, the warning that Fontane (1895) placed on the lips of the woman of Briest: "Not so wild, Effi, not so passionate" (*Effi Briest*, ch. 1). These two quotations bracket an entire epoch that rejected excessive arousal of emotions, especially in the behavior of women, as affected and unnatural. Modesty was demanded, even in body-language, and "natural" was thought to be what was already "regulated by self-repression."[13] Emotions are important in human upbringing; they are useful as a counterweight to monotonous work; but they must remain "exceptional, out of the ordinary, and excluded from sober bourgeois daily life."[14]

The required modesty also covered the intellectual activity of women and girls. Their reading was restricted to "virtuous" books and left art and philosophy to men, as another member of the Brentano family explained. Twenty-one-year-old Gundel (Kunigunde Brentano, later the wife of Savigny) wrote to Clemens, "See, a girl like me may not say 'in Schlegel and Goethe,' for that is contrary to the respectability that is proper to someone like me."[15] This expression was not meant ironically; it contrasts the eccentricity of Clemens and Bettine's siblings with what is "normal."

Women at the beginning of the nineteenth century were ordered to maintain their "natural" qualities to be, for example, "gentle, loving, caring, modest, tender, virtuous, patient, rejecting what is instinctive." Their life's duty consisted in subjection to their husbands and in motherhood. "Clearly and unambiguously evident behind this ideology stands the sex-specific division of labor . . . that was, of course, given an idyllic explanation."[16] The sisters, Gundel and Bettine, were related to that program as rule and exception. Bettine would remain an exceptional figure who lived according to her own rules. She would not even submit to her beloved brother; she commented on his educational program half in wrath and half in ridicule: "You are drawing a tiny drop of morality out of your brotherly affection."[17] Perhaps she also suspected the deeper cause of her brother's concern: Clemens and Bettine were kindred souls; the brother criticized in his sister what he sensed as a danger to himself— deviation from bourgeois order—and he reproached in her what he would depict decades later as "possession" in his image of Magdalene.

A woman who goes outside the lines, who does not behave as her station demands, who gives passionate expression to her emotions, who has little regard for the reputation of her family, who prefers to busy herself with art and philosophy rather than cooking and cleaning—such a woman is possessed by evil spirits and must (like Bettine and Magdalene) be brought back to her daily obligations. Of course all that was true only for women, for Clemens himself, thanks to his paternal inheritance, would never undertake a bourgeois lifestyle (something that distinguished him from other poets of his time!).

The Conversion of Women

Magdalene's dramatic conversion scenes are foreshadowed by the conversions of other women similar to her. Some of these are biblical figures; others are invented and provided with appropriate biographies. Only a few can be listed here. A *widow* who is freed from her demon after being healed at a distance repents, enters a life of penance, and distributes her fortune to the community of Jesus' followers: "She was like Magdalene in many things, except that she had been married" (I, 72–3). *Dinah,* the woman of Samaria, is depicted, like Magdalene, as a cultivated and noble lady. She had five husbands who were "gotten rid of either by sorrow or by her lovers"; another feature from Magdalene's life is here introduced, namely that one of her lovers is killed by another. "Dinah had much in common with Magdalene, but she had sunk still deeper" (I, 469–70). After her conversation with Jesus she calls the inhabitants of the town to the gate where Jesus speaks to them for a few minutes and tells them "they should believe everything the woman has told them" (I, 470). The Samaritan woman as missionary to her town is a surprising feature that has otherwise been emphasized only in feminist theology.

The story of *Mara of Suphan* is told in special detail (II, 154–60, 237–9). On the outside she is expensively dressed and adorned with pearls, but inside she carries five devils—one from her husband and four from her lovers. Jesus frees her of the demons and forgives her sins. In gratitude she and her children bring costly spices as a gift for Jesus, an action that calls forth the objections of the Pharisees; later, at a meal, she pours "a bottle of perfume over his head" (II, 239).

While the gospels tell of only two "sinful women" (Luke 7:36-50; John 7:53–8:11), the fate of many such women is described in the *Lehrjahre.* Their disordered lives stand in sharp contrast to the "holy women" around Jesus, which is why he does not merely teach the people in general terms about chastity, asceticism, marriage, and decent dress, but in the case of the sinful women also puts their marriages in order and has them send away their illegitimate children.

"Sin" for women is almost exclusively in the sexual sphere and is manifested as illness or possession, either in themselves or in their children conceived in adultery; that is why for women conversion and healing are always coincident.

Magdalene as a Type

When Jesus meets Dinah, the Samaritan woman, the people around him are described as "a complete image of a whole genus of humanity" (I, 463). Therefore when the conversion of individual sinners is narrated the most varied kinds of conversion are described. In a vision of sick people who had already sought out Jesus many times it is explained that these are tepid, sluggish sinners who are harder to convert than the great sinners: "Magdalene repented through struggle, after many times falling back, and then with great violence; Dinah of Samaria converted swiftly; Mara of Suphan desired it for a long time, then achieved it suddenly. All the great woman sinners repented very quickly and strongly; so did the powerful Paul, as if by a stroke of lightning . . ." (II, 381). Magdalene's story of sin and repentance is thus an "image" of all sinners whose conversion takes place in stages.

Brentano's conviction that the gospels do not contain the whole history of Jesus but omit a great deal that was useful only for a certain time and report nothing but what would be useful for all ages was especially true of Magdalene. From this point of view the evangelists' selection was oriented not to their interest in the persons depicted as individuals but to their usefulness for people at a later time. To put it another way, they were useful to the extent that they "describe a certain genre within the Church." Hence the many sinful women in the historical life of Jesus "are represented solely by the story of Magdalene" (II, 360).

Conversion as Process

Brentano was also convinced that the gospels only report briefly and in summary important processes that took place over a long period of time: the conversion that Luke summarizes in a single scene (Luke 7:36-50) takes place in Brentano's "reconstruction" in a number of steps.

Magdalene's first encounter with Jesus is carefully prepared beforehand. From the statement that "until now nothing had yet" been said of her "in Jesus' presence" (I, 128) the narrative proceeds by way of conversations between Jesus and Martha (Magdalene "will certainly come," I, 132–3) and the silent Mary (she will make everything all right, I, 201) to the first reference to Magdalene's internal unrest and longing for rescue (I, 230). Persuaded by Martha, she travels to the place where Jesus is supposed to be, but this first attempt at a meeting with Jesus comes to nothing. Nevertheless, soon afterward Jesus says, in a conversation with Lazarus, that "a spark of salvation has already entered her" (I, 302). On the advice of her relatives and friends Magdalene means to make a second attempt to see Jesus and perhaps even to hear him. In fact she sees, through a window of her lodging, that Jesus is passing by; he looks at her. This glance "struck so deep within her soul and so wonderfully shamed and confused her" that for a time she is deeply shaken (I, 311–2). However, her internal emotion does not lead to conversion because she is still deeply enmeshed in her vain life: "She did not put aside her adornment" and does not wish to dress herself "so meanly" as other women (I, 313). The curve of her sinful life even moves downward: she "had fallen very far . . . and had sunk still farther" (I, 427). Nevertheless, we hear repeatedly from the lips of Jesus that the ultimate outcome will be good and that she will be an example to many.

The shift between "being moved" and "sinking down" after the first, indirect encounter with Jesus will be repeated a number of times. Magdalene is persuaded by Martha to travel again to meet Jesus and finds herself among the audience of a Sermon on the Mount on the subject of sin and punishment. This speech is reflected in Magdalene's body-language and mood: she moves from proud self-assurance through shivering and weeping to making a step forward. The result is a kind of secret dialogue between Jesus and Magdalene:

> But Jesus, when he knew how Magdalene was touched, immediately responded with comfort as he continued: "If even a spark of penance, regret, love, faith, or hope has fallen, through his words, into a poor, strayed heart, it will bear fruit. . . ." These words consoled Magdalene; she felt them through and through, and seated herself again with the Other (II, 366).

After this experience Magdalene seeks Jesus' immediate presence and follows him (despite the disciples' concern) on the way to the hall where Simon has prepared a feast. During the meal, humble and veiled, she approaches Jesus, pours ointment on his head and strokes his hair with her veil. Here it is clear why there was such repeated reference to "hand veils" in connection with dance scenes: Magdalene is very close to Jesus but (differently from the New Testament anointing scenes) there is no bodily contact between them! Jesus tells her she is forgiven, and she, touched and deeply moved, leaves the house. But her conversion is not yet complete, for she does not travel with the others to Bethany; she returns instead to Magdala.

After this first direct encounter with Jesus her emotional shifts are repeated: Magdalene falls again and sinks still deeper. "Satan now attacks her still more strongly because he has seen that he may lose her" (II, 447). Her possession expresses itself as physical convulsions, cramps, and fainting fits.

At the climax of her relapse (she is now possessed by seven devils) it is again Martha who restores contact between Jesus and her sister. This second meeting is supposed to take place in Azanoth in Galilee; both the carefully tended place and the good weather are described in detail. Into this peaceful scene comes the fantastically adorned and possessed Magdalene. Again she appears at a talk by Jesus, but this time not "at some distance": instead, she comes "forward, boldly, freely, and contemptuously" (II, 528), and again Jesus begins "a great and strict teaching" in the course of which he mentions the Queen of Sheba who came to listen to Solomon's wisdom. After this coded reference to Magdalene he speaks more plainly: "Among other things I recall that Jesus, thinking of Magdalene, said that when the devil has been driven out and the house swept, he returns with six companions, and the case is worse than before. I saw that this deeply frightened Magdalene" (II, 529).

Then Jesus commands the devils to leave those who long to be free. As the conversion/healing of Magdalene has previously proceeded in stages, so also this last stage is played out gradually. Three times she is seized by fainting and cramps, and dark figures flee from her. Her siblings bring her into the lodging; she is shaken but "not yet completely healed." Later in the day she appears at another teaching session with Jesus, "no longer so boldly dressed . . . she was also veiled"—an external indication of at least a partial healing. A third time Jesus teaches "that she is obliged to listen" and again an evil spirit leaves her. Finally she tears herself from her companions, runs like a madwoman to Jesus, throws herself at his feet and begs to be saved. Jesus sends her back into the lodging with some words of comfort (II, 529–31).

In the midst of this second direct encounter between Jesus and Magdalene the portion of the *Lehrjahre* thus far published breaks off.

Hints of the Future

The description of Magdalene's sinful life has been shot through from the beginning with predictions of her future life. At the beginning of this chapter we said something about hints of her spiritual fruitfulness. The depiction of the four siblings is also marked by an ambivalent description of the youngest sister: Lazarus, Martha, and the silent Mary are mentioned positively while of Magdalene, who is here given her true name, it is said that "the youngest sister, Mary, has gone astray, but she will turn back and will stand higher than Martha" (I, 99). Later the silent Mary, who is described in a way befitting a saint, will call her sister "one of us, one of us" (I, 201), thus in anticipation giving her a place among the other saints. Jesus also, in conversation with her siblings and friends, shows that he always already sees the converted woman in the sinner.

In an especially charming scene the holy women play a game in which a pearl is lost; when it is finally found, after long search, Jesus interprets the event in a parable expressly interpreted to apply to Magdalene: "a pearl more precious than many others" (I, 451).

From time to time the author puts aside the chronicler's mask and speaks for himself; one of these instances is a note on the sinners Dinah and Magdalene (I, 469). He says of them that, through their families, they had "grown up in the law of true faith" and he summarizes the ups and downs of their lives in the image of a garden:

> Magdalene grew up sheltered and tended in the garden of the law among the noblest plants, but through vanity, an aberrant thirst for knowledge, and a drive to shine she twined herself on a fragile reed, crossed over the wall, and sank down, with all her glorious blossoms, into the mud, until she embraced Jesus' feet, poured her sweet aroma over his head, and climbed up by way of the cross of redemption into the light.

This, Magdalene's way, served "those outside" as a parable: if the way of sin that leads downward ends with sinking at the feet of Jesus, it opens the way of redemption that leads upward to the light.

The fact that Magdalene represents the "genus" of sinners, that she serves as a "parable," and that the story of her life and conversion stands as a model for all sinners' biographies was true in particular for the poet himself, for in her image he was reworking his own religious experiences.

Magdalene in the Desert

In a key text about Magdalene, the silent Mary says of her sister: "the maiden is in the dreadful wilderness where the children of Israel were, at the evil place of darkness where no human foot has trod, but

she will come forth into another desert where she will repair everything with penance" (I, 201). In the legends Magdalene lived in the
wilderness, in a deserted place, but not in the "desert." This word belongs more properly to the legend of Maria Aegyptiaca,[18] but is more
closely related to Brentano's lyricizing of his own life. For him, too,
the desert, with its twofold aspect as a place of terror but also a place
where everything can be made whole, became a symbol of life endangered and rescued.

In his autobiographical poem of 1816, "Ich bin durch die Wüste
gezogen" (I journeyed through the desert),[19] the desert is first of all
a place of despair and death. In the image of a journey through deadly
drought and desert heat he wrestles with the despair of his life: the
death of his beloved wife and children as well as the inner unrest of
his being and his spiritual homelessness:

> I scratched out a grave in the sand
> and sank down in despair,
> Oh, for I found no water . . .
> The well was dry and dead. . . .

Even the death that he encounters in the desert evades him and refuses him redemption with the words:

> For to die—that means to find rest,
> Therefore you can neither live nor die,
> Your thirst has no end.
> Your portion—no, that I do not desire to inherit.

In the depths of his despair the "angel of the desert" comes to meet
him and answers his question about the water:

> Then he said: "The one who would do penance faithfully
> Stands on the brink of the fountain."

Then the image of the desert changes; it becomes a place of redemption:

> Then I saw the heaven seem to open,
> O God! coolly flowing down
> Came grace, came a wave of blessing;
> Then at last I, too, could hope
> In my Redeemer's blood.

The speaker recognizes in retrospect that

> The desert was the birthpangs
> In which my life was wavering,

but now, through tears and repentance, it has become "a garden full of blessing" where the spirit feasts on "unforbidden fruit."

Besides Brentano's own "desert" situation we find here other motifs that play a part in the Magdalene aspects of the *Lehrjahre*: the desert as place of straying and sin, as place of penance and repentance, as a place where the cross opens a new opportunity for life. When the text speaks, with regard to Magdalene, of the transformation of "the terrible desert" into "another desert" it reflects the turn in the author's own life, and hope for the rescue of the constantly endangered life of the author is evoked. The extensive description of Magdalene's sinful way of life (sexual disorder and engagement with the arts!) as well as the repeated references to her later rescue were an existential necessity for the poet. This "invented" biography proves to be not simply the product of an unbridled fantasy; it also served Brentano as a reinforcement of his conviction of his own salvation.

3. Additions from the *Life of Jesus* (1858–60)

The information on Magdalene that follows her conversion in the *Life of Jesus*[20] is abundant enough, but no longer so detailed. Jesus' saying "she was a great sinner, but she will be for all ages the model for penitents" (2.265) shows the direction in which all further references to her will go. She is the *former sinner* who motivates other sinners to conversion (2.273) and the toleration of whose presence causes malicious gossip about Jesus (2.296). She is the *grateful penitent* who either sits in Bethany in a "mourners' corner" (2.323, 427) or goes to Jesus in secret to embrace his feet in gratitude (2.298, 425–6). She is the *anointing woman* who on various occasions anoints his head or his feet, the last time at a farewell dinner before his death (3.411, 413, 433–40). After her conversion she is frequently mentioned among the holy women who meet Jesus in a number of different places (2.279; 3.143, 237); the witty and intelligent lady who was accustomed to associate freely with men and women alike has now taken her place in the group of demure women around Jesus: "The women sat separately at the end of the room. . . . The women did not speak to Jesus until he addressed them, and then taking turns" (3.143).

From this time onward Magdalene, in her life of penitence, is pale and careworn; she has lost her former beauty (3.144). She plays almost no role in the life of Jesus after this, not even on the occasions that are narrated in such detail in the gospels (the raising of Lazarus and the scenes on Easter morning). After Jesus' death she remains with the holy women in Bethany; in her sorrow she appears to be mad; when Jesus appears during a love-feast of the apostles she is present, but more or less as an "extra," while the apostles on this occasion are inducted into their offices. Magdalene has no apostolic role in the community; instead she is occasionally depicted at her feminine activities: sewing, embroidery, weaving, braiding straw, etc. (3.493, 536). Brentano and the nineteenth-century editors turned the proud Magdalene into a busy little housewife in accordance with the ideas of the period, when a woman had to bring her workbasket with her even when she was invited out in the afternoon—a custom that left its traces even in twentieth-century cookbooks and etiquette manuals.

The observable tendency to restrict Magdalene, in the context of a description of the life of Jesus, to the role of sinner and penitent and to retouch her Easter role in favor of male apostles (who are consecrated bishops in a solemn ceremony) is even more strongly evident in an appendix to the *Life of Jesus* (with "images" from the lives of the apostles and contemporaries of Jesus). For the feast of Mary Magdalene (July 22) in 1820 the saint's later life is sketched: the great missionary achievements of Lazarus and Martha are praised, but with regard to Magdalene once again only the penitential aspect is described; her preaching, her daily levitations, and her nourishment with heavenly food are as much ignored as her miraculous last communion (3.627–33). The suppression of the story of this communion and the almost casual mention of her first communion on a previous occasion (3.503) could be connected with the fact that any advancement of Magdalene to the rank of apostle had to be avoided, since it is said of the mother of Jesus that after her solemn first communion she was closer to the circle of the apostles and "herself became like an apostle" (3.491).

4. Brentano's Magdalene in the Context of the Quest for the Historical Jesus

What distinguishes Brentano from other nineteenth-century authors of lives of Jesus with regard to Mary Magdalene is not so much his express identification of the sinful Magdalene, the anointing women, and Mary of Bethany (3.627) as the emphasis on her role as sinner and the simultaneous suppression of her importance for the beginnings of the Church. Among the rationalist and liberal authors discussed by Albert Schweitzer in his overview of the literature, by contrast, it is most often Magdalene who recognizes Jesus, awakened from his swoon or apparent death and dressed in a gardener's clothes, and who announces to his disciples that he is alive (K. F. Bahrdt, K. H. Venturini, H. E. G. Paulus, F. E. D. Schleiermacher).[21] Finally, in Ernst Renan's book she becomes the sole author of the belief in the resurrection. According to his account she is, indeed, "a very hysterical person," but at the same time "the most superb instrument through whom faith in the resurrection originated." Of course, her powerful imagination played the major role in these events: "O divine power of love! sacred moments in which the passion of a visionary woman gives to the world a resurrected God!"[22]

The "Catholic" depictions of the life of Jesus that appeared at almost the same time (Brentano's posthumously in 1858–60, Renan's in 1863) could not be more different with respect to Magdalene: in Renan we see the forward-looking visionary who set Christianity in motion, in Brentano the penitent woman at her embroidery, who eventually retires from the world for good.

Books, too, have their destinies: Renan's poetic *Life of Jesus* landed on the Index of Forbidden Books while Brentano's equally poetic and fantastic work received ecclesiastical approval from the bishop of Limburg, with the express statement that it contained nothing offensive to Catholic faith or moral teaching (according to the title page verso). Brentano's picture of Magdalene fit seamlessly into the nineteenth-century ecclesiastical image of women, an image that portrayed women far more in terms of humility than of self-assurance.

Notes

[1]From an unpublished version by Father Schmoeger, quoted in Wolfgang Frühwald, *Das Spätwerk Clemens Brentanos (1815–1842). Romantik im Zeitalter der Metternich'schen Restauration* (Tübingen, 1977) 194.

[2]One example of the internal censorship: in a "parable image directed to the present" the *Education* mentions different forms of idol worship as practiced by priests, people of quality and education, entire congregations, and religious professionals; finally it says: "Indeed, I myself saw in Rome, among cardinals and great religious personages, figures of ancient idols like Moloch, Baal, and others standing on the table and holding sway among the books; yes, even offering them mouthfuls" (II, 231). This sentence was sim-

ply excised from the *Leben Jesu;* in turn, a reference to the reformed Church was more sharply emphasized (*Leben Jesu,* 2.22).

[3] Clemens Brentano, *Lehrjahre Jesu* part I, edited by J. Mathes (*Sämtliche Werke* 24, 1) (Stuttgart and elsewhere, 1983), quoted as "I"); part II (*Sämtliche Werke* 24, 2) 1985, quoted as "II." The remaining volumes have not yet been published. For the complicated history of the text see Frühwald, *Spätwerk,* 189–298.

[4] The *Lehrjahre,* together with the *Marienleben* and *Bitteres Leiden,* were conceived as the central section of a trilogy covering the whole story of Jesus' human development.

[5] Albert Schweitzer, *The Quest of the Historical Jesus,* translated by W. Montgomery, with an introduction by James M. Robinson (New York: Macmillan, 1968) 110: "If Brentano had published his notes at the time of the excitement produced by Strauss's Life of Jesus, the work would have had a tremendous success."

[6] Cf. Frühwald, *Spätwerk,* 278–83. The degree to which the "pious" Brentano was also influenced by the ideas of the time is evident from his rational explanation of miracles, according to which Jesus did not break the laws of nature (to use the Church's formula), but manipulated them through his greater knowledge (*Lehrjahre* II, 286).

[7] Cf. Frühwald, *Spätwerk,* 286–8.

[8] Lujo Brentano, *Mein Leben im Kampf um die soziale Entwicklung Deutschlands* (Jena, 1931) 70; quoted from Frühwald, *Spätwerk,* 197.

[9] This small detail shows how much of the thinking of his time Brentano introduced into his depiction of the life of Jesus; cf. the motif of mirrors and the *Doppelgänger* in Romantic poetry, as well as the division of the world into I and not-I, or subject and object, in the philosophy of the period.

[10] *Clemens Brentanos Frühlingskranz, aus Jugendbriefen ihm geflochten wie er selbst schriftlich verlangte* (1844) (Munich, 1967) 129–30.

[11] Ibid., 171.

[12] Ibid., 52.

[13] Ilsebill Barta, "Der disziplinierte Körper. Bürgerliche Körpersprache und ihre geschlechtsspezifische Differenzierung am Ende des 18. Jahrhunderts," in eadem, ed., *Frauen—Bilder—Männer—Mythen* (Berlin, 1987) 84–106, at 88–9.

[14] Ibid., 97.

[15] Quoted from Klaus Günzel, *Die Brentanos. Eine deutsche Familiengeschichte* (Zürich, 1993) 118.

[16] Barta, "Körper," 91.

[17] *Clemens Brentanos Frühlingskranz,* 185.

[18] Brentano mentions these saints in *Lehrjahre* I, 26 and II, 211; he also described their lives in a major poem (Christian Brentano, ed., *Clemens Brentano's Gesammelte Schriften I: Geistliche Lieder* [Frankfurt, 1852] 229–31).

[19]Wolfgang Frühwald, Berhard Gajek, and Friedhelm Kemp, eds., *Clemens Brentano: Gedichte,* dtv 6069 (Munich, 1977) 348–61 (various versions and recompositions).

[20]*Das Leben unsers Herrn und Heilandes Jesu Christi. Nach den Geschichten der gottseligen Anna Katharina Emmerich aufgeschrieben von Clemens Brentano,* vols. 2 and 3 (2nd ed. Regensburg, New York, and Cincinnati, 1880).

[21]Albert Schweitzer, *Quest,* 43 (Bahrdt), 47 (Venturini), 54 (Paulus), 64–5 (Schleiermacher).

[22]Ernst Renan, *Das Leben Jesu.* Authorized German edition (4th ed. Leipzig, 1880, following the 16th ed. of the original) 178, 397.

Chapter Eight

The Fallen Woman, the Noble Courtesan

1. Patron and Protector of "Fallen Women" and Infanticides

On March 13, 1846, a play was given its first performance in Königsberg; it had already been rejected by the General Intendant in Berlin and forbidden by the censors in Vienna. That play was Friedrich Hebbel's *Maria Magdalena*.[1] It was a tale of the seduction, pregnancy out of wedlock, and suicide of a young girl. After the first performance in Königsberg the ladies of society said that "a lady of reputation could not join in viewing a play whose heroine was 'a seduced woman,'" while four weeks later at the first performance in Berlin many female members of the audience left the theater "ostentatiously" once the heroine's pregnancy became known.[2] It was not only the official censors and a portion of the public that found the piece immoral; even the actress Auguste Stich-Crelinger, whom Hebbel had originally foreseen for the principal female role, rejected the part on the ground that the poet, in depicting an obviously pregnant heroine, had offended "the tender laws of morality."[3] Hebbel's references, in his letter of reply,[4] to other "immoral" figures like Gretchen (in *Faust*) and Klärchen (in *Egmont*) were justified to the extent that the motif of the seduced or fallen maiden had been a fixed element in German stage literature for decades.

While Emilia Galotti, Lessing's heroic protagonist, preserved her virtue at the cost of her life, it was the poets of *Sturm und Drang* who brought the "fallen" maiden to the stage. (Examples include J.M.R.

111

Lenz, *Der Hofmeister,* 1772/1773; F. M. Klinger, *Das leidende Weib,* 1774.) The motif was ultimately refined so that the girls not only lost their virtue and thus maneuvered themselves into social limbo; in their desperate efforts to conceal their situation through abortion or child murder they also came into conflict with the law and were punished by death. (Examples of this include H. L. Wagner, *Die Kindesmörderin,* 1776; cf. also Schiller's youthful poem "Die Kindesmörderin.") The most significant presentations of this motif before Hebbel are found in Goethe's *Faust* poems and in Brentano's "Geschichte vom braven Kasperl und dem schönen Annerl" ("History of the Good Kasperl and the Beautiful Annerl"), probably written between 1815 and 1817.

In all these poems the special tragic character arises out of the circumstance of the seducer and seduced belonging to different social classes, with the consequence that the conflict can never be resolved by marriage but (almost inevitably) requires the death of the girl. These guiltless-guilty girls cannot match the ideal of female virtue because society does not recognize their right to integrity. Virtue is the privilege of the upper classes; it is simply presumed that girls from the lower classes are at the disposal of the gentlemen of the higher orders.

Beaumarchais, who posed a critical challenge to the feudal structure, using the example of the *ius primae noctis* in his comedy *The Marriage of Figaro* (1784; Mozart's opera appeared in 1786), is not unreasonably regarded as one of the spiritual forerunners of the French Revolution! But of course that did not solve the problem. As money replaced noble ancestry there were also consequences for female virtue, as the young Rilke formulated in a one-act drama first produced in 1896: "You know, when a woman has enough to nosh on she can also enjoy the luxury of keeping up that kind of virtue(!), just like other people who keep a dog or a canary . . . but . . . you . . ."(!)[5] Virtue has now become a privilege of the rich.

When Hebbel began to conceive the "bourgeois tragedy of Klara" in 1841 he thus seized upon a familiar motif; superficially, at least, he altered it only in one respect: he did without a noble seducer and allowed the play to proceed consistently within the middle-class milieu, for the collision "of the third order with the second or first in love affairs" was for a nineteenth-century poet sad at most but no longer tragic, as he explains in his foreword. His tragedy arose out of the changed attitude to moral values like honor and shame, which were no longer important in themselves but had been made conditional on one's reputation among one's fellow citizens.

Meister Anton, Klara's father, is a representative of this bourgeois morality. Violations of norms by his children (supposed theft by his son, the unwed pregnancy of his daughter) take away his honor and with it the very basis of his existence: "I cannot bear to live in a world where people have to pity me unless they want to spit at me instead" (II, 1). In the end, however, it is not the father who is ruined: he endures, though "helpless," while ruin befalls Klara, the girl seduced and abandoned.

A morality inimical to life—embodied by men (father, fiancé, youthful friend) who are accustomed to see through the eyes of their fellow citizens—drives Klara to her death. Her tragedy is that she herself has internalized these externally imposed norms. She remains caught in the rigid attitudes of her environment, delivered over to its hard-heartedness with no chance to take charge of her situation on her own initiative. Her circumstance cannot be defined with words like "sin" and "repentance"; the issue is rather fear of shame and the loss of social reputation. For a fallen woman who has brought shame on her family there is no future either for herself or for her unborn child. The way out of the conflict cannot lead to a life-sustaining solution, but only to suicide, although in order to avoid questions about motive even the suicide has to be disguised as an accident. The only "help" that comes to Klara in this play, therefore, is her brother's request for a glass of water that gives her a reason to go to the well at a late hour: "Now they will say: 'She had an accident! She fell in!'" (III, 8). The fact that Klara's sacrifice was in vain because in the end neither her pregnancy nor her suicide can be hidden intensifies the mood of sorrowful gloom that lies like a veil over the play. Into this closed world of self-righteous morality falls not a ray of grace; pardon is not to be expected (as is demonstrated by the father's attitude to his son); there is no hope of mercy. Even Christianity, that much-acclaimed religion of love, holds no consolation for the unfortunate woman here.

This is evident in the very first scene, when the mother recognizes her own failure in the image of the heavenly wedding banquet: "So gracious was he . . . not . . . to those seven (!) virgins in the gospel" (I, 1). While the image of the stern divine judge was an incentive for the mother to renew her pious resolutions, its effect on the daughter is purely destructive. She can draw from religion neither strength for her life nor consolation in death.

Klara's final words evoke only the wishful dream of a merciful God from whom she expects no real help, for she knows that for a suicide who thus becomes simultaneously a child-murderer nothing remains but departure into a "fearful eternity" (III, 4). The dominant mood here is quite different from that found in Brentano's work a few decades earlier; he had bathed the guilt of seduced women and child-murderers in a rosy light of grace: the beautiful Annerl was executed, of course, but then she was buried with cross and pall in an honorable grave, and in Brentano's brothel romance a child (aborted or killed after birth?) appears with the message "God is appeased," for Jesus, himself a "murdered child," redeems through the power of his blood.[6]

Goethe, too, who seals Gretchen's fate in the original *Faust* with the words "she has been judged," gave a reconciling ending to the final version of *Faust I* when the "voice from above" proclaims Gretchen's salvation—to say nothing of her apotheosis at the end of *Faust II*.[7] Hebbel himself had attempted in two rather sentimental poems, a few years before his *Maria Magdalena,* to find a Christian-glossed solution. In "Versöhnung" (1836) the last verse reads:

> Gentle mother, mother of grace,
>   Bend down and acquit her;
> Her reconciler and her mediator
>   is the child in her womb . . .
> And so all her sins are abundantly
>   paid, and in full.

In the other poem, "Auf eine Verlassene" (1838) we find:

> And if anyone will revile you,
>   Show him, silently, your lovely child . . .
> Then ask him gently
>   If he can forgive the fact that it lives.[8]

Nevertheless, in the tragic play in which Hebbel had found his own voice such appeasing notes are no longer to be expected. There is no mercy for Klara, for religion is only a part of the milieu described and embodies the compulsions in which people entangle themselves. Thus Hebbel wrote a tragedy in which everything moves toward its bitter end with fateful necessity. Unlike ancient tragedy, however, here the acting (or suffering!) persons no longer understand their super-human destiny, for in fact their destiny lies hidden within their own character, and whereas ancient tragedy left the audience moved and "cleansed" *(katharsis),* Hebbel's audience feels more depressed than anything else.

In the years before the writing of this drama Hebbel had given a good deal of thought to the motifs of seduction, shame, and suicide; at length the plan for the "bourgeois tragedy of Klara" emerged, with a title that was intended to point to the figure in the drama who stood at the center of a complicated web of relationships. Nevertheless, even while it was being written he called it "Maria Magdalena."[9] Since the name of the central character remained unaffected by the new title, and since there are no references to Mary Magdalene in the play itself, one must ask what the relationship between the title character and the principal figure in the drama may be, and what image of Mary Magdalene is thereby presumed.

Hebbel gave his play a biblical name and in doing so awakened corresponding expectations, but he did not write a biblical play. He took from the Bible the figure of a morally vulnerable woman rejected by society: nevertheless he altered the character of that woman from what traditional ideas had made it out to be. Now she is not the actively seductive character (the sinful woman, the *magna peccatrix*) who ultimately seeks to change her situation on her own initiative, but instead one who is passively seduced, over whom fate inexorably rolls. Klara is indeed the principal figure because everything revolves around her, but she does not act; she suffers. Both in the prehistory and in the play itself she is the passive victim and her "guilt" consists in letting something happen to her and not opposing her own will to that of another (her father, her lover). The only act to which she brings her own initiative is her self-destruction, something the twenty-one-year-old Hebbel had feared for himself: "the situation destroys the person if the person is not able to destroy the situation."[10]

In the biblical story repentance leads to action and opens a future; Klara's desperation only brings her to a dead end. The sinful woman is returned to life; Klara—as Hebbel wrote while he was working on the first act—is "forced out of the world";[11] hopelessness drives her into the abyss, and that can be taken quite literally: she throws herself down the well. The important words of pardon and encouragement in Luke 7, provocative for hypocrites of all ages, are broken off: for this poet in the mid-nineteenth century such a "happy ending" is unimaginable.

German literature of the eighteenth and nineteenth centuries is full of the tragedies of fallen girls and women, but Hebbel was the first to connect them with the biblical motif of the sinful woman. On the basis of his reflections on the theory of art the temporary title, "a bourgeois tragedy," would have been more enlightening, but the new drama was intended to carry forward the previous tradition of "women's dramas" *(Judith, Genoveva)*, and yet at the same time it would not, like those others, give the name of the principal female figure in the title; it would have a "symbolic title"[12] that pointed to the problem featured in the content. That Hebbel struck on the figure of Mary Magdalene in his search for such a symbolic title for his tragedy of a woman, that he quite as a matter of course equated her with the "great sinner" and thus made his thought intelligible even to a secularized audience, again shows the degree to which this equation was part of the general fund of knowledge. The title was only possible because the author and the audience combined the same associations with the name: some kind of bad behavior in the realm of sexuality. Other aspects (the saint, the disciple, the Easter witness) were obscured. What remains is the dingy eponymous patron of fallen women who are destroyed by a merciless world.

When Hebbel chose the name of Mary Magdalene as synonym for a fallen woman he could count on his contemporaries' understanding, but what people did not follow was the naturalistic depiction of the shamed woman that he associated with the name. For his contemporaries Mary Magdalene had other aspects: she was the "beautiful sinner" who appeared in countless paintings, and also in the light literature of the period.

In a tale by the then best-selling author Carl Heun (1771–1854) published in 1824, the physical charms of a young girl named "Magdalis" or "Lenchen" (!) were described (her lovely body, the tender curves, the swanlike breast); they were concealed only by her long, loose hair and inevitably recalled a painting: "I really thought I was seeing the saintly Magdalene in the picture that hung in the master's bedroom."[13] That this lascivious picture hangs in a gentleman's bedroom underscores still more the character of the offensive beauty. When social convention (fashion!) and political censorship conceal the female body in public, art serves as a vent for male fantasies that are expressed in the intimate private sphere.

People who spontaneously associated lustful ogling of female charms with thoughts of Mary Magdalene were necessarily alienated by Hebbel's version of the tortured, suffering woman. In light literature aimed at a wide audience his ideas made no impression.

The novel *Ferien vom Ich* by Paul Keller, published in 1915 and soon a bestseller, still used all the fixed formulae that belonged to Magdalene's image: the "unfortunate, beautiful girl whose beauty was her curse" and who ultimately becomes an adulteress and "sinner" adopts (in her penitence) the name of "Magdalena" after her looks have already evoked associations with Mary of Magdala, the friend of the Savior.[14]

For a broad readership in the nineteenth century Mary Magdalene was interesting only in the role of beautiful sinner and sorrowing penitent. This explains the reservations evinced by Hebbel's contemporaries toward his play. They were irritated: they expected frivolous dalliance and what they got was bitter social and religious critique.

Hebbel made the "sinful" Mary Magdalene the patron and protector of fallen women, but he was not the first or the only one to make the connection; before and alongside him there were other poets who cautiously brought her into play. We recall Clemens Brentano's fragmentary novel "Der schiffbrüchige Galeerensklave vom toten Meer" ("The Shipwrecked Galley-Slave of the Dead Sea") or Georg Büchner's (1813–37) play *Woyzeck*. Of course, when Hebbel's *Maria Magdalena* appeared these works were not yet in print, nor would they be for a long time.

In Brentano's fragment,[15] parts of which were published in 1852, 1921, and 1949, appears the will-o'-the-wisp figure of Perdita, a little whore, beautiful, godless, and bad; and yet the cavalier whom she has just deceived and robbed says that she is "really a good kid." That is not a contradiction, because to be really "bad" she would have to be able to distinguish good from evil, but Perdita is amoral. Nothing is serious for her; she makes a game of everything: love, from which she makes her living; religion, where "the little child Jesus" is the highest authority; her dead mother, for whose supposed burial she swindles herself some new clothes. Not even she herself can be pinned down: within a few hours the image of the shamelessly shameful girl shifts until one suspects that even her coy gestures were only an insolent game. Perdita's is a kind of brilliant godlessness that, in its genuineness, can really be called religion, which is why she can say: "I don't want to become a Catholic; I have too much religion already." This creature is more genuine in her own way than the cavalier's next lover, a woman actor who is used to playing many roles while Perdita in her touching and insouciant way plays only herself. Nothing better describes this girl, whose fate is already foretold in her name ("the lost"), than the mendaciously pious words with which she asserts her "innocence": "O you heavenly stars, witness to my innocence! Never again will I receive the body of the Lord, never shall the little child Jesus forgive me my sins, never shall the holy Magdalene pray for me if this jealous accusation is true." The picture of the saint is reflected in the nature of the speaker, for whom sin has become second nature. The holy Magdalene whose solidarity is evoked with a wink in this frivolous game was herself one of the "lost" and is now, in heaven, responsible for girls like Perdita.

In Büchner's *Woyzeck* (written in 1836–7, first performed in 1913)[16] the issue is also virtue and morality, but at the end Woyzeck kills his Marie not because of lack of virtue but out of jealousy, for "virtue" is something the two of them cannot deliver, as Woyzeck says in the first scene ("At the Captain's"): "Look here: we common folk don't have any virtues. . . . There must be something beautiful about virtue, Captain! But I am just a poor slob!" The same is true of Marie also, of course; in a long scene ("In Marie's Room") she leafs through the Bible and comes across the story of her namesake: "Lord God! Lord God! I can't!—Lord God, just this much, just let me pray . . ." (striking her breast) "Quite dead! Savior! Savior! I want to anoint your feet!" Marie has read the savior's words of forgiveness, but they remain nothing but paper; they are not a reality for her. Woyzeck, whose life she destroys, will destroy hers as well. The sinner in the Bible and the woman who bears part of her name merge into a single image: the saint is the whore who, unlike Marie, has rescued a happy destiny from her lost state.

Both Brentano and Büchner relate their very different female figures to the sinful Magdalene. The reference to her expresses a hope, however forlorn, for a new opportunity for life. A few years later, in Hebbel's work, Magdalene is only the primitive image of the "lost" woman, and as reflected in the dramatic heroine she is a tragic figure.

However, Klara is only one of the many "Magdalenes" in nineteenth-century literature because the "fallen" woman who, by her wicked behavior, endangers the fragile honor of the man and therefore is rejected by society (and often pays with her life) became a favorite figure in literature (Effi Briest, Madame Bovary, Anna Karenina, etc.). Wherever a heroine of drama or novel violates the moral laws the Magdalene motif is unmistakably in the background, even if it is not always expressly noted. Theodor Fontane in *Effi Briest*, his best known depiction of this theme, avoids any play on the biblical model; in other novels he refers at most indirectly to the "penitent Magdalene": Melanie in *L'Adultera* (ch. 16) does not desire to be a "penitent Magdalene"; in *Cécile* (ch. 8) the major figures in the action view a gallery of portraits of noblemen's mistresses and describe it as a "gallery of Magdalenes." The poet calls all these women his

"Magdalenes," and loves them "not for their virtues, but for their humanity, that is, for their weakness and their sins."[17]

When society punishes in women what it admires or silently accepts in men, its attitude arises out of a subliminal fear of sexually active women, a theme treated on the one hand in the ballads (and operas)[18] that appeared at the time and on the other hand in theoretical works on female education and upbringing.[19]

In contrast to the authors mentioned in this section who use the name of Mary Magdalene in a metaphorical sense in order to initiate a critical discussion of a current theme, the authors in the next section undertook a historical retrieval of the biblical sinner in order to glorify her as a noble courtesan.

2. The Noble Courtesan

Around the turn of the century there was stiff competition over Magdalene material.[20] Under cover of a biblical figure it was possible to treat themes that otherwise would not have passed the censors or found entrée into middle-class bookcases: after all, this was a woman who gave expression to her sensuality and called into question the rules of the double standard. Mary Magdalene here appears as an unusual woman who sought her happiness outside the norms of society. She thus matches the "image of the courtesan as someone damned by predisposition and fate to be an outsider,"[21] who like many of her literary relatives is elevated by her inner nobility above "normal" women. Two authors in particular, both of them quite famous in their own time, gave literary expression to the theme in this sense: Paul Heyse and Anna von Krane.

(a) Paul Heyse (1830–1914), winner of the Nobel prize for literature in 1910, in his drama *Maria von Magdala* (1899), unlike Hebbel not only used the biblical figure for his title but also made her the hero of a five-act play.[22] The place of the action is Jerusalem in the last days before Jesus' crucifixion, with flashbacks to the life of Mary and a flash forward to the resurrection on the third day. Jesus himself does not appear as an active character, which is why the encounter between him and Mary is narrated in the form of the witness's message; his gentle and saintly image is also visible only as reflected on by other persons.

Mary from Magdala is presented as a noble courtesan with moral and nationalist principles: she is not a prostitute who sells herself to anyone at all; instead she chooses one whom she can love, and she has sworn not to open her house to any Roman (cf. I, 4).

The drama plays itself out between two almost identical exclamations by Mary: "He is not coming" and "He will come again" (I, 1; V, 6). The first refers to Judas, Mary's lover, and signals the beginnings of her separation from him; the second refers to Jesus, who now dominates Mary's thoughts and feelings. Between these two exclamations the drama unrolls before the audience: not only is there a change in the two men who are thus respectively awaited; the woman who speaks these words is also altered. The drama tells of the change in Mary and its flashbacks reach farther back into her biography, for her way of life ("just to satisfy the hunger of our senses, to taste all the joys of youth") is explained in terms of her past. As a fifteen-year-old girl she was married against her will to a rich old man. Three years later she fled with another who pretended to want to rescue her from her unbearable marriage, but really wanted only her money. Disappointed, she lived from then on only for pleasure. When she had had enough of callow youths she chose a lover who was "raw and violent," Judas, from whom she is beginning to separate as the drama begins.

From Judas and the Roman Flavius, both of whom are vying for Mary's affections, she hears for the first time of the holy man from Nazareth. (The name "Jesus" is never spoken during the play.) She feels drawn to him and wants to see him, not as Messiah and Savior, but because "he had never touched a woman" (I, 7). When her wish becomes known another temptation is offered her: the high priest promises her thanks and great honor if she will use her beauty once more as a tool. She is to employ all her wiles to expose that hypocrite; his power over the people would be at an end if they could see that he too is "powerless against the sorcery of sin" (II, 5).[23] What might at another time have enticed Mary as a means to recover her place in society now makes no impression on her; she feels herself too much drawn to the prophet whom she thus far knows only from hearsay.

When she finally comes into his presence she is recognized by the crowd as "the woman from Magdala, the adulteress, the whore." But it is not the sword of Flavius that rescues her from stoning; instead it is the word of the holy man that saves her (II, 7, 8). Mary is transformed. She seeks his presence a second time without heeding the danger involved. The events in the house of Simon are depicted in three scenes. First Hananiah, a noble stranger, reports that "she strode through the people who scattered to the sides, and approached the prophet. When he silently raised his eyes to her she sank at his feet.

She was carrying an ointment vase in her hand but she anointed his feet with the tears that broke from her eyes like a flood, and dried them with her long hair" (III, 9).

Judas sees the same scene with the eyes of a rejected lover. As Mary washes Jesus' feet with her tears he reads in her eyes: "You are my Lord and ruler; you shall rule over me, for I am thine with soul and body" (III, 10).

Mary counters this with her own view of the events. After Hananiah's rather sober account and Judas' mockery her depiction is heightened by the stage directions: "ecstatically blooming." (The same directions are found only for her closing words at the end of the play.) While at their first meeting Mary found Jesus' gaze judgmental and destroying ("Who will save me from these eyes!" II, 9) at the second meeting she experiences the same gaze as like a fire that burns "all vanity and sinful desire to ashes" and "warms and brightens the soul" (III, 10). She tells Judas he is right to suppose that she loves this man, but in a way that she has never loved a man and unlike anything Judas can comprehend: "Therefore I will love him . . . with a love that is pure as sunlight, that desires nothing more than to look up to him forever and to thank him for having blessed this straying, lost woman with his heavenly grace" (III, 10).

Judas mistakes the holy man's intentions just as he misreads Mary's behavior, and he thus finds himself unwillingly in the company of the Romans who misunderstand the man from Nazareth as someone who will aid them in oppressing the people and want to send him to Rome when his work is completed so that they may reward him for his services. Mary has her place in this scheme as well: "Perhaps you can go with him, and it may be that his beautiful girlfriend will decide to make the journey as well. She can make her fortune in the capital of the world" (III, 12).

Judas's and Flavius's speeches present an image of Mary that belongs to the past and refuses to recognize her transformation. For Judas she is one of the "weak and craving types" (III, 10); for Flavius she is the courtesan who can "make her fortune" with her beauty and willingness to please. These misunderstandings about the love of the changed Mary are carried on by the serving woman for whom this new love is to be treated according to the rules of the same old game: "If that miracle-man has awakened love in your heart, why not send him a message by me: 'Come! for Mary is longing for you'?" (IV, 1).

After the Savior is arrested and condemned Mary is confronted with a second blackmail attempt: while previously she was supposed to seduce the holy man in order to expose him as a false messiah, now she is tempted to surrender to Flavius's enticements in order to secure his release (IV, 2).[24] The woman who had just thought herself freed from all impurity is asked to drink again from the cup "that Eros wound with roses" (IV, 2). She decides to be "a sacrifice for the Holy One," but not without at the same time recognizing the outcome: she will save herself "in the eternal night that buries all shame" (IV, 3). Judas also gives her a choice: flight with him or death at his hands. This shows her the way she is to go: she will submit to Flavius and then willingly die at Judas's hand. But in the hour of decision she remembers Him and cannot open the door to Flavius.

Mary has not committed sin; she has not soiled her body. She has preserved her soul in purity and is by that very fact—according to her own interpretation—guilty. After the crucifixion she appears "behaving like a madwoman" and cries to the people: "Do not look at me, men and women of Jerusalem. I did it; I drove your Lord and Savior to his death" (V, 5). Flavius, who sees in her "the fever of a death-wish" (V, 6) wants to save her from herself. But she is not planning suicide; she has other plans: "I will hide myself in the wilderness, and there immerse myself in thoughts of my Lord and Savior . . ." (V, 5).

Only the statement of Simon, in whose house she had experienced the decisive transformation just a few days previously, that the dead man had spoken of his return and resurrection, brings about another transformation in her. Her final words are again designated "ecstatic" in the stage directions: "He will come again? Oh, what a promise! Let us adore and give thanks!" (V, 5). According to the last stage direction for the drama, all the people present do as she says.

The transformation of Mary from the proud, self-confident woman to the penitent and ultimately to the leader of the faithful people is emphasized by the poet's detailed directions for her appearance. At the beginning Mary is a woman well aware of her value, one who as mistress masters others. Her hairstyle corresponds to this attitude: "her rich hair is done in braids" (I, 4). In contrast, the penitent's inner state is made visible by her loosened hair (cf. the description of the scenes in IV, 1, and V, 5).

Something similar may be said of the clothing the poet prescribes for Mary. Before her encounter with the prophet she is described by her admirers and opponents as beautiful and proud, and is distinguished by corresponding attire: her grey headdress is "shot through with gold" (I, 4); she appears "in striking garments, richly jeweled" (II, 4). After her first encounter with the holy man the poet prescribes a black gown for her, and her face is to be covered with a grey veil (III, 3). The penitent woman wears a "simple, yellowish woolen robe without decoration" (IV, 1), in which she also appears at the execution (V, 5). Special attention should be paid to her "grey" head covering in the first act and her "grey" veil in the third; this color is deliberately chosen: Mary is no ordinary whore, but from the outset an "honorable woman"[25] who through no fault of her own has fallen outside the norms of society.

Heyse's drama *Maria von Magdalena* was an anachronism even at the time it was written: its idealizing historical depictions ignored the major literary currents of Realism and Naturalism. That it was nevertheless a success shows how much the image of the exciting sinner answered public taste; it also explains in retrospect the shock that Hebbel's tragedy created in many of those who saw it. A similar picture—combined with attacks on a bigoted Christian morality—was sketched by the next author.

(b) Anna Freiin von Krane (1853–1937), a much-read author at the beginning of this century, had special success with her Magdalene novel, *Magna Peccatrix* (1908).[26] In it she describes the life of Miriam of Bethany, called Magdalene from the place where she lived.

The novel's exposition depicts a woman who lives in luxury as mistress of the Roman legate Proculus; he had taken her from the narrow world of her house in Bethany and educated her in all the arts of Greco-Roman culture. Foreigners call this celebrated dancer the "star of Magdala" (p. 10), the "pearl of Magdala" (p. 9), but her Jewish compatriots despise her as an apostate.

A look from Jesus as he walks past her villa changes the life of the proud woman and ultimately leads her to the arduous search for the Master, after she has first rejected the offer of the noble Roman Fabius to stabilize her social position once and for all by marrying him. Her turn to Jesus comes to a preliminary climax in the foot-washing scene, which culminates in a flaming appeal against narrow-minded morality: "Thus the Lord smashed for all time the narrow-minded, short-sighted, and proud, who take from the fallen ones every hope, regarding their repentance, their shame, their suffering, their tears as nothing and letting them, despite all their penances, stand forever as soiled and branded!" (pp. 156–7).

Magdalene's life is described in emotion-filled scenes and metaphorically interpreted through the fate of the white dove: in Magdala Mary, already transformed but still entrapped in her sinful luxury, sent forth her snow-white dove with the message of her desire and repentance and saw with joy that it flew to Jesus (p. 56); later it returns trustingly to her as heaven's answer (p. 101). Long before she herself is able to sink at the Savior's feet his sacred hands have healed her wounded dove (p. 132); the dove's gratitude anticipates her own reaction to the encounter with Jesus: "in its love and fidelity it knew not what to do" (p. 133).

The proud Magdalene has here become a humble dove: she is allowed to accompany Jesus, care for his modest needs, and stand with the other women under the cross. At this point the poet breaks off the thread of the action in order to give a principled interpretation of the events: "It was the woman's greatest day of honor! In these fearful hours the new Eve beneath the cross of her Redeemer made restitution for the sin that the first Eve had brought upon the human race!" (p. 197). Out of the depths of her pain over the dead Jesus arises a vision in which Magdalene beholds the victory of the glorious Christ over Lucifer and the rescue of the souls of the dead. Before she returns to reality she hears a mysterious voice: "But be consoled! In the morning, in the spring garden, you will see me again!" The melody of these words accompanies her to the tomb and resounds again in the garden (pp. 218, 220, 222) until it flows into the dialogue: "'Mary!' 'Rabbuni!'" "For in the spring garden there was a most blessed woman on her knees; she laughed and wept for holy desire and stammered forth with lips that trembled for joy: 'The Lord is risen!'" (p. 223).

Magdalene's later life (the persecution of Lazarus and his sisters, their journey in a rudderless ship, the sisters' preaching in Marseilles, and Magdalene's retired life in a grotto) is narrated in a conversation with Fabius by Peregrinus, the guise assumed by the legate Proculus, now converted to Christianity. For the Gentile Fabius, Magdalene is "a priest of your faith," while for the Christian Peregrinus she is "a saint of God" (p. 251).

The novel ends with the apotheosis of Magdalene: the recognition scene and the dialogue in the garden are repeated in Paradise at the heavenly wedding feast. When Magdalene mourns that she cannot give her Lord the lilies of the virgins she hears: "You brought me the red roses of penitence!" and the angels place "a wreath of dark red roses on her head" (p. 258). Later Maximinius, the bishop of Marseilles, finds her body in a cave filled with tender light and the scent of roses.

Anna von Krane's novel, which from a present-day perspective passes the bounds of kitsch in many places and, because of its anti-

Jewish clichés, represents a questionable document of Christian belles-lettres,[27] nevertheless dared a considerable forward movement in the "woman question." Together with her condemnation of the socially sanctioned double standard and the rehabilitation of Eve the author also takes a position on contemporary questions such as the right of self-determination, the right to think for oneself, and the right to have one's own opinion:

> The Lord has thus shown us men that woman has a different position than the one we previously allowed her. . . . Jesus Christ taught us, and not least through Magdalene, that a woman is also an independent, thinking, and feeling being, equal to us, although different in many ways. He has shown us that a woman also has a right to self-determination, that she is independent of us, a being gifted with soul, intellect, and reason, who finds her own path on the way that leads to blessedness, and who is regarded by God as our equal! (pp. 247–8).

The description of a woman as a being gifted "with soul, intellect, and reason" is, of course, attached to Magdalene and thus is a gift of grace, not a natural right; nevertheless the theme is present, the key words that point toward the future have been written and were also seen by readers who would have given the voices of active promoters of women's rights not the slightest hearing.

3. Mary Magdalene on the Twentieth-Century Stage

Hebbel's configuration of the Magdalene material was more "modern" than that of the later authors just described, but his critique of religion and society was deliberately misunderstood, something that changed only in the twentieth century when art was no longer interested in imitating the beautiful, but instead took on a social-critical function. Only then did *Maria Magdalena* become Hebbel's most frequently performed play.

At the same time, and in direct connection with major stagings of the play, the question arose whether the problem treated in it was still a live one. While some think that the problems that destroyed Hebbel's characters are for us "only historical, and only understandable in retrospect" (F. Luft), matters "about which people today, however, think very differently" (P. Hoffmann), others discern behind the apparent antiquarian interest of the play the great humanity that can still be expressed on today's stage: "It is a story of yesterday with a lesson for today" (G. Hensel).[28]

After Hebbel's tragedy had achieved its success on the stage, other social-critical authors took up the material, but unlike Heyse or von Krane they did not start with the biblical story; instead they began with Hebbel's version of the theme and transposed his drama into their own present.

First among these we should mention Ludwig Thoma (1867–1921), who took over Hebbel's title and the framework of action for his popular piece, *Magdalena*.[29] Thoma, however, adapted his heroine's name, "Leni," to the title and transferred the action from the North German Protestant milieu into the Catholic rural culture of his chosen home near Dachau. The farmer's daughter Leni, in the city in search of a better life, goes "bad." The shameful thing she has done is never openly mentioned, but a variety of hints allow the audience to guess that, after being deceived by a swindler who promised her marriage, and after the loss of her savings, she has fallen into prostitution. The police force her to return to her village, and conflict results because she, unlike Hebbel's Klara, cannot properly estimate her situation ("She still doesn't have a clue what the problem is." [II, 4]) The hypocritical morality of the village, embodied in the priest, the mayor, and the young men, demands that the girl must disappear: "we have nothing to do with anyone who earns her living by her shame" (III, 9).

Thoma uses contrasting figures to make clear what honor and morality are worth: the honorable mayor, whose own daughter has a child born out of wedlock and nevertheless lives unmolested in the village, uses the "scandal" in the family of the small farmer ("We're shocked at this scandal, that someone like her is in this village," II, 5) in order to buy the farmer's land cheaply; the priest, with no compassion for human misery, leaves the dying farmer's wife when he hears that the disreputable daughter might come home at any moment.

The title word "Magdalena" stands, as in Hebbel's work, for the fallen girl, but differently from Hebbel the issue is only superficially her fate; in reality Thoma, the liberal member of the Bavarian legislature, is aiming at a reckoning with the political and ecclesiastical authorities whose hypocrisy he attacks in the attitudes exhibited toward the by no means sympathetic heroine. While in Hebbel's play it was the father's rigid concept of honor that drove the girl to her death, for Thoma it is the hypocritical morality of the good citizens that the father internalizes and that becomes the cause of the girl's death. Thoma also deviates at a crucial point from the biblical model; there is no place for kindness, consideration, or mercy. The representatives of the village demand of the father: "you've got to get rid of Leni!" (III, 8)—which he then in fact does, even more radically and finally than the village community had demanded: in a helpless rage he strangles his daughter who has undermined his honor and therefore his place in the village. Leni, like her predecessor Klara, receives no help from outside, nor is she, as a passive heroine, in a position to take charge of her situation on her own initiative.

In Hebbel's petit-bourgeois world, as in Thoma's rural society, the daughter's false step brings on a family catastrophe; for both authors such a situation offers the material for a tragedy of the bitterest kind. In the meantime, however, the world has changed: in the age of the pill when pregnancy "happens" to a young woman she is not a tragic figure; she is merely seen as stupid. The tragedy has become farce. At any rate that is how Franz Xaver Kroetz (b. 1946) sees it in his masterful adaptation of Hebbel's tragedy. In the subtitle of his *Maria Magdalena*[30] and in the final speech of the printed version he expressly acknowledges his debt to Hebbel's model, which he has translated down to the last detail into the present, the Augsburg of the late 60s. The people in this comedy take nothing quite seriously because they are indifferent to everything: the breaking of a coffee pot is depicted with the same intensity as the sudden death of the mother (I, 8). These people allow nothing, not even death, to put them on the spot: while the mothers in Hebbel's and Thoma's works think about death in terms of an often scrupulous piety, for this mother there is nothing

> . . . worth pining over.
> I'm Catholic, and I've done
> what I could.
> What more do you want? (I, 1)

There are no values outside the banal world of everyday life, no demands from a higher court, no God and no religion, and therefore also no sin. "Sin" is no longer defined in terms of God, but in terms of what everyone does (I, 3):

> You'd better look out
> or you'll put your foot in it!

God is no longer responsible for everything, but only for practical matters, as Marie, who does not believe in God, expresses in a "prayer" (I, 4):

Dear God,
let me miscarry this child.
Be reasonable, dear God, please!

In this world there are no values, only status symbols; no morals, only careers; only one goal: carrying off as much as possible from the table of the economic miracle. Leo gives precise expression to this way of thinking when he rejects a marriage without dowry: "I am a normal human being" (I, 6). This Leo is not an immoral person (he doesn't even know what that is!) but he can count: after all, marriage costs money. Even a pregnancy out of wedlock is evaluated on these terms: "It's not bad luck, as it used to be; it's just stupidity" (III, 13) says Marie, and soon afterward she gives a reason (III, 15):

> For Petra Schürmann a child when she's single
> is cheap publicity.
> And for me it is
> a real bump in the road.

The men affected by Marie's pregnancy take exactly the same view: her father ("clumsy stupidity": III, 16), her boyfriend ("you dope": II, 12), the child's father ("but an illegitimate child is not such a big deal nowadays": III, 13). There is no place for tragedy here. In the end they all meet, not for a duel (Hebbel), but for a game of Skat: Leo, who left the girl in the lurch; Peter, who would only marry her if she were divorced; her father, who doesn't care at all; and her brother, who will later give her some help and consolation. Nobody is responsible for Marie and her baby: what her father says is true for all of them: "I look out for myself and I survive" (III, 17). Consequently, no one lets himself get upset when Marie threatens to kill herself (III, 17):

> Well, when you're really dead
> we'll believe you! . . .
> Get y'self a beer, that's a lot smarter.

No one would have been upset if she had really poisoned herself; it would just be unpleasant and would break up the fun of the Skat game. And Marie plays the same game as the rest of them: she gets herself a beer. She does not die; she has just ruined her life. When nothing matters, suicide would be too final a solution.

Kroetz's comedy evokes laughter that dies in one's throat. It masquerades as a peasant farce full of stupid dialogue, but it is a deathly sad story reflecting an entire epoch of postwar Germany: this is true not only of the men who are utterly incapable of taking responsibility, but also of the woman who, in her lethargy, simply takes whatever comes instead of taking her life into her own hands. Marie does not have to take poison because everything in this meaningless world is poisoned. There is no contrast between boundless suffering and redemptive concern, as in the Bible, no tragedy arising out of the failure of anyone to help, as in Hebbel's work; there is neither a strong sense of guilt and repentance nor any salvation. Resolution of conflict or, in religious terms, salvation no longer reaches the deepest levels of the person. Financial security for Marie and her child would suffice, as she, for example, fantasizes in a daydream in which her father kills himself and she inherits the family condo (II, 2).

Hebbel, Thoma, and Kroetz use Mary Magdalene's name as their title but do not write plays about her. The playwrights can feel confident that their readers' imaginations will follow the right course. The name fulfills a function: the reader or theatergoer is prepared for a theme involving a woman and a seduction, the "weakness" of the woman and the "success" of a man.

While for these three authors the reference to Mary Magdalene is only indirect, by way of the title, other authors' allusions are more direct:

Daphne du Maurier (1907–89) subtly connects Mary Magdalene with prostitution when she has a vicar say of Jesus, in an ironically broken sermon, that he had human feelings and even "understanding for poor Magdalene." The same vicar will shortly thereafter intimidate a pregnant girl with the accusation that she is a prostitute and drive her to her death![31]

For Isak Dinesen (Baroness Karen Blixen-Finecke, 1885–1962), whose stories with remarkable frequency work with material drawn from biblical passages and who repeatedly refers to Mary Magdalene, she is also a former sinner. She speaks of her as "the highly-ranking saint of heaven" who was not lacking a certain "earthly . . . experience," and the characters in her stories always refer to Magdalene in the context of the social game of seduction and susceptibility.[32]

The path sketched by a number of authors from the eighteenth to the twentieth century has shown that in this period many standards changed, but apparently not the fact that women were easily made victims of the dominant (moral?) ideas. Klara (in Hebbel's drama) kills herself to prevent her father's shame; Marie (in Büchner's work) is stabbed by her husband and Leni (in Thoma's play) by her father, not as requital for a crime but simply out of helpless rage in order that the men may improve their own positions. The reasons for the women's deaths vary, but their fate remains the same: Gretchen (in Goethe's *Faust*) or the lovely Annerl (in Brentano's story) must die because they have killed their infants; Kroetz's Marie is reviled because she forgot to take the Pill and then waited too long to think of an abortion.

The authors no longer present the women (as in the baroque theater) as heroic martyrs, but as broken figures: seduced, pregnant girls, fallen women, whores, adulteresses—women with a blemish, despised by society and destroyed by it spiritually and physically. And apparently for these authors and their audiences such women have a strong affinity to Mary Magdalene.

The Church's image of Magdalene as it had developed in the Middle Ages and in the baroque period was solidified in its secular reception: Mary Magdalene is nothing more than the fallen sinner. But while in the Church's tradition her pardoning was always part of the story, that aspect vanished from the secular literature. Mary Magdalene is now only the woman lying prone on the ground, without a halo. When her story is recalled it is as protest against a society in which there is no place for the victims of a morality gone deadly, as Hebbel formulated it in a letter[33] that Kroetz quotes as a final speech in his play:

> This Klara
> disturbs me profoundly
> in the way she is hustled
> out of this world.

Mary Magdalene reflects the fate of women who stand hopelessly on the margins or even outside society, passive women who internalize the judgments of others and accept their situation. Magdalene has not yet become synonymous with the strong women who take charge of their own destiny, demand their rights, and provoke society.

Notes

[1]Friedrich Hebbel (1813–63), *Maria Magdalena. Ein bürgerliches Trauerspiel in drei Akten, mit Hebbels Vorwort.* Reclams Universal-Bibliothek 3173 (Stuttgart, 1992).

²Karl Pörnbacher, *Friedrich Hebbel. Maria Magdalena. Erläuterungen und Dokumente.* Reclams Universal-Bibliothek 8105 (Stuttgart, 1991) 66, 75.

³Letter of 6 January 1844 to Hebbel. For the divided reception of the play and its stagings in the nineteenth century, see Pörnbacher, *Erläuterungen* 57–75; the quotation is on p. 58.

⁴Letter of 23 January 1844 to A. Stich-Crelinger; cf. Pörnbacher, *Erläuterungen*, 60.

⁵Rainer Maria Rilke, "Jetzt und in der Stunde unseres Absterbens," quoted from Wolfgang Lappmann, *Rilke. Sein Leben, seine Welt, sein Werk* (Bern and Munich, 1993) 74.

⁶Clemens Brentano, "Geschichte vom braven Kasperl und dem schönen Annerl" in idem, *Erzählungen.* Selected and introduced by Walter Flemmer. Goldmann TB 1459 (Munich, 1964) 169–97; Clemens Brentano, "Ich kenn' ein Haus, ein Freudenhaus" in idem, *Gedichte,* edited by Wolfgang Frühwald, Bernhard Gajek, and Friedhelm Kemp. dtv 6069 (Munich, 1977) 332–5.

⁷Erich Trunz, ed., *Goethes Faust: Der Tragödie erster und zweiter Teil. Urfaust* (Hamburg, 1963).

⁸Quoted from Pörnbacher, *Erläuterungen*, 36–8.

⁹Ibid., 32–44.

¹⁰Quoted from Hayo Matthiesen, *Friedrich Hebbel mit Selbstzeugnissen und Bilddokumenten,* rowohlts monographien 160 (Hamburg, 1970) 22.

¹¹Letter of 26 March 1843; cf. Pörnbacher, *Erläuterungen*, 46.

¹²Letter of 11 December 1843, ibid., 57, 84–5.

¹³Carl Heun, *Der Fastnachtsball,* quoted from H. Kunze, *Lieblingsbücher von dazumal,* dtv 947 (Munich, 1973) 128–9. While Carl Heun was a successful author whose books were published in large editions, Hebbel's publisher sold only 114 (!) copies of *Maria Magdalena* in the year it was first staged: cf. Pörnbacher, *Erläuterungen*, 66.

¹⁴Paul Keller, *Ferien vom Ich* (Stuttgart and Hamburg, 1951 [original ed. 1915]) 7, 132.

¹⁵Clemens Brentano, "Der schiffbrüchige Galeerensklave vom toten Meer," in *Erzählungen* 80–91. All quotations are from the section entitled "Morgenstern, der freundliche freigebige Kavalier [Morgenstern, the Friendly, Generous Cavalier]" 80–5.

¹⁶Georg Büchner, *Woyzeck,* in idem, *Leonce und Lena. Dantons Tod. Woyzeck,* with an afterword by Klaus Ziegler, Exempla Classica 59 (Frankfurt and Hamburg, 1962) 125–52.

¹⁷Quoted from Gotthard Erler, "Die gefährliche Liebschaft von Kessin," in *Die Welt,* 14 October 1995.

¹⁸The woman is depicted as a demonic force of nature and her powers of sexual attraction as a deadly danger for the man; cf. the popular ballad motif of the Lorelei in its various guises: mountain, water, or forest spirits (Clemens

Brentano, Heinrich Heine, J. von Eichendorff), daughter of the Erl-king (J. G. von Herder), or Lady Venus in Tannhäuser material (K. Gerock, Richard Wagner).

[19]In particular, girls' early introduction to fancywork served not only for their general disciplining but also helped "to suppress their sexual needs," cf. Dagmar Ladj-Teichmann, "Weibliche Bildung im 19. Jahrhundert: Fesselung von Kopf, Hand und Herz?" in I. Brehmer, J. Jacobi-Dittrich, E. Kleinau, and A. Kuhn, eds., *Frauen in der Geschichte* IV (Düsseldorf, 1983) 219–43, at 225.

[20]The most important works of the Jesus- and Jesus-Magdalene literature have been collected by Elisabeth Frenzel in her article, "Maria Magdalena," in *Stoffe der Weltliteratur* (8th ed. Stuttgart, 1992) 496–9.

[21]Elisabeth Frenzel, "Die selbstlose Kurtisane," *Motive der Weltliteratur* (3rd ed. Stuttgart, 1988) 434–51, at 435.

[22]Paul Heyse, *Maria von Magdala. Drama in fünf Akten*. In idem, *Gesammelte Werke* I, 5 (Stuttgart, Berlin, and Grunewald, n. d.) 597–669. The fact that this work at the time appeared suspicious to the censors (cf. Frenzel, *Stoffe* 499) is something we can scarcely imagine today.

[23]Mary is given the same assignment as Kundry: the holy and pure one is supposed to be destroyed by the charms of a sinful woman. Caiaphas and Klingsor thus agree that no man (neither the pure Parsifal nor the holy Jesus) can resist the temptations of the flesh. But in both cases the one to be seduced becomes the "savior" of the woman.

[24]Heyse seems to have been the first to introduce a connection between Mary Magdalene and a Roman into literature; at the beginning of the twentieth century such relationships appear several times: cf. Frenzel, *Stoffe*, 498–9.

[25]In the novella *Jorinde* (1875) the servant is depicted "in a respectable grey dress": idem, 289–394, at 292.

[26]Anna Freiin von Krane, *Magna Peccatrix. Die große Sünderin. Legendenroman aus der Zeit Christi* (27th–31st eds. Cologne, n. d. [1930]; 1st ed. 1908).

[27]Cf. the alienating counterpositions in the God-image (the understanding helper and the cruel tyrant, p. 142) and the image of Jesus (the white figure of Jesus before the dark mob, p. 151), as well as the different descriptions of Galilean and Judean physiognomies (the slender figures "with direct gaze and regular features, fundamentally different from the sharply hooked noses and restless eyes of the true Israelites," p. 168).

[28]Cf. Pörnbacher, *Erläuterungen*, 78–9, 82.

[29]Ludwig Thoma, *Magdalena. Ein Volksstück in drei Aufzügen* (Munich, 1912).

[30]Franz Xaver Kroetz, *Maria Magdalena. Komödie in drei Akten frei nach Friedrich Hebbel*, in *Oberösterreich u. a.* Edition Suhrkamp 707 (Munich, 1972) 217–75.

[31] Daphne du Maurier, "Ich rufe mit meiner Stimme zum Herrn," in *Ihr ergebener Diener und andere bisher unveröffentlichte Erzählungen.* Knaur TB 60 199 (Munich, 1993) 7–47, at 29 and 35.

[32] Isak Dinesen [Karen Blixen], "The Dreamers," in *Seven Gothic Tales* (New York: Harrison Smith and Robert Haas, 1934) 271–355.

[33] *Erläuterungen,* 46; quoted from the instructions for the printer in Kroetz, *Maria Magdalena,* 275.

Chapter Nine

The Woman at Jesus' Feet:
Mary Magdalene
in Modern Spiritual Poetry

From a certain distance in time the epochal shift from the medieval to the modern period may appear to represent a sharp break, but when we look at it closely we can discern gradual transitions at many points. Magdalene's role in spiritual poetry represents one such transitional move. She remains the great saint and model for those who pray; they can orient themselves to her life as an example and dare to hope that in imitation of her they will find the same blessedness that is already hers, but they can also turn to her directly, for she is an advocate and helper. These motifs in the medieval veneration of saints (exemplification and advocacy) were retained in spiritual poetry of the early modern period: for example, in the work of Angelus Silesius.[1] This is particularly true of German hymnody, which from the time of the Reformation and the Catholic reform movement became an essential expression of piety. Following the model of Martin Luther, poets and theologians not only taught the faith but sang it into human hearts.

Anyone who depreciates lyrics composed for such practical purposes should consider that in the past spiritual poems that were the objects of reflection during household devotions or in the hours of prayer conducted by religious societies, and church hymns encountered again and again at divine worship had an enormous influence on Christians. For many, well into our century, hymns, alongside the Bible, the catechism, and the calendrical stories, were the only literature of any kind ever encountered; this was the sole opportunity not only to learn the content of Christian faith but to process it emotionally. This last was a task completely outside the capacity of the catechism.

It is therefore especially interesting to see how people encountered the figure of Mary Magdalene in such texts: that is, how her image developed out of the text for believing readers. We will see that, while she managed to salvage her significance as the great medieval saint, from the eighteenth century onward her appearances in spiritual poetry decline to a striking degree, or only partial aspects of her self are retained.

1. Mary Magdalene in Religious Poetry and Poetic Cycles

Mary Magdalene appears in all the principal poetic works of the Schlesian Johann Scheffler (1624–77), better known as Angelus Silesius; she is, in fact, the saint most frequently mentioned. This is true of his *Heilige Seelenlust,* a collection of spiritual songs in which Christ and Psyche (that is, the soul) express their longing and love as shepherd and shepherdess, and also of his *Sinnliche Beschreibung der vier letzten Dinge,* but especially of his collection of proverbs, *Cherubinischer Wandersmann,* which contains advice for a successful life.[2] The traditional image of the saint is presupposed: this is not always expressly stated, but it is indicated by certain verbal signals (tears, anointing, feet of Jesus, etc.). Especially in the eight-strophe poem "Lob der Heiligen Maria Magdalene" [Praise of Saint Mary Magdalene] in the collection *Heilige Seelenlust* we find all the elements of Bible and legend that have marked her image for centuries: she is the sinner who does public penance, the anointing woman who lives on in the memory of Christians, Mary of Bethany who chose the better part, the woman beneath the cross who is then the first to be permitted to see the Lord, and finally the visionary who lives for thirty years without food, rapt in the vision of God. Since Angelus Silesius takes the unified image as his starting point, Magdalene is almost necessarily the embodiment of the tearful-beatific penitent.[3] Tears, remorse, penance, and love are interchangeable concepts that, especially in the "pilgrim" sayings, point to the saint's function: the reader should "like Magdalene" weep, do penance, and love in order to be blessed as she is:

> No sinner ever died so well and so blissfully
> As the one who, like Magdalene, has gained the Lord's favor.[4]

Of course it is not a question of automatically effective grace, which is why readers are warned against a too-hasty identification with the saint:

> Ah, sinner, do not feel too secure because you see
> How Magdalene goes forth from the Lord,
>   consoled and comforted.
> You are not yet like her; if you desire
>   to enjoy this consolation,
> First prostrate yourself, as she did, at his feet.[5]

But anyone who follows the example of the great penitent may hope to be consoled as she was and in the consummation of all things to attain eternal blessedness there where the "strict penitents" are accorded a very prominent place. As the visitors to a baroque church allow their gaze to wander from the symbols of *vanitas* in the nave to the heavenly scenes in the cupola, so the readers' gaze is drawn from their own sinful and therefore fatally destined situation to Mary Magdalene and through her to the vision of heavenly glory. Hence she has great significance for the readers who immerse themselves in the contemplation of her repentance, penance, and pardon, especially for people who are driven by a strong sense of their own sinfulness, but in most instances it is also restricted to this aspect—and that restriction appears to us today as altogether questionable.

The same is true of another aspect of her depiction: the theme is constantly that of the individual relationship between the one praying or reading and the saint. Mary Magdalene is the model for an individual reader, not for the community of believers, and her outstanding place, which is undeniable, is tied to her individual story. She is great in her personal reception of pardon, but even a strophe whose content is the narrative in John 20 centers on her *private joy,* the reward for her fidelity, and not her *apostolic mission:*

> Hence also he desired
> To gladden your face first of all
> And grant to you to behold
> His risen light.[6]

Mary Magdalene's function for the disciples at that time and for the later Church is not acknowledged.

These critical remarks must be supplemented by an observation that illuminates the poet's image of Magdalene from an entirely different side. Angelus Silesius was not only a convert and priest in the

Counter-Reformation Church, he was also, as the sayings in the *Cherubinischer Wandersmann* particularly attest, a mystic according to whose world view the primary issue was the individual human person's (or soul's) relationship to God. This God is not available in holy places or institutions, but must be sought within the soul itself. The human being must ascend above the world of things, of desires, and of deeds; only those who have abandoned individual things will be able to find, behind the ephemeral things of time, the pure Nothing that is God:

> The tender divinity is a Nothing and More-than-Nothing.
> O human, believe, the one who sees nothing in all things sees this.[7]

In the pure nothingness of the Godhead they recognize true perfection. John and Mary Magdalene attained this highest condition: John "flies" to the breast of Jesus in order to "cradle" there in secret desire; Magdalene "runs" to the feet of Jesus in order to kiss them with eternal surrender.[8] For both of them movement releases into endless rest. John and Mary Magdalene are the prototypes of the person who has attained the goal:

> John on the breast, Mary at the feet,
> Both of them doing nothing but enjoying God.[9]

Thus Angelus Silesius's image of Magdalene is not exhausted in the portrait of the great penitent as she is known to us from the plastic arts of the baroque era; it gains new contours through the mysticism of surrender. It is not the "doing" of the penitent, but the "not-doing" of the one who reposes that describes her perfection. John and Mary, man and woman, are equally capable of this perfection, this "divinization."

While Mary Magdalene plays a major role in the work of Angelius Silesius and other poets of the high baroque era her significance was altered in the very next generation, as shown by the example of the lyricist Johann Christian Günther (1695–1723), in whose work one may search in vain for a text or even an allusion to Mary Magdalene. In comparison, for example, to Andreas Gryphius (1616–64) this is especially significant, since both poets wrote texts for the feast of Mary Magdalene.[10] While Gryphius, using the text of Luke 7, contemplates the miraculous transformation of the sinful saint, Günther's poem honors Frau Magdalena Sparr on her name day; the name appears both in the title and as an acrostic in the text. But as the title indicates ("On the Occurrence of the Name Day of Frau Magdalena

Sparrin, born Mentzelin, In Accordance with Her Motto: 'Lord, According to Thy Will'"), the text is not concerned with the saintly patron, but with the life motto of the woman being honored.

The development that announces itself here can be observed in other Protestant poets of the early eighteenth century. This is connected with the fact that the threefold figure of Magdalene was gradually dissolving, but also with the circumstance that spiritual lyrics from the "awakening" movement were oriented to a personal relationship to God and scarcely required any saintly models for the purpose. This is true both of the poems of Count Nikolaus Ludwig von Zinzendorf (1700–60), the founder of the Herrnhut Brotherhood, and of those of Gerhard Tersteegen (1697–1769), the most important lyric poet of the period.

In the Count's penitential lyrics and spiritual dialogues there are indeed references to the tears of the penitent sinner but they are no longer connected, as they had been in the "Catholic" past, with the model of the weeping sinner, Mary Magdalene. The women who previously contributed to the image of Magdalene remain individual figures without connection to her. This is true especially of "the defamed woman" in whose case Jesus' secret wisdom was demonstrated, the poor prostitute who is "a miserable human being" and yet was "received in grace."[11] Other women who in the past had contributed positive features to the image of Magdalene are newly evaluated, or rather devalued, such as Mary of Bethany, who is criticized because she, together with Martha, buried her brother before Jesus came,[12] or the anointing woman from the Passion narrative who performed "an action that in itself deserved rebuke," and was not condemned only because the Savior regarded not her deed, but her "desire to do," that is, her good intention.[13] Mary Magdalene, in contrast, is restricted to a partial aspect of her role on Easter morning:

> With Mary I will implore,
> Go early to the tomb
> And see him with the eyes
> Not of the body, but of the soul.

The fact that the one who prays here is reflecting elements of a biblical figure is only an apparent contradiction to what was said above, for the "Festive Greeting to the King of Heaven" from which this verse is drawn is a translation of the Latin poem by Bernard of Clairvaux, *Jesu dulcis memoria dans vera cordis gaudia.*[14] When the hymn was adopted in the hymnal of the Herrnhut community it was because, as this fifth verse reveals, it expresses some ideas typical of Zinzendorf's own piety.[15] Mary's journey to the tomb exemplifies the theme of the fourteen-verse hymn—joy at the presence of Jesus and longing for him to remain—as well as the longing of the Christians who had joined the community at Herrnhut. Nevertheless, one should not give too much weight to this reference to Mary Magdalene, which was prescribed by the Latin original. Mary of Magdala was no pietist saint.

These observations are confirmed by Gerhard Tersteegen's song and sayings cycles. Mary of Bethany and the sinful woman are mentioned there as individual women.[16] While Mary of Bethany is frequently mentioned in the songs because the one who prays wishes to be like her, despising the many and seeking only the one thing, sitting at the Lord's feet and listening to his word,[17] Mary of Magdala's importance declines. Her sole, almost incidental mention occurs in an Easter hymn:

> I throw myself with Mary,
> My Lord and God, at your feet,
> And if I dared, I would with her
> In humility most tenderly kiss you.
> Speak also a word with power into my heart,
> So will I see you, so will I rejoice in you![18]

More important than her gestures is the word of Jesus that the one who prays "also" implores for his or her own heart. What is really important is this "heart," the petitioner himself or herself, the desire for the presence of Jesus, as the closing lines make clear:

> You are not far away; the one who loves you purely
> Can in spirit be with you in heaven.

It is quite clear that Mary of Magdala plays no further role in the piety of the awakening, for not only her function as model, but still more her significance as an advocate before God have vanished. This business of doing without a female saint is, of course, made easier by the fact that God is given feminine attributes: in the presence of a motherly God whose maternal heart turns tenderly to human beings there is no longer need for an advocate, either male or female, before the throne of God.

Eighteenth-century pietism was the last great spiritual movement in which religious and secular life mutually saturated one another. The increasing secularization of all areas of life and the separation between Church and society also had consequences for the spiritual poetry of the nineteenth century and still more that of the twentieth: the authors of lyrics for practical use in particular religious communities are no longer to be sought among the great poets of the era, as had been the case with the authors of sixteenth- or seventeenth-century hymns, most of them powerful wielders of language like Luther and Spee.

In turn the important lyricists who devoted themselves to Christian poetry (Clemens Brentano, Annette von Droste-Hülshoff, Gertrud von le Fort) no longer found entrée into congregational song, or did so (as in the cases of Jochen Klepper and Rudolf Alexander Schröder) only with great difficulty. These poets, male and female, who were formed by the Church either from childhood or through a deliberate attachment, understood their work as a religious action and further underscored their ecclesiastical ties by orienting their poetry collections to the course of the religious day or the Church year. In these spiritual cycles, but among the other poems by these authors as well we may seek the traces of references to Mary Magdalene.

First we will consider two authors who, despite the great differences in their character and origins, reveal many common features precisely in their attitude toward religious poetry: Annette von Droste-Hülshoff, deeply marked by the harsh environment of her Westphalian homeland, and Clemens Brentano, a man driven by his Italian heritage. Both wrote poetry cycles on the Sunday gospels but withheld them so long that they were published only after their respective deaths.[19] Both had reservations about their dangerous talent, which they described with words like "sin" and "time wasting," and both saw their salvation in spiritual poetry that combined artistic effort with religious engagement.

Annette von Droste-Hülshoff (1797–1848) completed in the fall of 1820 the fair copy of the first part of her poem, *Geistliches Jahr* ("The Spiritual Year"), based on the Sundays and holy days from New Year's Day to Easter Monday according to the calendar of 1820; at the urging of her friend and spiritual mentor Schlüter she resumed work on the cycle in 1839. From that year there are two passages in her letters according to which "this book is perhaps the only one that gives me joy," while all her other work seems "foolish." In the same letter she reflects the dilemma of every dedicated artist, here the tension between the demands of art and religious conviction; the poet expressly emphasizes that she gives only so much consideration to "beauty of form . . . as is possible without detracting from the object, and no more."[20] She understands her work as a religious duty whose obligation is solely to the claims of truth and may not be controlled by any other considerations; that in this she is deceiving both herself and her readers is clear from a passage that at least indirectly had consequences for her depiction of Magdalene as well.

Mary Magdalene is mentioned in two poems from the Easter cycle of the Church year. In the poem "Am Christi Himmelfahrtstage" ("On the Day of Christ's Ascension") the introductory verses look back on the earthly life of Jesus and recall his encounters with Martha and Magdalene, the latter appearing as a mixture of the sinful woman from Luke 7 and Mary of Bethany (Luke 10:38-42; John 12:1-3).

> With Magdalene I would have wanted to kneel,
> My tears, too would have to have glowed
> On your foot, perhaps then, oh perhaps
> Your blessed word would have reached me, too:
> "Go, your sins too are forgiven!"[21]

The image of the sinner remains, at first glance, entirely within the bounds of the conventional portrayal. But here we must note, anticipating some other observations, that the poet, identifying with Magdalene, makes no statement about the kind of sins from which she wishes to be delivered as Magdalene was before her.

Information on this subject is found in the text for the first Sunday after Easter,[22] based on the pericope John 20:19-31, as Droste expressly states in a prose passage set before the poem: "Jesus passes through closed doors and says 'Peace be with you!'" The first and last lines of the poem take up the word "peace" and interpret it as a desire of the poetic persona, which has no peace. Its situation is described as "of little faith" and full of "sins," and is more closely characterized by its petition: "Let love prevail, for faith is weak."

The word pairs faith/sin and faith/love, which mark this poem, are at the same time the leitmotifs of the entire cycle. Its ground bass is a strong consciousness of sin, meaning here not moral faults but a lack of faith. Reason (negatively portrayed) stands in the way of faith.[23] The poet—and here one may shift from the poetic to the personal level—suffers under the burden of insufficient faith and also of fear of becoming otherwise vulnerable to doubt and thus to sin; only if love is accepted as a substitute for faith is salvation possible:

> If it is only faith that you promise,
> Then I am dead . . .
> I have it not.
> Oh, will you not accept love in place of faith . . . ?[24]

In the dedicatory letter of 1820 to her mother the poet herself offers some information about the relationships described: her book is not for the simple and childlike, for it contains "traces of a much pressured and divided mind." It addresses itself to "the secret, but undoubtedly very widespread sect of those whose love is greater than their faith."[25]

The theme of the cycle is thus summarized in the poem for the first Sunday after Easter as if it were placed under a magnifying glass. The Lord who stands before the closed door of the doubting soul lacking faith is asked to accept love in place of faith and with his word of peace to step through the closed door (of the soul); at the end of the poem, then, one would expect a corresponding reference to the apostles seated behind the closed door and to Jesus' words. (See the prefatory prose statement.) Instead, contrary to the gospel narrative, Mary Magdalene is introduced:

> So speak, my Father, speak also to me
> With that voice that called Mary's name
> When she, unwitting, turned about weeping,
> O say: "My child, peace be with you!"

The New Testament plural "Peace be with you!" is shifted to the singular: the addressee of the greeting is now the loving Mary Magdalene, behind whom the poet's own persona is concealed. She thus becomes an embodiment of hope: Christ does not look at faith, whether strong or weak, but at overwhelming love. In Magdalene we see the magnitude of the divine care for human beings by which even sinners weak in faith can from now on raise themselves up. What an irony: the deeply believing disciple of Jesus has become the model for Christians weak in faith. (This shift is assisted by the fact that Droste no longer interprets "faith" as an act of the whole person, but rather in neoscholastic terms as an act of the intellect alone; this point cannot be pursued here.)

Thus the day of the Ascension (see above) also sheds light on Magdalene: Droste, because of her equation of reason, doubt, and sin, can only partially outfit the image of Mary Magdalene with the traditional features. She is a weeping sinner at Jesus' feet, but she is not depicted as a morally depraved woman.

Of course one must ask why Droste developed her depiction of Mary Magdalene on this point contrary to the Church's tradition. The answer can scarcely be comprehended by present-day readers: the poet, in everything she published, had to take into account the society's opinion of her family (to the extent that her strict mother permitted her to publish anything at all!). On this point the poem "Am Feste vom süßen Namen Jesus" (On the Feast of the Sweet Name of Jesus) is especially revealing. In the critical edition of 1971[26] we find the following lines:

> And I, O dearest Jesus mine,
> Shall be the fallen one, faithless to all duty,
> And yet the heiress of thy Name:
> God! You do not will the death of the sinner!

When Droste had already released this text for publication she wrote to Schlüter, who had been entrusted with the printing, that he must, without fail, change the words "the fallen one" because this "expression has always evoked great scandal, and that among my closest relatives, those who I am least willing to distress"; the relatives found the word "improper and ambiguous," and the poet understands that it can "certainly by no means be pleasant for them to leave its interpretation completely open to the whole public."[27] How, that is, could she propose to her relatives and friends that they identify with a morally "fallen" Magdalene?! Mary Magdalene remains the sinner, but her sin must be socially acceptable. . . .

If this poet models her image of Mary Magdalene on the social ideas of her fellow members of the nobility, such considerations were not necessary for the romantic poet Clemens Brentano (1778–1842); nevertheless it is to be feared that his statements about Mary Magdalene have also been subjected to certain corrections. It is very well known that parts of the family and some of the owners of his manuscripts destroyed some things and revised a great deal in order to be able to stylize the image of the "saintly Clemens." This is true both for manuscripts from his Dülmen period and for the *Collected Writings*[28] published by his brother Christian, the first volume of which contains his spiritual poetry. For a poet who in all phases of his creative activity mixed religious and sensual-erotic language the absence of such echoes in the Magdalene verses is more than surprising.

In considering his spiritual poetry one will think first—again much like the case of Droste—of the cycle *The Sunday Gospels* from the years 1826–7 (see n. 19 above). These were fifty-seven poems on the gospel texts for the Sundays and holy days; unlike Droste's *Spiritual Year*, Brentano's cycle follows the Church year, beginning with the first Sunday of Advent, and in content as well he assumes less freedom: while Droste used the gospel texts as occasions for spiritual contemplation Brentano remains strictly tied to the biblical model, which he paraphrases in verse, although certainly his usual magic with words is lacking. The poet himself, in a letter in which he refused publication of these poems, called them "hard and stiff."[29] The fact that here—again differently from Droste in the same years—the poet rejects any kind of personal tone corresponds to Brentano's attitude at that time, when he even purified already completed poems of anything too personal so that one might read them "without becoming too familiar with the author."[30] A natural consequence is that Mary Magdalene appears only on the fringes of this pericope cycle, especially since the order of readings for the Church year provides for no text specifically focusing on Magdalene.

Individual poems the author could shape more freely. Especially important in this connection is the poem "Magdalene Goes to the Tomb."[31] The principal strophes are presented as a monologue by Mary Magdalene, who, in the manner of a gospel harmony, tells of the events on Easter morning; in contrast the second strophe, which also has a different rhythm, is an appeal by the poet to an otherwise unspecified "thou."

The poem begins, much as with Friedrich Spee, whose poems Brentano had edited and published a few years earlier, with an indirect indication of time: The night is indeed past, but it is not yet full daylight:

> The anxious night has fled,
> But still no one can make out another's face,
> Still can I flaunt my tears
> And steal silently to the Master's tomb.

The depiction of the morning twilight corresponds to the mood of the "I," who in what follows makes herself known as Mary Magdalene; important points of reference are the linguistic signals like "anxious night," "tears," and "tomb."

This poem is linked in many ways both to the poet's corpus of lyrical poetry and to his particular interests during the time of its composition. This is true especially of the individual lines of the principal strophes, which interrupt the thread of the gospel narrative by introducing Mary Magdalene's reflections (cf. also the fourth strophe):

> So I wander in the grey morning
> To the tomb where my love rests;
> I will bedew him with tears,

For he gave me all his heart's blood.
To lift the stone from my heart
My whole delight went down to death.

The blood symbolism and the mystic formulae of exchange (my tears/his heart's blood; the stone before the tomb/the stone from my heart) are found in countless poems. In two there is even an express reference to Mary Magdalene, or to the penitent woman:

(a) The poem "Vor dem ersten Aderlaß, am Tage vor dem Abend-mahl" (Before the First Bloodletting, On the Day Before the Last Supper) from the time of his general confession introduces the blood of the one speaking, which flows from the lancet, into a mysterious and mystical exchange with the blood from Jesus' wounds, the blood ultimately given and received at the Lord's Supper:

That your blood may unite with me
My own makes room for it today . . .
Let it be that all (= the blood) slip away . . .
And replace it in spirit once again
Tomorrow for me with your blood.
Before you I will then sink down, purified,
Where the penitent woman rests.[32]

(b) The poem dated "22 November 1835" that in some places reads like an echo of the Magdalene poem also has in its eighth strophe the exchange between tomb and heart:

With Magdalene, as the day grows grey
I wander to the tomb where Jesus lay,
O heart, who will lift the stone from you,
O heart, when will he enter under your roof?[33]

One can see how closely the apparently naïve, narrative Magdalene poem is united in its deeper structure with the rest of Brentano's spiritual poetry. At the same time it recalls Brentano's activities as writer and recorder for the stigmata-bearing nun Anna Katharina Emmerick (1818–24).[34] This is true especially of the second strophe, which acts as an interjection interrupting the thread of the narrative:

Let go of the world,
The bright tent,
The deceptive form,
Jesus is coming soon!
He will give a friendly greeting;
Sink at his feet,

> Seek him, seize him, hold him,
> Sigh, speak, lament:
> "O Jesus, stay, stay with me!"

We find one of the poet's deepest concerns expressed in these strongly appellative verses: rejection of the world, judgment of it as fleeting ("tent") and deceptive, the sevenfold challenge to encounter Christ— all this is not only an echo of Brentano's preoccupation with baroque (and neopietistic) poetry and devotion, but corresponds at the deepest level to his mood in the period after midlife when Jesus' mysticism and retreat from the world characterized his life. This was expressed both in his rejection of poetry and his turning to the Catholic Church[35] as well as in his change of location from Berlin to Dülmen. The retreat from the world demanded by the Magdalene poem is both literary topos and biographical reality. Magdalene's journey to the tomb concentrates the motif of the poet's life: the pilgrim passage from the world to the place "where love rests." Magdalene is thus not only the vehicle of a central idea but also a reflection of the entire painful existence of the internally divided poet.

We find it thus to be true of Brentano as it had been of Droste that Mary Magdalene is an important figure even though she seldom appears in the spiritual poetry of either: she is someone onto whom they can project their own life crises. On the road of faith, on the route toward encounter with Christ she embodies for people at the beginning of the nineteenth century whose unbroken faith has been lost the ideal of a Christian strong in faith. The woman in whom all women at the feet of Jesus (the sinner, Mary of Bethany, Mary Magdalene at Easter) are united becomes the embodiment of a longing to find rest and comfort in religion. From the contexts in which both poets place their Mary Magdalene—not the biblical figure, but that developed by the Church—it is also clear that the Biedermeier period only lightly veils what has begun to move beneath the surface. The traditional values are being questioned in society, politics, and the sciences. The evocation of the repose that Mary Magdalene finds at Jesus' feet is only the obverse of the general unrest that caused both poets so much suffering.

We may add to these observations, as was already noted in regard to the baroque poets, that the poems relating to the Easter appearances to Mary Magdalene break off before Jesus' crucial words: the commissioning and sending of the apostolic witness, her assignment to the world—none of this is acknowledged. Even the missionary-minded Brentano overlooks this feature in the picture of the biblical Mary Magdalene. The world of both poets was confined to the interior spaces of the soul. Their Magdalene is a child of the nineteenth century embodying the visionary ideal of an existence to be developed apart from social realities in an artificially maintained "Catholic" paradise.

What had crystallized in the work of Droste and Brentano can be observed also in that of Guido Maria Dreves, a scholar of hymnody and author of hymns who in 1886 published a collection of spiritual songs oriented to the Church year and, according to the author's statement, "conceived and composed by me as songs for the Church."[36]

The fourth song for Easter was related to John 20, as had become customary; its final verse still further heightened the previously observed tendencies:

> Mary, your desire
> Is far too hot and hasty,
> You shall indeed embrace me,
> But first in Paradise.[37]

Not only is Mary's commission to the Church in the world erased; she is completely directed to the world beyond. Mary has no significance for the disciples and the beginnings of the Church. Correspondingly the author celebrates only male saints in his songs (except for the virgin Mary, who is elevated to an unreal plane) and even in the contemporary Church he acknowledges the existence only of "sons" of the Church who, "like young lions," engage themselves in the service of their Lord.[38] Mary Magdalene, who in the Bible and still in the medieval Easter songs had a duty to fulfill as messenger of Easter joy, is shoved into the non-binding heavenly paradise that places no obligations on the present-day Church and society.

A glance into the imposing spiritual work of Rudolf Alexander Schröder (1878–1962) yields a different picture. As a Christian humanist poet Schröder took an early interest in religious poetry; his attitude toward National Socialism and his adherence to the Confessing Church (from 1934 onward) only strengthened this tendency. In the years of darkness and silence he, like Reinhold Schneider on the Catholic side, became a mouthpiece for many others.

A major part of this body of lyric is quite consciously written to strengthen and comfort the community, something encouraged also by the form of the traditional Church hymn. Schröder preferred morning and evening hymns or songs to accompany the seasons of the Church year.[39] The scope of his poems extends from the individual assurance of salvation for believing sinners, who find consolation in gazing at the crib and the cross, to metaphors that are to be understood as veiled responses to the inbreaking of the forces of ungodliness and finally (after the war) as personal acceptance of guilt. Nevertheless, the individual concern of the one praying for his or her own salvation or return to the circle of the community remains dominant.

Mary Magdalene is encountered in two thematic areas: the Easter poems and the many that feature the figure of a pardoned sinner. Since Schröder writes from an emphatically male perspective and traces sinners' involvement in sin to Adam (not Eve!) it would seem natural that he would have recourse to a male figure also for the experience of justification and grace. Instead, in the poem "Ich hab ein Wort gefunden" ("I have found a word")[40] he has chosen a female reference with whom the male "I" of the speaker identifies:

> I have read a word
> About one who sinned,
> You were her beloved
> And you announced her salvation.

The sinful person who reads her story can also discover from her fate that the "word" that freed the sinful woman from the compulsions of guilt can also be salvation for him or her since it is true of everyone who prays that "I have greatly sinned" (fourth verse).

Schröder's verses read like variations on Droste's poem on Ascension Day in which the poet desires to place herself at Magdalene's side:

> . . . oh, perhaps
> Your blessed word might have come to me:
> "Go, your sins too are forgiven!"

Both dispense with a description of the sins, something as easily understood in the case of the young noblewoman as for the man from the upper middle class, all the more so as the accent in both cases lies less on (past) sins and more on the word of forgiveness they hope to hear. Thus the topos of Mary Magdalene as the pardoned sinner who is for all sinners a comforting image of grace survived for a millennium while the other sinful saints of the New Testament have for the most part vanished from Christian collective memory.

The other image of Mary, that of the Easter witness, appears twice in Schröder's spiritual poetry: in the *Osterspiel* ("Easter Play,"

1937) and in the poem "Es war die Zeit vor Morgengrauen" ("It was just before the grey of dawn," 1946). In the *Osterspiel*,[41] which is in the tradition of the old mystery plays, Jesus' mother and Mary Magdalene sit to right and left of the sealed tomb. The thoughts of both women wander back: "So I held him . . . ," "So I anointed him. . . ." Mary Magdalene recalls situations in which Jesus, humble and merciful, turned to other human beings: besides his loving gesture of washing feet and his words to the crucified bandit it is primarily her own story that she tells. The whole action of salvation in Jesus' life is summarized in his mercy to the woman who washed his feet, anointed them, and dried them with her own hair:

> But he did not see my shame,
> He saw me according to the sickness of my will.

In the third part of the play the three Marys go to the tomb in the early morning. While at first all three are seized by sorrow, Mary Magdalene separates from the group and becomes active: she is the first to see the transformation of the tomb and goes to announce what has happened. After the angel's speech this constellation of events is repeated: while two Marys retire, consoled, from the stage, Mary Magdalene remains behind; the angel's word has not penetrated her consciousness; she is disturbed and despairing. She stands "in a bright circle of light" beside which another circle appears with the Risen One in its center. In a short dialogue incorporating motifs from John 20 (confusion with the gardener and mutual address, Jesus' forbidding her to touch him and sending her as his messenger) Mary is distinguished by her mission, directly derived from Jesus: "Go you now also and report." She quickly leaves the stage, but in a different direction from that taken by the other Marys before: Mary Magdalene, the one sent, the apostle, goes her own way, not that of private consolation but that of apostolic service.

The same connected motifs are taken up again in the double poem "Ostern—Joh 20" ("Easter: John 20"), the first part of which[42] is entirely devoted to Mary Magdalene. In the seven-verse poem the encounter between Jesus and Mary culminates in the fulfillment of her sending:

> Full of joy, she follows his command,
> Comes to the disciples, says in haste
> What the Lord instructed her.

In contrast to Mary, Jesus' messenger who gives her testimony before the disciples and whom Jesus commissions, the disciples remain "intimidated and despondent" (v. 7). Here again Mary's activity is contrasted with the behavior of another, initially passive group.

In the context of the whole collection of almost four hundred spiritual poems the reference to Mary Magdalene is certainly not overwhelming. On the other hand, apart from Mary the mother of Jesus there is no other biblical figure who stands out so clearly. The twofold figure of Magdalene the pardoned sinner and Mary the faithful Easter witness, as it had developed in the tradition, also fascinated the man who renewed Protestant hymnody: in Mary Magdalene believers find the entire scope of their own Christian existence modeled for them.

2. Mary Magdalene and the Middle-Class Image of Woman

In a review of this small selection of spiritual poetry we are struck by several traits that are found throughout the series:

(a) On her way to the present, Mary Magdalene has lost the traits that still shaped her image as late as the work of Angelus Silesius: she is no longer the ecstatic penitent or the desert saint of legend; the poets orient themselves (apparently correctly!) to the depiction in the New Testament.

(b) The active features in her image are lost: through her equation with Mary of Bethany and/or of the sinful woman she becomes the woman who, sunk within herself, sits or lies at Jesus' feet; she is the image of an inwardness that emits no power from within but remains fixed in passivity.

(c) The same is true for the Easter scene according to John 20, where the text does *not* speak of sinking down (Brentano: "I sank at my Jesus' feet"), but of becoming active (Jesus' commissioning and sending).

(d) While the drama of this period sees Mary Magdalene as the sinner in Luke 7, with the reconciling conclusion broken off and the stage heroine meeting her demise, the spiritual poetry of the same period is oriented almost exclusively to the Easter narrative; still, the latter is also used only in part because the crucial element—Jesus' commissioning of Mary Magdalene—is for the most part not received.

Both movements—the retraction of the active and emphasis on the passive features—correspond to the simultaneous change in women's roles in society: the more private life and economic activity moved apart from each other (including spatially), the more were women assigned to the "interior" space of the house, as Friedrich Schiller in his "Lied von der Glocke" ("Bell Song") prescribed as norm for an entire epoch:

> The man must go out
> Into hostile life . . .
> And within governs
> The diligent housewife . . .

In these verses, which once belonged to the standard education of middle-class society and were not even questioned, the existing distribution of roles is quite clear; it was considered to be natural (rational reason) or God-given (religious reason). That before and alongside this situation (especially in the lower social classes) there were other role models for women was not even acknowledged.

In medieval artisanry, for example, a woman was neither "employed" nor did she have a "private life," for the two were interlocked. She had her own competences, was independently responsible for all the needs of the household and the life of her husband, children, members of the household, journeymen, and apprentices; the same was true of farm women. Husband and wife divided the direction of the economic unit of the "household." In the modern period, when "interior" and "exterior" life broke apart, this role of household management existed, if at all, only for (ruling) noblewomen, farm wives, or (in a different fashion) for women of the lower social classes. The women of the newly arisen bourgeois middle class (or those within the nuclear family) in the nineteenth century, which must be extended in this sense to the outbreak of the First World War, undertook only the duties of the internal, "private" sphere, while the more highly regarded external activities of "employment" or "professional life" were reserved for men. Since in bourgeois society only work for pay outside the household was regarded as employment, with its associated prestige, women's work became invisible: the husband works, the wife stays at home (and thus does not work!). This new devaluation of women's household work changed the relationship between husband and wife into a hierarchical one. The husband is active, that is, he works, has responsibility, cares for the family; the wife is passive, that is, she does not work, she is taken care of. Thus the wife responsible, together with her husband, for the needs of the economic factor "house" or "household" became the husband-fixated "only a housewife." Her status was no longer soberly calculated according to what she actually did, but (by ideological prescription) by the professional and social status of her husband. Self-realization through work, something that was a matter of course for men, was forbidden to women.

The relationship between Gustav and Alma Mahler may stand as representative of many: Gustav Mahler forbade his wife, Alma Schindler, who had been a composition student of the composer Zemlinsky, to do any musical work of her own: "Gustav Mahler demanded in a letter that I immediately give up my music. I must live only for his. He thought that the marriage of Robert and Klara Schumann, for example, had been a 'ridiculous thing.' I was required to choose."[43] "He was indignant that anything in the world could be more important to me than writing to him. He sent me a long letter in which he forbade me to continue composing."[44] This "long letter" in which Gustav Mahler formulated the conditions for marriage was not published word for word by Alma either in her autobiography or in her book of recollections accompanying the first publication of Mahler's letters (1940; German edition 1971). It was published in full for the first time in 1995![45]

According to this letter Mahler took the loving expressions of his young bride when she said that she wanted to be entirely what he wanted and needed as a literal program for married life. A married couple who were both composers was ridiculous to him, especially if one considered the practical side: "What would happen if you were really 'in the mood,' but you had to take care of the house, or something that I needed right away?" The wife should not, of course, be "her husband's housekeeper," but she must accommodate herself, or rather subordinate herself, to his needs. Alma's attempts at composition are for her "pleasure," while his activity as a conductor and composer is "work." Her "profession" (namely, serving the happiness of her husband) is private; his "profession" is public. Hence the roles must be properly distributed: "And so the role of 'composer,' of the one who 'works' belongs to me, and to you that of the loving companion. . . ." Toward the end of the letter Mahler summarizes his thoughts once more: "You must give yourself up to me *unconditionally* [emphasis in original], [and] in your heart make the shaping of your future life in all its details dependent on my needs. . . ." (The letter-writer calls these demands "almost without measure"!)

In spite of her inner reservations, Alma consented to the marriage, but she never succeeded in the surrender of her own self-realization. Her ambivalent attitude toward Gustav Mahler runs like a guiding thread through her books of memoirs: alongside the desire to make him happy stood her sorrow at the loss of her own purpose in life.[46] When Gustav Mahler demanded of his wife that she completely surrender her own life, her own creativity, and unconditionally give herself to his work he was not expecting anything unusual according to the canons of the period, but was projecting the image of a "normal" middle-class marriage.

Against this background—the wife without responsible activity, dependent on her husband, captured in the image of a woman at a man's feet—the dominant picture of Magdalene in spiritual poetry acquires a new meaning: Mary is the mirror of the bourgeois ideal of the woman that restricted a woman's activity to the interior sphere of house and family and prevented any effective influence outside.[47] Thus it could not be that Mary Magdalene had played an active role in the origins of Christianity; she sinks down at Jesus' feet, her place for all time (and it was not without reason that Church and theology, often against their better knowledge, maintained the identity of Mary Magdalene and Mary of Bethany!)—or she is banished to Paradise, where she cannot cause any disturbance. It is apparently no accident that R. A. Schröder, who had lived through the social revolutions after the First World War, was the first poet to refer again to her old commissioning as the one who gave impulse to the Christian movement.

Notes

[1] Angelus Silesius, *Heilige Seelenlust oder Geistliche Hirten-Lieder* in idem, *Sämtliche poetische Werke*. 3 vols. Edited by Hans Ludwig Held (3rd, newly revised ed. Munich, 1949) 2.105, 230.

[2] Angelus Silesius, *Sinnliche Beschreibung der vier letzten Dinge* and *Cherubinischer Wandersmann*, in *Sämtliche poetische Werke*, 3.

[3] *Seelenlust*, 228; *Wandersmann*, 84.

[4] *Wandersmann*, 89.

[5] Ibid., 89.

[6] *Seelenlust*, 229.

[7] *Wandersmann*, 19.

[8] *Sinnliche Beschreibung*, 293.

[9] *Wandersmann*, 113. Angelus Silesius alternates use of the names "Maria" and "Magdalena," but the overall context yields the identity of Mary Magdalene.

[10]Andreas Gryphius, "Am tage Mariae Magdalenae. Lu. 7," in idem, *Sonn- und Feiertags-Sonette.* Reprint of the first edition of 1639 with the alterations of the last edition of 1663, presented by Heinrich Welti (Halle, 1883); *Johann Christian Günthers Sämtliche Werke 2: Klagelieder und Geistliche Gedichte, in zeitlicher Folge,* edited by Wilhelm Krämer (Darmstadt, 1964 [reprint of the Leipzig edition of 1931]) 248–9.

[11]Nikolaus Ludwig von Zinzendorf, "Die fünfte Rede" 110–1, and "Die sechste Rede" 159–60, in *Hauptschriften,* vol. 2, ed. Erich Beyreuther and Gerhard Meyer (Hildesheim, 1963).

[12]"Rede über Luc. 21, 25-36," ibid., 203.

[13]"Rede über Marc. 14, 8," ibid., 297, 299.

[14]*Geistliche Gedichte des Grafen von Zinzendorf. Eine Auswahl,* ed. by H. Bauer and G. Burkhardt (Leipzig, 1900) 112–4. For the sources see the historical-critical notes on p. 232.

[15]Heart of Jesus mysticism, or the statement that earthly eyes cannot see what is essential, are found in many songs including some not incorporated in the hymnal: cf. *Geistliche Gedichte* 37–8: Jesus' heart is the "Wound-cave / That cries aloud for grace for us," the "Motherly heart" that bears us up, but certainly not to the earthly eye; it is reserved for the eyes of the enlightened.

[16]*Gerhard Tersteegens Geistliches Blumengärtlein inniger Seelen mit der Frommen Lotterie und einem kurzen Lebenslauf des Verfassers* (2nd printing of the new ed. Stuttgart, 1969); cf. No. 95 (pp. 539–41) in which New Testament men and women are listed; among those named is Mary of Bethany; among those without names is the sinful woman.

[17]Cf. ibid., 193, 220, 374, 494, 592, 597.

[18]Ibid., 365–7.

[19]Annette von Droste-Hülshoff, *Geistliches Jahr,* in Karl Schulte Kemminghausen and Winfried Woesler, eds., *Liedern auf alle Sonn- und Festtage,* 2 vols. (Münster, 1971). The first publication was by C. B. Schlüter in 1851. Clemens Brentano, *Die sonntäglichen Evangelien,* in Christian Brentano, ed., *Clemens Brentano's Gesammelte Schriften 1: Geistliche Lieder* (Frankfurt, 1852) 275–362.

[20]For the history of composition see *Geistliches Jahr,* 2.176–80.

[21]*Geistliches Jahr,* 1.73–4. The main part of the poem alludes to the time of the Prussian-Rhenish *Kulturkampf* and can remain out of consideration here.

[22]Ibid., 63–4.

[23]"My knowledge had to kill my faith," ibid., 67; cf. also pp. 84 and 142, where he speaks of "reason's curse."

[24]Ibid., 79.

[25]Ibid., 1–2.

[26]Ibid., 9–10.

[27]*Geistliches Jahr,* 203.

[28]For the destruction see Wolfgang Frühwald, *Das Spätwerk Clemens Brentanos (1815–1842)* (Tübingen, 1977) 145–50; for the edition of the *Gesammelte Schriften* see ibid., 22–5.

[29]Quoted by Frühwald, *Spätwerk*, 158.

[30]Letter to L. Hensel, 6 June 1829, ibid., 140. The reluctance to surrender one's inner self to the public had, of course, begun earlier, as an 1810 letter to the painter Runge shows; Christian cites it with agreement in his introduction to volume 1 of the *Collected Writings*, p. x.

[31]Ibid., 70–2, and Clemens Brentano, *Gedichte*, edited by Wolfgang Frühwald, Bernhard Gajek, and Friedhelm Kemp (Munich, 1968). Here cited from the dtv edition (no. 6068, 1977) 441–3. All quotations from this edition.

[32]*Gedichte*, 407–9.

[33]Ibid., 606–7.

[34]The poem "Magdalene geht zum Grab" was written, according to Emilie Brentano, in 1816, but in the opinion of recent researchers it was composed after 1824: cf. *Gedichte*, 750.

[35]As representative of many others see the poem "Zweimal hab ich dich gesehn" (ca. 1821/1822, *Gedichte*, 449–55): "Poetry, the painted girl / Took my faith, hope, and prayers" (ll. 165-6). Only one thing was salvaged in the new phase of life: the art "of planting a Catholic cross" (ll. 172).

[36]Guido Maria Dreves, *Kränze ums Kirchenjahr. Geistliche Lieder* (Paderborn, 1866) 5 (letter of dedication).

[37]Ibid., 77–8.

[38]Ibid., 120.

[39]Rudolf Alexander Schröder, *Die geistlichen Gedichte* (Berlin, 1949); these are texts from the years 1917–48.

[40]Ibid., 289.

[41]*Das Osterspiel*, ibid., 176–203.

[42]"Es war die Zeit vor Morgengraun," ibid., 170–1.

[43]Alma Mahler-Werfel, *Mein Leben*. Fischer Taschenbuch 545 (Frankfurt, 1963) 31.

[44]Alma Mahler-Werfel, *Erinnerungen an Gustav Mahler. Gustav Mahler: Briefe an Alma Mahler,* edited by Donald Mitchell (Frankfurt and Berlin, 1971) 47.

[45]Henry-Louis de La Grange and Günther Weiss, eds., *Ein Glück ohne Ruh'. Die Briefe Gustav Mahlers an Alma* (Berlin, 1995) 104–11 (Letter 14). The following quotations are from this edition.

[46]"I had completely obliterated myself, my being, and my will" (*Erinnernungen* 144). "Gustav lives his life, and I must also live it" (*Mein Leben* 34).

[47]We know today how much women with artistic talent in particular suffered under this assignment of roles: Annette von Droste-Hülshoff, Bettine von Arnim, Fanny Mendelssohn. . . .

Chapter Ten

The "Sinful Magdalene of Bethany": The Confused Image Today

At the beginning of the twentieth century the so-called Magdalene question played an important part in Catholic exegesis. Well-known scholars like Marie-Joseph Lagrange in France or Peter Ketter in Germany[1] separated Mary of Magdala from the sinful woman or Mary of Bethany and advocated a revised picture of the disciple. This discussion, however, did not reach the public either within or outside the Church. The confused image of Mary Magdalene had long since become a matter of course. Nineteenth-century art and literature had cemented the image of the fallen woman as fully as liturgy and preaching had perpetuated the picture of the repentant sinner. Anyone, even today, who wants to see something different in Mary Magdalene is quickly put on the defensive.

Certainly many authors are eager to describe her significance, but they believe that the New Testament evidence yields too little information; hence the evidence is "enhanced" by making the connection to other women. In particular, authors who seek an honorable rehabilitation of the "sinful woman" indirectly strengthen the image, as the following examples will show. The confused picture is "used" as a means of pursuing various ends (emancipation of women, esoteric interests, spirituality, etc.). Hence it is worthwhile to inquire, in every case, about the motives of those who attack this image and what image of women is in the background.

1. Sin's Fascination: Spiritual Interpretations of Mary Magdalene

The mixed image of Mary Magdalene as sinner and saint, originating in preaching (Gregory the Great) and spiritual contemplation

(Odo of Cluny), has lost none of its fascination in this sphere even today. If secularized forms of this image of Magdalene have left stronger traces on public consciousness than have exegetical corrections, this may be understandable against the background of a post-Christian society. But when religious literature—preaching (Eugen Drewermann), spirituality (Heinrich Spaemann, Walter Nigg), meditations (as found in church papers) and so on—take scarcely any notice of the biblical picture of Mary from Magdala or deliberately reject it (Walter Nigg: "even though a hundred objections may be brought") we must be permitted to raise questions about the function of this Magdalene.

Eugen Drewermann attempts a very sensitive approach to the figure of Mary Magdalene. He speaks of her in a number of books drawn from his preaching experience. His image of humanity includes the great damage done to life by fear that cripples the person and prevents his or her development as a mature human being. Even when people try to act "rightly" their deeds are drawn into the current of evil because they do not really choose freely, but live in "the ghetto of fear."[2] Only if the fear-ridden person comes under the influence of an anxiety-free, truly human person can he or she be "redeemed."

For Drewermann, Mary Magdalene is a lovely example of an evil-beset and then healed person: in the encounter with Jesus she escaped from the alienation and powerlessness of her life and found her true self. Her condition is clarified by the example of a schizophrenic patient: the ego is divided among multiple non-egos and collapses into fragments; the inner self turns to stone in the "ghetto of pure fear."[3] Thus Mary Magdalene, ultimately, is depicted as "the perfect prey of pure fear," the "inhuman product of sheer inhumanity."[4] Her incarnation as a true human being happens in her encounter with Jesus, which is why she is able to continue to live in his presence. His death is a catastrophe for her, or better, a near-catastrophe, for Mary and the other women at the cross do not harden in their pain, like ancient Niobe, but have learned from Jesus that deadly fear is overcome by God, that one can rise from sorrow to life.[5]

This picture of Mary Magdalene is one possible interpretation of her illness and healing, even though the assurance with which the picture of illness as demonic possession is equated with a modern mental illness is at least questionable. Has Mary Magdalene here perhaps assembled too many key terms from the patient files of the therapist and not enough from the findings of the exegetes? But if we agree with the psychologists that there is no such thing as a "normal" human being,

"The Penitent Mary Magdalene"
Marius Vasselon (1887). Museum of Fine Arts, Tours.

that everyone suffers some kind of deficiencies, Mary Magdalene can take the role of a model: in identifying with her we can gather hope and strength for our own lives. This functionalizing of the biblical figure is legitimate if the Bible is understood as the book of life and word of salvation.

More problematic than Mary as "sick" is her approximation to the "sinful woman." It is true that Drewermann repeatedly emphasizes that the New Testament offers no basis for identifying these two figures,[6] and yet he agrees that art and legend have correctly understood, in the overall dimension of misery and sorrow, the relatedness of the two women; he joins them by way of the novelistic figures of Sonia (in Dostoievski's *Crime and Punishment*) and Lara (in Boris Pasternak's *Doctor Zhivago*): Mary Magdalene is drawn through association with Lara into the field of "sexual exploitation and prostitution," through Sonia into the themes of "saint and sinner."[7] In the triangular relationship of Sinful Woman—Mary Magdalene—Sonia (or Lara), Mary Magdalene is silently made the type of the "pardoned whore"[8] who has loved much and to whom much is forgiven. The identity of the two biblical women is rejected with rational arguments and simultaneously maintained by suggestion: Mary Magdalene acquires her fascination through the proximity of sin.

This association is still stronger where religious literature uses the sinful Mary Magdalene to emphasize fundamental concepts of the spiritual life such as faith and love, pardon and penance. A clever combination of biblical passages ultimately yields the image of the woman "who had such a turbulent life behind her, who loved so much, and whom Jesus so richly pardoned," as one could still read in 1993 in the Easter meditation in a Church paper.[9]

How hard it is to unravel this equation (which is so seldom questioned) is illustrated by the process played out in another Church paper where the author of a spiritual meditation on Luke 7 carefully avoided any reference to Mary Magdalene but the editors completely thwarted this good intention by inserting an illustration with the caption "Christ and Mary Magdalene."[10] At any rate, this sequence of events evoked the criticism of a woman reader: "The caption under the picture might have been regarded as correct at the time it was created, but with the current state of knowledge of the Bible the combination is no longer appropriate."[11]

Can the touching encounter between Mary and Jesus as developed in John 20 really be understood only against the background of a sinful past? Is Mary's love only able to keep alive the memory of the one she loved through the night of the grave because she had been acquainted with the abyss of a chaotic sexuality? Do the authors of spiritual texts see the deeper levels of a soul with special clarity, or do they have to regard this "Magdalene" as they do so that she can be useful as a demonstration of the way from sin to faith and (purified) love? The suspicion of such manipulation cannot be dismissed out of hand when we look at the next two interpretations, both of which without the (artificially created) identity of the sinner and the disciple would collapse completely.

For Heinrich Spaemann the common name of the Marys (Jesus' mother, Mary of Bethany, Mary of Magdala) is a sign of their symbolic identity: all three are figures of faith. Common to all of them is their openness to Jesus as the revealer of God, but each illustrates in her special way what faith means. In this threefold symbolic figure of faith Mary Magdalene embodies dependency on God's mercy and the mystery of pardon. However, such a perspective is only possible if she is expressly regarded with the sinful woman as "*a single* figure of faith."[12] From her we can see how a person is transformed in the encounter with Jesus and, washed clean by the tears of penitence and gratitude, is able to enter the garden of the tomb as a Garden of Paradise.

Spaemann's method of reading, sensitive to underlying tones and the arcane language of significant texts in salvation history, comes to some noteworthy results: he takes up the topos of the new Eve, who no longer transmits death but, at Jesus' commission, gives life, and he derives from John 20 as a divinely inspired document the dignity of humanity and the apostolate, because Mary, like the apostles and before them, had "seen the Lord." It is all the more astonishing that John 20 is regarded only as a pendant to Luke 7. The two texts, like the two sides of a coin, must be seen together to give the whole picture of Mary Magdalene. This combination is not suggested by the texts themselves; it is only required if one is to carry through the program of a threefold figure of faith and (in the one case) dependence on forgiveness. In the same way the statements about the liberation of women and the dignity of her humanity are all the more powerful if they are based on a woman who previously was given over to the denigrating or lustful regard of others.[13]

Far more problematic is the image of Mary Magdalene in Walter Nigg's book on the great penitential figures of the West.[14] Here Mary Magdalene is the beginning and primeval figure of all penitents; in her life are reflected all other sinners and penitents: the pathos of vice and that of the life of penance necessarily belong together. Gregory the Great and the legends present us—correctly, according to Nigg—with the "symbolic image of Mary Magdalene" that is indispensable even today. Therefore all modern attempts to divide this unified figure into several persons are vehemently rejected as examples of a subversive exegesis. According to Nigg's idea, Mary Magdalene was "a woman alluring in her physical charms and given over to evil," "a woman surrendered to lust" who "experienced the joys of whoredom with all her senses" and "enjoyed the lusts of the flesh to the point of swooning."[15] These statements, referring to the disciple in Luke 8:2 (!), depict Mary Magdalene as the *magna peccatrix*. But then the picture changes: she is also the anointing woman (not, however, regarded in the perspective of Easter, but as the anointing sinner!), the preacher, the penitent, the contemplative soul who conquers her past.

Mary Magdalene as prototype of all penitents illustrates Nigg's thesis that repentance is a form of self-healing and that the gift of conversion is one of the great mysteries of life. Penance is not the enemy of life, but is creative: it opens up opportunities for life. Precisely because words like repentance, conversion, or penance have a negative overtone today, while the reality behind them cannot be dispensed with, the image of the sinful and penitent woman must be maintained. The lovely phrases that describe Mary Magdalene as one of the invisible companions and eternal partners of life, however, are questionable if they are only made possible by the erotic and fantastic features of the sinful woman.

2. Mary Magdalene and the Founding of the Church

The unified figure of Mary Magdalene is especially well developed by Wilhelm Hartke,[16] whose image of Mary Magdalene can only be briefly described. In order to substantiate his hypothesis of the origins of the apostolic Church from four "parties" he combines very disparate statements in the New Testament into a new picture, beginning with a change in the text of Luke 24:10 where he makes the name "Joanna" the genitive of the masculine name "John." The two (instead of three!) women at the tomb are therefore Mary Magdalene, the mother of John, and Mary, the mother of James.

For Hartke, Mary Magdalene is the mother of the Beloved Disciple and evangelist John Mark (for the double name see Acts 12:12). After her adultery (John 7:55–8:11) her son cannot bring himself to receive his mother, thus shamed, into his home, which is why she lives with relatives in Bethany where she later anoints Jesus' feet. Only beneath the cross do the mother and son encounter one another again and become reconciled through Jesus' words, "Mother, behold your son. . . . Behold your mother" (John 19:26). Thus the woman addressed by Jesus in this scene is not his own mother, but Mary Magdalene, the mother of the Beloved Disciple who is also standing by the cross.

After Easter, Mary Magdalene's house becomes the home of the original Galilean Christian community in Jerusalem (Acts 12:12). Later, in the time of the emperor Hadrian, this house was the only church in Jerusalem; on its site, ca. 340 C.E., the Church of Zion, the mother of all churches, was built.

From her Jerusalem period Mary also knows Paul, with whom she has a faithful relationship and who confirms in a letter to Ephesus (Rom 16), where she was then living, that he owed her a great deal (Rom 16:6). In Ephesus, after torture and martyrdom, she was buried.[17]

Through her contacts with Jesus, John, and Paul, with the Galilean and Jerusalem communities, with Pauline and Johannine Christianity, Mary Magdalene stood at the nodal point between these groups and was thus able to advance the process of the Church's coming together. The historian's interest is thus not in her as a person but in her function as a connecting link among different directions in the primitive community.

While in this monumental work Mary represents only a tiny stone in the mosaic and serves to underpin a historical thesis, in the works of the following authors she moves more strongly toward the center.

In connection with the boom in esoteric Jesus books Mary Magdalene has also become a marketable quantity and has been connected in a fashion that appeals to public interest (as Jesus' wife!) with the beginnings of Christianity.[18] The canonical depictions of Jesus and the origins of Christianity are thus "revealed" as having been "misunderstood" or even falsified, as in Barbara Thiering's book or the work of Lincoln, Baigent, and Leigh.

In Barbara Thiering's *Jesus von Qumran* Mary Magdalene (as her name is written throughout) was married a second time, to the Davidide Jesus.[19] According to Thiering the gospels speak openly of Mary and her "chaperone," Martha, but in a kind of secret language, for she is also the bent woman (Luke 13:10-17) and the doorkeeper Rhoda (Acts 12:13). That is, Thiering understands the gospels to be "superficial tales" for the general public while the "underlying stories" were intended only for initiates. With this method of reading she makes the claim to be the first person able to understand the "real" content of the New Testament texts.

Thiering's book is about money, power, betrayal, and efforts to achieve world dominance on the part of Davidides, Herodians, Romans, and Essenes, with all the threads "somehow" leading to Qumran. In this fantastic fabric Jesus, more a tool than an actor, plays a special role from time to time as priest and crown prince. For dynastic reasons he married Mary Magdalene and had a daughter and two sons with her. Since Mary had different spiritual and political priorities than her husband they ultimately divorced. Jesus founded a new family and accompanied Paul on his journeys. When the Christians developed their own separate identity Mary was declared a non-Christian. The most that can be said of her later fate is that through her daughter Tamar (the Phoebe of Rom 16:1-2) she became Paul's mother-in-law.

Thiering's "disclosures" attempt to explain the figure of Jesus and the beginnings of Christianity in terms of purely human forces; hence she cannot do without a dynastically necessary wife for Jesus.

Michael Baigent, Richard Leigh, and Henry Lincoln follow a similar tendency in their book, *Holy Blood, Holy Grail,* which discloses a relationship between Mary Magdalene and her descendants and the whole of western history.[20] In the first half of the book she appears a number of times: as "a mother goddess," Magdalene "of the celebrated vase" (p. 75) without her significance for the context becoming apparent. The references to her having landed in Marseilles with the Grail according to an old tradition remain as mysterious as the emphatic assertion that she took "the Grail" with her and not a "vase" (pp. 284, 316). The reader does observe that in the opinion of the authors the Grail is connected with the *"sang réal"* of the Merovingians (". . . the aura about the throne and the royal bloodline was quite unique," p. 215), and the descendants of that dynasty are said to play a role, in secret fashion, even today in European history, but at first one cannot make any sense of such references. Only little by little do all the speculations of this Grail research form themselves into a "hypothesis":[21] Mary Magdalene was married to Jesus, an aspirant to the throne in Jerusalem; this marriage is said to be the one mentioned in the Fourth Gospel as the "wedding at Cana." Through marriage with a socially superior woman Jesus came a little closer to his goal of ascending the throne for, through the probably well-thought-out ritual of anointing, his wife had made him the "true Messiah," and her family, especially Lazarus the Beloved Disciple, and their influential friends provided for the necessary support among the people.

When Pilate got rid of this dangerous pretender to the throne, Jesus' adherents were determined at least to rescue his dynasty, which they succeeded in doing by inveigling the release of his son (!) Barabbas. After the death of the husband it was important that his wife and children, the "royal blood," should be rescued through flight to Gaul. After that the Jesus movement split: the family held fast to the human king Jesus and pursued their dynastic goals while the remaining followers were interested only in his message and made the earthly priest-king into a god with universal purposes.

For these authors Mary Magdalene and the Grail, that central mystical symbol of European history, belong together, for the Holy Grail is the "royal blood" and at the same time "the vessel that received and contained Jesus' blood. In other words it would have been the womb of the Magdalen—and by extension, the Magdalen herself."[22] It is not the Church but the secret descendants of Mary Magdalene, the Merovingians, the legendary Grail kings Parsifal and Lohengrin, the crusader Godfrey of Bouillon, and many European noble houses who are the true heirs of the Davidide priest-king Jesus and his wife Mary Magdalene, and they await their historic hour to rebuild his kingdom.

Anyone who thinks that this work is the summit of all speculations about Mary Magdalene, however, is mistaken—as we shall soon see.

3. Daughter of Wisdom, Priestess of the Goddess

The new interest in Gnosticism and esoteric ideas arising in the last decades has led to some fantastic new editions of the mixed figure of Mary Magdalene, now understood sometimes as the representative of male philosophy, sometimes as the embodiment of female wisdom. The breadth of the spectrum of such interpretations is evident when we consider as examples such different authors as Raymond-Léopold Bruckberger and Christa Mulack,[23] both of whom see Mary Magdalene as a representative of Wisdom who initiates others into Wisdom. From a masculine perspective (Bruckberger) she is the symbol of unredeemed paganism, the daughter of Wisdom who encounters in Christ, one infinitely superior to Plato, eternal Wisdom itself. From a feminine perspective (Mulack) she is the priestess of a matriarchal religion, the representative of the Goddess who initiates Jesus as Messiah-Christ. In both interpretations the anointing sinner plays a key role, with the emphasis falling either on her conversion (Bruckberger) or on the act of anointing (Mulack).

In their search for motives for the "fragmentation" of this woman in the Bible and modern exegesis the two authors go in opposite directions: while Bruckberger makes the enemies of the Church and orthodox faith (that is, the Gnostics) responsible for the silence about her, Mulack is convinced that she has been hushed up because of her true significance as Jesus' life-companion and priestess of the Great Goddess.

A sentence from the introduction to Bruckberger's book captures the complete picture he paints of Mary Magdalene: "Christ converted Phryne and made of her a Christian and the great saint Christianity knows" (p. 7). According to this Mary Magdalene is a courtesan, a great lady of society who lives in Tiberias at the Herodian court—perhaps as Herod's lover, perhaps hired by Herodias to seduce John the Baptist. She is acquainted with Greek philosophy and had learned from Plato that the way to wisdom leads beyond pleasure and the enjoyment of bodies and their beauty. In her "conversion" she recognizes that Christ is Wisdom itself. She represents ancient Greece in its finest female figures, for before her conversion she was "Phryne," the free, educated woman; after her conversion she becomes a Christian "Antigone" who watches over the corpse of the one who is Wisdom, and she survives as "Diotima" (cf. the promise in Mark 14:6-9): "As Socrates in the *Symposium* associated his wisdom with the name 'Diotima,' still more than Socrates did Christ attach his gospel to the name and fame of Mary Magdalene" (p. 126).

The converted courtesan plays for Gentiles seeking Wisdom the same role as John the Baptist played for Jews standing in the prophetic tradition; she herself becomes a symbol for redeemed paganism, which Christ led back to God. Of course, this connection can only be made by holding fast to the mixed figure of Mary Magdalene; the New Testament passages are not sufficient to support this kind of ideological superstructure.

A similar objection can be made about Christa Mulack's thesis that Jesus was initiated into the mystery of the Goddess. In this conception it was women who made Jesus what he in his own time was—a feminine man—as well as what he became and remained—the Messiah-Christ. Only in the patriarchal tradition did Jesus become a "man" in order to serve as a guarantee of male claims to power, while in the same moment his life-companion was eliminated, or simply defamed as a converted prostitute, so that the feminine experience that (physical) death cannot put an end to inner contact with Jesus was made into a (masculine) means to power and its legitimation. In reality Jesus had a great affinity for women,[24] who saved him from contempt for women (the Syro-Phoenician woman), liberated him as Messiah (the Samaritan woman), and anointed him (the anointing women). Women helped him to understand himself and his calling: as Messiah he was "affirmed by the woman in the anointing ritual, so that he thenceforth received from the female sex his official commissioning to communicate feminine wisdom to his fellow males with the authority of one anointed" (p. 131).

This wisdom also includes knowledge of death as it is experienced in nature as a part of life and thematized in the matriarchal religions: the son-beloved of the Great Goddess dies a cultic death as Nature's representative and returns to life with Nature. For matriarchal consciousness "life and death are not absolute contraries" (p. 269), for death is not the end but the transition to a new life. Hence the anointing woman and Jesus work within the circle of matriarchal myth when she anoints him as Messiah and he interprets it as an anointing for death, while the men reject both the anointing (Simon the Pharisee, Judas) and Jesus' death (Simon Peter). In this decisive act of anointing Mary Magdalene becomes Jesus' partner, even though the gospels refuse to name her. Since anointing and resurrection are the central events in the transformation of the historical Jesus into the mythic Christ this internal relationship allows us to conclude "that the first proclaimer of the Easter message was also the initiator of the anointing and bestowed on him his consecration as Messiah" (p. 121).

In order to assert that Mary Magdalene had this central place in the matriarchal context of anointing, death, and resurrection Mulack must dissolve her into a single figure with the women in the anointing stories and Mary of Bethany; the final result is an image of the priestess of a matriarchal cult who maintained a school for the mysteries at Bethany where she, as the representative of the Great Goddess, anointed the Chosen One as Messiah, released him to death, and helped him to enter into new life; thereby she both founded a new mystery religion and elevated Jesus to one of the slain and risen women gods. This is Mulack's thesis.

Both Bruckberger and Mulack want to replace the "falsified" image of Mary Magdalene with their own genuine image, and each is guided by his or her own image of women. While Bruckberger is fascinated by the Greek idea of Eros in all its shadings between sensuality and spirit, and interprets the revelation of the beautiful body of Phryne as an epiphany of the divine, Christa Mulack proceeds on the basis of an idea of the feminine that does not recognize an equality of the sexes but asserts the superiority of the feminine over the masculine: only the feminine is the fullness of humanity.

It is obvious that these reconstructions are not mere matters of historical speculation but have consequences for the self-concept of women, especially Christian women today. For Bruckberger Mary Magdalene, as Mary of Bethany, is the central figure at the Christian-Platonic symposium, the mystical hearer and the model of contemplative souls. This assigns to her, and to women in general, precisely the role of passive listener that Christa Mulack vehemently rejects for the presider over the mystery school at Bethany and the proclaimer of the Christian Easter message—and thus also for Christian women today—as a role assigned to women by men, whereas the true, original commission of Mary Magdalene and all women rests in the proclamation of the word.[25]

4. Magdalene/Miriam: Woman Between Myth and Emancipation

Writing a novel about Mary Magdalene also always means writing about the image of women or their place in society—to paraphrase a statement of Luise Rinser.[26] For behind the figure in the novel the author's time-conditioned view of women can always be discerned; in the case of the novels to be discussed here it is strengthened by the particular roles of the authors as men (in a world shaped by myths and traditions) or as women (in a society ruled by enlightenment and emancipation). The woman between myth and emancipation: these are the poles between which Magdalene/Miriam has had to seek her place in recent fiction (Kazantzakis, Rinser). Of course she is never the principal figure; she has her place in the literary approaches to Jesus.

Something similar can be observed in musical treatments of Jesus, Magdalene, and Thomas, as shown by the rock opera *Jesus Christ Superstar* and its now-famous song by Magdalene, "I don't know how to love him."[27]

Probably best known, especially through its cinematic version, is the Jesus novel *The Last Temptation of Christ* by Nikos Kazantzakis.[28] The author works independently and with great creativity, recreating biblical tableaus and motifs and combining them in freely imagined scenes. The landscapes of Israel are more the product of the author's imagination than of geographical reality; the characters in the novel are shaped by Greek philosophy, not biblical thought, and yet the compact clarity with which everything is brought together in the novel gives it a compelling rightness: it is the fascinating world of the divine drama surrounding a young man named Jesus.

In deliberate analogy to the thirty-three years of his life, Jesus' story is described in thirty-three chapters: the tormented period before he forced himself to accept the calling he had long suspected, his encounter with the Baptizer and his testing in the desert, his joyful proclamation of the kingdom of heaven in images of springtime, feasting, and dancing, his reorientation toward preaching of judgment and fire, and finally the idea of the end of the ages that he, together with Judas, would have to bring about: "We two must save the world," the one as betrayer, the other as sacrifice. The plan succeeds: Jesus comes to the cross. He falls senseless and has a vision that paints a very different life before his eyes: the dream of blissful love with Magdalene, the dream of a happy family with the two women from Bethany, with children and grandchildren. . . . These last and ultimate temptations again end in oblivion as he wakes and dies on the cross.

This "Jesus" is neither a historical-scientific nor a naïve-pious redrawing of the image the gospels draw; he is a creation of the author, as is Mary Magdalene. Magdalene's father lived in a monastery as a young man, but then he surrendered to "temptation" and married. The child of this union, "his just reward," is Magdalene (p. 67), who as a child of sin appears predestined for (sexual) sin.

From the prehistory that plays a considerable role in the memories of all the characters the relationship between Jesus and Magdalene is clear. The two children grow up as neighbors in Nazareth. When Mary wants her twenty-year-old son to marry and for that purpose takes him with her to a wedding feast in Cana the fateful encounter with Magdalene occurs. The young man is carrying a red rose in his hand and tries to give it to Magdalene:

But as he did so, ten claws nailed themselves into his head and two
frenzied wings beat above him, tightly covering his temples. He
shrieked and fell down on his face, frothing at the mouth (p. 26).

The strict God has spoiled the peaceful, earthbound life of man
and wife. The man's life is confused and for a long time disturbed; the
woman becomes a whore and the man feels that the guilt is his.[29]
Later he admits to his uncle the rabbi that the guilt goes still farther
back into the past. The three- and four-year-old children had already
had a fateful, erotically-colored relationship. The adult recognizes in
their childish caresses not only joy, but sin as well, and confesses:
"From that time on Magdalene was lost; she was lost—could no
longer live without a man, without men" (p. 145). He drove her onto
the way of sin, made her what she now is and how she appears to his
inner eye: painted, bare-breasted, laughing and proud. His knowledge
of this guilt makes him unable to accept the calling he has long
sensed. He refuses the invisible, wrathful God's mission for the kingdom of heaven because he loves the earth and Magdalene, whom he
wants to marry even though through his fault she has become a
whore. He changes the commission laid on him by God: he will not
save the earth, but Magdalene. That is the point at which God and the
devil struggle within him, for the accusation he hurls at God in a
wrathful speech is the same pointed at him by the serpent in the
desert: what matters is not to save the earth, but Magdalene. And as
always, his temptation wears a religious veil; he is to take Magdalene
to himself as his wife as God took the whore Jerusalem, and as still
earlier the prophet Hosea the whore Gomer. Magdalene becomes the
embodiment of all sins that need to be redeemed. Yet Jesus puts aside
the temptation, and Magdalene's way is also a different one. After
Jesus' first visit to her house she is changed. While for the outside world
she remains the marked prostitute whom the mob wants to stone, Jesus
rescues her from the people's rage and acknowledges her here, as later
at a marriage feast; she glows with a new virginity (p. 214).

Magdalene stays with Jesus and travels with him, the disciples,
and old Salome to Judea, where in Bethany the sisters Mary and
Martha join the group. But the love between Jesus and Magdalene
cannot be consummated. In his dreams Jesus has long known this: as
he and Magdalene silently and gently fade away an old man (God?)
tells him that the Messiah loves the whole world and dies for it; there
is no place for an individual woman as his wife. But Mary has learned
the same lesson. When Jesus hints at his death and the men fail to

understand him, while only the women suspect what is coming, Magdalene produces a flask of costly perfume from among her possessions. She has brought it with her for the day when she will be able to anoint Jesus as her bridegroom, "but now behind her beloved's body she saw death—not Eros, death. It too, like a marriage, required perfumes" (p. 416). The harmony of their souls is revealed one last time: Jesus understands and accepts Magdalene's action as anointing for his death. In the end Jesus hangs alone on the cross between heaven and earth; none of his own is with him.

Who is Mary Magdalene in Kazantzakis's conception? She embodies a love that is sin. She was born a child of sin, and in her life sexuality and sin become interchangeable concepts. Her love means heaven and hell, despair and consolation; it bewitches and delights. In the dream images of Jesus' temptation this ambivalence is most strongly developed. In a waking dream he has in the desert a bird reveals to him the great mystery of the gates of Paradise and of hell, which are indistinguishable from each other. Both are beautiful and green (p. 280)—who can fail to think of the description of Magdalene's house, which has "a green single-leafed door" decorated with two intertwined serpents and, above them, a transfixed lizard (p. 84)? If the image of serpents holding themselves in a circle represents love and eternity, this is immediately retracted by the green lizard: the love that desires to be eternal cannot endure.[30]

Thus in reality the love of the converted Magdalene cannot find fulfillment. It will either be a temptation to the Crucified or it will be elevated to the super-personal level: when Jesus on his second visit to her house embraces her like a shy bridegroom she is, at that moment, not his real bride but the embodiment of the great idea that rules him: "It was not Magdalene . . . but the soul of man—and he was its bridegroom" (p. 329). This idea of the elevation of a concrete woman into a symbol is anticipated in the episode with the Zealots in Nazareth. In the night before his crucifixion Magdalene has crept to him; he only looked at her and she became the image of all his longing. The fighter who had thus far distanced his goal from the peaceful life of human beings experiences, in this night of his death, the other face of life that opens itself to him in Magdalene's tender presence: the soft body of the woman gives him a hint of a heaven "not . . . of angels and clouds, but as he wanted it, warm in winter, cool in summer, and made of men and soil" (p. 38). The comforting nearness of the woman that the Zealot can experience is forbidden to Jesus; the Tempter dangles the image of a love-encounter with Magdalene, but the picture dissolves into greyness: Magdalene is dragged from his side and, in a perversion of the dream, she is stoned as a whore and a martyr.

The Mary Magdalene of this novel is an "artistic creation" who has nothing in common with the biblical Mary from Magdala except her name. The real greatness of the model shown in the Easter traditions is here broken down; the negative features that have attached themselves to her tradition shape the portrait: Magdalene is the guilty-guiltless prostitute, the converted sinner—but also the mythical figure of the woman to whom the man is drawn by magic, in whose fathomless depths he desires to sink and from whom he flees in panic fear. Women who embody this image are only bearable if they can be denigrated as "whores" and "strumpets" (pp. 452–3); ultimately they are in fact unbearable, and must be stoned and ritually murdered like the widow in Kazantzakis's *Zorba the Greek*, like Magdalene in the Jesus novel. The descriptions of the murders of these two women are very similar: in both cases the men's fears are banished through religious vows: "In the name of the God of Abraham, Isaac and Jacob—strike!" the men cry as they kill Magdalene (p. 454); "In the name of divine justice!" and "In the name of Christ and the Panjia, lay on!" as they kill the widow.[31] Magdalene may not live even in the Crucified's dream. Significantly, the Jesus of the novel fantasizes about a peaceful family life in Bethany not with Magdalene, but with Mary and Martha, the housewifely women. Magdalene vanishes from memory.

The sparse information in the New Testament about Mary of Magdala is not adequate for a biography, and thus not for a biographical novel either. Anyone who attempts the latter therefore has recourse to legends and creative fantasies. Such is the work of Luise Rinser in her Jesus novel told from the perspective and in the voice of Miriam (= Mary), the titular heroine of the book.[32] Incidents from all four gospels are rearranged in the book in a kind of gospel harmony. Miriam is the medium with whose aid modern readers are to experience, vicariously, the fascination of Rabbi Yeshua. The excited expectations that are directed to him are personified in Yehuda (= Judas), the freedom fighter, and Yochanan (= John), the esoteric. The true significance of the rabbi is revealed, however, neither to the will of the one nor the intellect of the other, but only to the loving gaze of Miriam, who is at home in both worlds.

But who is Miriam? The answer comes from the place where we find our narrator: the caves of Provence, yet not the (penitential) caves of legend, for the men are recording foolish gossip when they later write that she "led a holy life of penitence there, holding a skull in her hands and bewailing [her] sins" (p. 10). The cave of her recollections is a symbol of her life without the rabbi, and at the same time the cave of Plato's parable: things are only real in the light of the divine sphere; when that light goes out all we see are "the shadows on the wall of the cave." The immortal Miriam in the cave has herself become a symbol: she is the living reality of "waiting for the reign of peace" (p. 332) that is to become reality in the hearts of human beings and from person to person.

Again, who is Miriam? The woman in the cave has a history in which—despite the explicit rejection of "foolish gossip"—topoi of tradition and legend play a part. She is the beautiful, wealthy, educated woman whose external and internal gifts prove to be her undoing. She rejects the role of a Jewish wife as well as that of a Greek courtesan. She wants to be free and unfettered; she curses men, tradition, and God. She is restless, searching for her destiny, and she appears to men like a demon:

> So I was alone in the big house that now belonged to me, young and beautiful and rich and without a husband. Something is wrong with a woman like that. "She is a demon," one said, "who forced me into a trap, until I put it to flight with nothing but my glance. She has serpents for hair and glowing coals for eyes . . . the demon" (pp. 14–5).

The demonic possession mentioned in the gospels is interpreted in the novel not as an illness but as rejection of typical female roles; her "sin" is not offense against individual ethical norms but breaking out of the restraints of patriarchal society. It is "the original sin of offense against absolute authority,"[33] something that must also be expected of modern women if they are to achieve a breakthrough to their full humanity. But whether women must renounce the security purchased with their sexuality in order to achieve identity is not men's problem; it belongs to the women who accommodate themselves.

Miriam reflects the modern woman who recognizes her social situation and rebels against it.[34] The sexual interpretation of this "sin" is attributed to the later (male!) reporters who transferred to it the myth of God and the whore, the pure and the impure: "I had to be a whore to fit into their mythical picture" (p. 15).

Before her encounter with Jesus, Miriam bears the attributes of her origin: as a proud daughter of the Maccabees she wears the Zealot's dagger; as a wealthy heiress she bears three costly alabaster flasks. At Yeshua's glance she throws away her dagger; she pours out the costly oil on him. At their first, crucial encounter she anoints his feet and hair, weeps out her past and hears the words: "With these tears you have washed yourself clean" (p. 53). The second anointing takes place before the Passion: "As often as people speak of me and my death, they will also speak of this woman" (p. 243). The third flask is not used: first the soldiers prevent the anointing of the corpse, and then the oil becomes superfluous at the tomb because the dead man has been transformed into a new reality. Through these three oil flasks all the anointings are attributed to Miriam and retold. At the same time they point progressively to the true image of Jesus: he is the savior of the restless woman, the redeemer ready to die for all humanity, the living Word of God.

Miriam is the only one of the disciples who recognizes him in the biblical sense: in spirit and love. In their last conversation, sealed with a kiss, Yeshua asks for her strength as he goes to his death and promises her his own strength beyond that death. Miriam is the true disciple who is always with him: at the Last Supper, when he washes the disciples' feet, as a watcher with him in the Garden of Olives, at his arrest, and beneath the cross. It is she who receives the commission to strengthen the others (cf. Luke 22:32, where this is said to Peter) and to proclaim the Living One;[35] she will preside over a congregation and is one of those persecuted by Saul; finally, with other male and female disciples, she escapes across the sea.

The very beginning of the novel already anticipates this ending. With the stylistic tools of epic portent her flight from the powerful persecutor Saul/Shaul is prefigured; it is especially the women, and among them Miriam above all, the proclaimer of the resurrection, that he wants to reach: "If we are to root out this new thing, we must root out these women" (p. 327). Shaul is the fanatic Jew, the self-righteous Christian, the Roman citizen captivated by the power and magnitude of the Roman empire. Miriam is deeply disturbed "that he, like the emperor Augustus, wanted to found a world power with Jesus as its emperor," and that he sought world domination on behalf of "what people were beginning to call Christianity" (pp. 329–30) and was accomplished by the emperor Constantine: the rule of Rome and Christianity.

In the passages about Paul the author's intent and the function of Miriam become clear: this is a critique of Christianity (Paul) and the Church in its historical form (Emperor Constantine). The figure of Miriam is developed on this basis; therefore she must have been a daughter of the Maccabees and a Zealot. Only because she has rejected violence can she criticize Paul and Christianity. The novel does not portray the biblical Mary of Magdala but a critique of the Church personified in Miriam: Miriam in her cave still dreams the dream of Yeshua's reign of peace, of the birth of the divine child in every person, even though his movement has long since been transformed into the authoritative and aggressive Roman state church. In Miriam and Shaul utopia and reality are contrasted: love and peace against domination and power, the community of siblings against male claims to absolute authority. History has trampled on Rabbi Yeshua, but as long as Miriam remains awake in her dark cave of memory there is hope that the "waiting for the reign of peace" with which the novel ends is not in vain.

Notes

[1] Marie-Joseph Lagrange, "Jésus a-t-il été oint plusieurs fois et par plusieurs femmes?" *RB* 9 (1912) 504–32; Peter Ketter, *Christus und die Frauen 1: Die Frauen in den Evangelien* (5th ed. Stuttgart, 1950).

[2] Eugen Drewermann, *Das Markusevangelium* (Olten and Freiburg, 1988) 2:10.

[3] Eugen Drewermann, *Die Botschaft der Frauen* (2nd ed. Olten and Freiburg, 1992) 162.

[4] Ibid., 163. For Mary's condition before her encounter with Jesus cf. also *Markusevangelium*, 2:627, 705–6.

[5] Drewermann, *Markusevangelium*, 2:640–1, 706; *Botschaft*, 181–2.

[6] Drewermann, *Markusevangelium*, 2:413; *Botschaft*, 180; *Tiefenpsychologie und Exegese* (Olten and Freiburg, 1984) 1:450.

[7] Drewermann, *Botschaft*, 180–1; *Tiefenpsychologie*, 1:450–2.

[8] Drewermann, *Tiefenpsychologie*, 1:451.

[9] *Katholisches Sonntagsblatt. Kirchenzeitung für die Diözese Rottenburg-Stuttgart* 15 (11 April 1993) 10.

[10] *Konradsblatt. Wochenzeitung für die Erzdiözese Freiburg* 24 (19 June 1994) 14.

[11] *Konradsblatt* 26 (3 July 1994) 17.

[12] Heinrich Spaemann, *Drei Marien. Die Gestalt des Glaubens* (Freiburg, Basel, Vienna: Herder, 1985) 7 (emphasis in original). Cf. p. 125: "Magdalene was a public sinner."

[13] For Mary Magdalene as a third figure of faith see ibid., 125–39.

[14] Walter Nigg, *Buch der Büßer. Neun Lebensbilder* (Olten and Freiburg, 1970) 33–56.

[15]Ibid., 35–6.

[16]Wilhelm Hartke, *Vier urchristliche Parteien und ihre Vereinigung zur apostolischen Kirche.* Deutsche Akademie der Wissenschaften zu Berlin, Schriften der Sektion für Altertumswissenschaft 24. 2 vols. (Berlin, 1961). The remarks on Mary Magdalene are summarized in Appendix 1, "Maria Magdalena und die andere Maria," 2:745–60.

[17]The tradition about the tomb in Ephesus is known in the West since Gregory of Tours (6th c.), but was subsequently suppressed by the Burgundian and Provençal traditions. The tomb at the entrance to the Grotto of the Seven Sleepers is regarded as that of Mary Magdalene.

[18]Mary Magdalene is not a central character for contemporary authors, but she appears more and more frequently as the most important "extra" in Jesus books: as a kind of girlfriend, as with Kazantzakis (see n. 28) or Rinser (see n. 32), or even as Jesus' wife, as for Thiering (see n. 19), Lincoln, Baigent, and Leigh (see n. 20), and in the most recent book by Weddig Fricke, *Der Fall Jesus. Eine juristische Beweisführung* (Hamburg, 1995) 193–4.

[19]Barbara Thiering, *Jesus von Qumran. Sein Leben, neu geschrieben* (Gütersloh, 1993). For Mary Magdalene see especially pp. 110–3, 180–1, 510–1; for Tamar/Phoebe see pp. 186–7.

[20]Michael Baigent, Richard Leigh, and Henry Lincoln, *Holy Blood, Holy Grail* (New York: Delacorte, 1982). The page numbers in the text refer to this edition.

[21]Cf. ch. 12, "The Priest-King who Never Ruled," 287–332.

[22]Ibid., 374. The cult of Mary Magdalene arose out of knowledge of these connections; she was honored as the "black Madonna" or "black Virgin" and the many Notre Dame churches are dedicated to her (p. 374).

[23]Raymond-Léopold Bruckberger, o.p., *Maria Magdalena* (Düsseldorf, 1954); Christa Mulack, *Jesus, der Gesalbte der Frauen* (Stuttgart, 1987). The page numbers in the text refer to these editions.

[24]On this see the section "Jesus, the Women's Pupil," 77–128. Even earlier (1983) Mulack proposed the thesis that Jesus, by his attitude toward Mary Magdalene, the representative of feminine emotionality against masculine rationality, had clearly taken a position "for the feminine and against the masculine." Cf. eadem, *Die Weiblichkeit Gottes. Matriarchale Voraussetzungen des Gottesbildes* (6th ed. Stuttgart, 1992) 302–7.

[25]Bruckberger, *Maria Magdalena,* 78, 81; Mulack, *Jesus,* 283.

[26]Cf. the opening sentence of her essay, *Unterentwickeltes Land Frau* (Würzburg, 1970) 5: "To speak of women always means speaking of society."

[27]Published 1970. Music by Andrew Lloyd Webber; lyrics by Tim Rice. Film directed by Norman Jewison, 1972.

[28]Nikos Kazantzakis, *The Last Temptation of Christ,* translated from the Greek by P. A. Bien (New York: Simon and Schuster, 1960). Film directed by Martin Scorsese, 1988.

[29]One of the first statements by the youthful Jesus in the novel refers to Magdalene: "if Magdalene becomes a prostitute, it is my fault" (p. 13).

[30]The green lizard also appears in the love scene with Magdalene that Jesus experiences on the cross (p. 425).

[31]Nikos Kazantzakis, *Zorba the Greek [Alexis Sorbas. Abenteuer auf Kreta* (rororo TB 158) 1963, 198–201].

[32]Luise Rinser, *Mirjam* (6th ed. Frankfurt, 1983). Mary of Magdala is not Martha's sister, of course, but she assumes her role as anointer (John 12) and is, by the author's own original interpretation, the anointing sinner in Luke 7.

[33]Rinser, *Land,* 14.

[34]Rinser's explanation of possession and sin is as time-conditioned (this novel appeared at the height of the women's movement) as is Drewermann's vehement rejection of this position; he sees the causes of the soul's deformity not at all in the social sphere, but in the individual: cf. idem, *Botschaft,* 223.

[35]"That was certainly the highest possible commission to a woman to teach, a *missio canonica* given by the highest possible authority." Rinser, *Land,* 37.

Chapter Eleven

Freed from
Sins, Demons, and Subjection

The path of the disciple Mary from Magdala from her own time to the present appears to have taken a fairly straight course: from the apostle of the beginnings to the saint of the Middle Ages and the penitent of the Baroque to the fallen woman—adulteress or prostitute—of the nineteenth century. In the course of it she was laden with ideas that are almost impossible to dislodge and yet must be removed if we are to discern the original picture of this woman.

1. Freed from Sins

First, of course, we must mention the still omnipresent sinner. Despite all the efforts of critical exegesis, Mary Magdalene has not been able to shed this identity that has fastened itself on her. On the sinner Magdalene whose way of life broke all the taboos of society are projected the desires and fantasies that "one" cannot actually bring oneself to realize. Her fascination comes from the erotic aura that surrounds her: her wild hair, her tender, feminine hands, the passion of the former whore—these are the fixed elements from which her image is made up even today.

We owe it to the patience and persistence of feminist authors (Elisabeth Moltmann-Wendel, for example) that gradually the many layers of overpainting are being removed and another image laid bare: the healed woman, the disciple, the apostolic witness.

2. Freed from Demons

But as tradition always pretended to see the former sinner behind the converted penitent, so the New Testament picture of the healed woman implies the one who was formerly possessed: the picture transmitted by Luke, a picture so mighty in its effects, is one of a woman broken by a demonic illness. Thus when we turn our eyes, now sharpened by an examination of the fantastic effects of this picture, back to the starting point we find in the passage where Luke (and he alone among the four evangelists!) speaks of the wealthy and respectable women who followed Jesus after they had been healed "of evil spirits and illnesses" that the first name is that of Mary Magdalene "from whom seven demons had gone out" (Luke 8:2-3).

This statement has always incited readers to produce "contemporary" explanations. Medieval theologians explained the seven demons as the seven deadly sins; Martin Luther translated the expression in an era excited by fear of the devil and belief in witches with "seven devils"; authors in our own time, a period influenced by esotericism and New Age ideas, read the biblical text as an echo of the seven steps of initiation in the cult of a mother goddess or as a coded reference to the fact that Mary Magdalene was really filled ("possessed") by the (feminine) Holy Spirit.[1] The "seven demons" have always been made functional for the current age in every era of the history of interpretation. This observation permits us nevertheless to ask what moved the evangelist himself to mention in the case of Mary Magdalene not only the "evil spirits" that cause illness but also these "demons." Was it sympathy with the tortured woman or the desire to emphasize the greatness of the miracle worker, or was he impelled by quite different motives? In order to answer this question we need to cite some other "woman" passages in Luke's two-volume work.

We recall that for the earliest evangelist Mary and other women were part of the Jesus movement from the beginning and fulfilled all the requirements of discipleship. Readers are permitted to suppose that women and men came to Jesus in similar ways, as exemplified in five "typical" call narratives (Mark 1:16-20; 2:14): they came immediately out of their daily lives and occupations. The process of consideration and discernment that lay behind such a decision is summarized in a single instant of choice. The disciples, male and female, were so deeply marked by this turn in their lives that they remained faithful to Jesus even when failure seemed inevitable; this was apparently even more true of the women than of the men.

With Luke it is quite different: women come to Jesus because they are in need; their discipleship is portrayed as grateful adherence and their service as good works. They are still present at Jesus' death, but not as the normative witnesses; they are "extras" in the scene who could be dispensed with. The role of the women, headed by Mary of Magdala, is altered in favor of the male disciples.[2] This statement is confirmed by a look at the same author's second book.

According to the Acts of the Apostles women were part of the primitive community (1:13-14; 5:14) and their presence is presumed in later local congregations (8:12; 17:4, 12, 21:5), house churches (12:12), or at the baptism of households (11:14; 16:15); they are also among those subjected to persecution (8:3; 9:2; 22:4). But when it comes to public appearances only men are named, and emphatically so; there is not a clue that could lead us to suppose the presence of women. For example, Luke tells of the descent of the Holy Spirit, whom "all" (2:1; similarly 4:31)—namely the men and women mentioned before this—receive in fulfillment of a prophetic word (2:17; Joel 2:28-29 [Hebrew 3:1-2]). But when the phenomenon is publicly revealed it is not "all," but only Peter and the other apostles (2:14) who appear. Men are the speakers (cf. also 15:1-35) while women have only a passive role. Should we really suppose that the Christian women neglected the commission to prophetic speech given them by the Spirit, or did Luke forget to tell us about it? Significantly, an active woman like Tabitha is not shown at her diaconal work; there is only a narrative recollection of it, while she herself is the "object" of Peter's miracle (9:36-42). A brief mention (21:9) is all that remains of the work of the prophetically gifted daughters of Philip the evangelist. Similarly, the godfearing women of Philippi, the first believers in Europe, are presented as "listeners" in an exclusively passive role (16:13-15).

The only woman who is shown as publicly active, giving witness for Paul, calling him "servant of the most high God" and his teaching "the way of salvation," is the slave woman in Philippi whose proclamation, "true" in itself, is given a negative qualification: it is a divining spirit that is speaking through her, and Paul silences it through an exorcism (16:16-18). Is it accidental that the woman who speaks in public is one possessed by a demon? Or to put it in more general terms: are the women disciples, teachers, and missionaries—Mary of Magdala, the Galilean women, the slave in Philippi—only imaginable for Luke as women possessed by demons?[3] Perhaps the search for Mary Magdalene must not only clear away the ballast of a long history of influence, but even seek in the New Testament for the true picture hidden behind some of the texts themselves. Was the "real" Mary perhaps not at all a sick woman ruled by demons, but—as the other evangelists suggest—a strong woman, a true disciple, a courageous follower?

3. Freed from Subjection

Anyone who has seen Mary Magdalene depicted (in paintings, stained glass, sculpture) knows her place: she lies, sits, kneels at Jesus' feet as the penitent sinner, the attentive listener in Bethany, the weeper beneath the cross, the woman overcome with joyful surprise in the Easter garden. Homilies, hymns, songs, and poetry show us the same picture: Mary is the woman "on the floor"—shamed, humble, deeply moved.

If today, for good reasons, we no longer connect the first of those two scenes with her, still the traditional portrait endures—unless we forget the internalized images and pay close attention to the gospel texts. Then we will have to imagine Mary *standing* both at the cross and in the Easter scene. While Mark 15:40 (*par.* Matt 27:55) says nothing about the women's posture, Luke 23:49 and John 19:25 clearly say that the women were *standing*. Similarly in the Johannine Easter scene Mary *stands* at the tomb and repeatedly turns, which presumes a *standing* posture (John 20:11-18).

Nowhere do the texts say anything about falling down or kneeling. The fact that nevertheless this image has so enduringly marked the Christian collective mind from the time of the Church Fathers until now is of course connected with the *status subjectionis* of woman—something in the meantime rejected even in Church documents as out of date. This means that gender polarity (male/female) was wrongly interpreted in the past in hierarchical categories (superior/inferior).

The woman's subjection to the man, according to the Vatican statement regarding the admission of women to the priesthood (*Inter insigniores,* 1976) is one of the statements "that modern thought would have difficulty in admitting or would even rightly reject."[4] The extent to which the idea of women's inferiority is present within the context of ecclesiastical arguments is evident from the emphasis with which the official commentaries defend *Inter insigniores* against this easily inferred (mis)understanding. Thus the Roman commentary explains that the earlier assertion of an ordering, subjection, or state of servitude of the woman with respect to the man (*quia mulier est in statu subjectionis*, as Thomas Aquinas wrote) was due to "the undeniable influence of prejudices unfavorable to women"[5] and constituted a flaw in the argumentation.[6] The German bishops published a similar aid to interpretation.[7]

Against the background of the earlier subordinate position of women derived from the order of creation it is easy enough to understand the stubbornly-held false depictions of Mary Magdalene, a woman standing upright, as she appears in texts and images: humble and bowed down.

The Misereor "Hungertuch" (hunger scarf) for 1990–91 bearing the work of the Indian artist Lucy D'Souza shows us what an appropriate portrayal of Mary Magdalene today could look like: Mary Magdalene, surrounded by the Easter light, strides toward the bewildered disciples who look expectantly toward the victorious messenger (see Plate 4). This Mary is not trying to hold onto the past (cf. the *Noli me tangere* motif), but is moving toward the future, or as the artist herself says: "Mary of Magdala . . . proclaims the invincibility of life. She is transparent for God's power and light."[8]

4. ". . . that the one who knows may teach you."

Mary Magdalene must be rediscovered. She no longer embodies the old roles of prostitute and saint; even the other roles in which the Church sees the great women of the past do not seem appropriate for her ("holy martyrs, virgins, mothers who have transmitted the faith to their children").[9] Even the ancient title *apostola apostolorum*, first rediscovered by feminist theologians and now adopted by the Pope, veils her significance, for the apostolic function that comes from "seeing the Lord" is restricted in the case of Mary Magdalene to the little circle of the eleven apostles and exercised within a very short time period (the transmission of the Easter message), while the same "seeing the Lord" in the cases of Peter and Paul led to universal and enduring apostolicity. Does this really represent essential equality of persons and rights for men and women?[10] Are not different consequences drawn from the same fact ("seeing the Lord"), and to the detriment of the woman?

Mary Magdalene must be rediscovered. In the important Magdalene text in John 20 there occurs an exchange of roles, or rather the reversal of the (more or less contemporary) prohibition on women's speaking.[11] Mary is *not* to be silent, but to *speak*; she is to *teach* her brothers by *speaking* of what she has experienced.[12] Only when the preconditions are created within the Church for Mary Magdalene to be able to carry out her commission will the vision of the one who gave it be fulfilled.

Mary Magdalene must be rediscovered. She is not just the sinful saint from whose vision the people of the past derived new hope. She is a biblical saint who represents modern virtues: *solidarity* with the dying, *sympathy* with the tortured, *fidelity* to a person and that person's cause beyond death, *courage* for (public) *mourning*, but also *imagination* that helps in overcoming personal resignation and global fears, *endurance* when new insights must be defended convincingly and patiently. . . . When we understand that, she can become the woman of Kurt Marti's dream,[13] the prophet of a Magdalenian age.

Notes

[1] Thus Christa Mulack (*Jesus, der Gesalbte der Frauen* [Stuttgart, 1987] 122–4), affirms and expands the corresponding suggestions of O. Eberz and Baigent, Leigh, and Lincoln.

[2] This can be observed in more recent Church documents; cf. the reference to Luke 8:2-3 in *Mulieris dignitatem* (15 August 1988): "Sometimes the women whom Jesus met and who received so many graces from him, also accompanied him as he journeyed with the Apostles through the towns and villages" (*AAS* 86).

[3] A little later this procedure was introduced into the polemics against heresy, as the defaming of the anonymous teacher and prophet in Thyatira shows; she is accused of Satanism (Rev 2); cf. Ingrid Maisch, "Isebel. Autoritätskonflikt—nicht nur in Thyatira," in Karin Walter, ed., *Zwischen Ohnmacht und Befreiung* (Freiburg, Basel, and Vienna: Herder, 1988) 163–72.

[4] *Declaration on the Question of the Admission of Women to the Ministerial Priesthood* (*Inter insigniores*), *AAS* 117 § 7.

[5] Ibid., § 6.

[6] Ibid., § 6.

[7] "Erklärung der Pressestelle im Sekretariat der Deutschen Bischofskonferenz," ibid., 59–60.

[8] Misereor Hungertuch "Biblical Portraits of Women, Guides to the Reign of God," *Arbeitshefte zum Hungertuch*, Misereor, ed. (Aachen, 1989) 22.

[9] Apostolic letter of Pope John Paul II "On the Reservation of Priestly Ordination to Men," 22 March 1994, in *AAS* 117 (quoting his own words in *Mulieris dignitatem* no. 27).

[10] *Mulieris dignitatem* 16, *AAS* 86. In comparison to the statement about the "unnatural equality of women with men" in the papal encyclical *Casti connubii* of Pius XI, of course, all the more recent documents regarding women represent progress. For the changes and deficiencies in the Church's image of women cf. Wolfgang Beinert, "Theologie und kirchliches Frauenbild," and "Die Frauenfrage im Spiegel kirchlicher Verlautbarungen," in Wolfgang Beinert, Herlinde Pissarek-Hudelist, and R. Zwank, eds., *Frauenbefreiung und Kirche. Darstellung—Analyse—Dokumentation* (Regensburg, 1987) 51–76, 77–97.

[11] Cf. 1 Cor 14:34-35; 1 Tim 2:11-12.

[12] For this general topic see Hildegard Gollinger, "Das Weib schweige nicht in der Gemeinde," in H. Gollinger, J. Maier, and J. Thierfelder, eds., *Dem Frieden nachjagen* (Weinheim, 1991) 13–26. In antiquity the role of the "teaching" woman belongs to a goddess; cf. the Sophocles quotation in the subtitle (from *Aias* 5.13).

[13] Kurt Marti, *Geduld und Revolte: Die Gedichte am Rand.* With a Foreword by Ingeborg Drewitz (Stuttgart, 1984).

Index